POWER-PACKED
DIRECT MAIL

ALSO BY ROBERT W. BLY

Targeted Public Relations
Selling Your Services
The Copywriter's Handbook
Secrets of a Freelance Writer
Business-to-Business Direct Marketing
The Elements of Business Writing
The Elements of Technical Writing
The Advertising Manager's Handbook
How to Promote Your Own Business
Ads That Sell
Creative Careers
Dream Jobs
Create the Perfect Sales Piece
Keeping Clients Satisfied

▼ ROBERT W. BLY

POWER-PACKED DIRECT MAIL

▼ HOW TO GET
MORE LEADS AND
SALES BY MAIL

HENRY HOLT AND COMPANY ▼ *NEW YORK*

Henry Holt and Company, Inc.
Publishers since 1866
115 West 18th Street
New York, New York 10011

Henry Holt ® is a registered trademark of Henry Holt and Company, Inc.

Published in Canada by Fitzhenry & Whiteside Ltd.,
195 Allstate Parkway, Markham, Ontario L3R 4T8.

Library of Congress Cataloging-in-Publication Data
Bly, Robert W.
    Power-packed direct mail: how to get more leads and sales by mail/
    Robert W. Bly.—1st ed.
        p.   cm.
    Includes index.
    1. Direct marketing—United States.   2. Mail-order business—
United States.   I. Title.
    HF5415.126.B584   1995
    658.8'4—dc20   94-32821
                                                        CIP
ISBN 0-8050-3505-2

Henry Holt books are available for special promotions and premiums.
For details contact: Director, Special Markets.

First Edition—1995
Designed by Victoria Hartman

Printed in the United States of America
All first editions are printed on acid-free paper. ∞

10 9 8 7 6 5 4 3 2 1

To Cynthia Vartan—
editor and friend

Contents

Acknowledgments

As the years go by, more and more people—clients, friends, and colleagues—contribute to my education in direct mail. I learn something new almost daily.

The result is that I don't dare try to acknowledge those who contributed their know-how, information, and experience to this book. If I did, I'd surely leave many out and inadvertently offend a great many direct mail professionals I admire.

So instead, I say, "thanks, folks"—to all of you. You know who you are.

Special thanks to my longtime editor, Cynthia Vartan, for publishing *Power-Packed Direct Mail*. Additional thanks to my agent, Bonita Nelson, for her continued enthusiasm for my career and my books. Without these two wonderful people, my opportunities for helping businesspeople through books would be fewer and farther between.

Introduction

What kind of response should I expect from a sales letter designed to generate sales leads?"

"Is it worth going to the trouble of personalizing my direct mail, or can I get good results by mailing a form letter?"

"Where can I get mailing lists, what will they cost, and how can I tell a good list from a bad one?"

"Should I put my direct mail piece in an envelope, or send it as a self-mailer?"

"Can I succeed with a single mailing, or do I need to develop a series of mailing pieces? And must they comprise a campaign with a consistent look, tone, and feel?"

"Is a plain letter or circular good enough, or do you need some crazy, far-out gimmick to attract attention these days?"

"Why do so many send out those lengthy, four-page letters? Isn't it true that people don't read today and so copy should be short?"

Do these questions sound familiar? They are some of the most common things I and other direct mail copywriters and consultants are asked by our clients. Naturally, you'll add some of your own to the list. *Power-Packed Direct Mail* was written to give you the answers.

Who is this book for?

If you're new to direct mail, or you're thinking about getting into direct mail for the first time, *Power-Packed Direct Mail* will answer questions, eliminate confusion, and give you step-by-step instructions on how to make every mailing pay off.

If you already use direct mail, *Power-Packed Direct Mail* will help you avoid common mistakes, make better decisions about what to test, improve your offers, create more effective mailings at less cost, and generate more inquiries, leads, sales, orders—money!

Most direct marketing books target experienced direct mail users—companies that sell directly through mail order and that mail volumes in the hundreds of thousands or even millions of pieces per year. But there is another group ... the *average* businessperson, using direct mail as an adjunct to other marketing and sales tactics such as radio commercials and press releases ... whose objectives, activities, and needs are different from the major direct response players'.

Recognizing this, I've worked hard to make *Power-Packed Direct Mail* accessible and relevant to this second group (as well as the first), because I perceive that the majority of my readers fall into this category: people in companies that have limited direct mail knowledge and experience, and that mail in modest volumes. These companies include:

• manufacturers of a wide variety of products, especially products sold to business and industry;
• retailers who are using mail to attract large numbers of people to their stores;
• service businesses ranging from real estate and insurance agents, to caterers and lawn-care services, to doctors, lawyers, dentists, therapists, accountants, and consultants; and
• high-tech companies—firms involved in computers, software, electronics, communications, office automation, and other technology industries.

These businesses range from small and medium-size companies that count every penny spent on marketing (as I do), to

Fortune 500 firms and other big corporations that have invested millions in television and print advertising but are just beginning to explore what direct mail can do for them.

Regardless of where you fit into the picture, *Power-Packed Direct Mail* will teach you techniques that have generated millions of dollars in sales for traditional direct response marketers. It will show you how to adapt proven methods to increase response to your own mailings, whether your goal is to bring in orders, distribute sales literature, generate leads, answer inquiries, educate customers, announce new products and services, sell upgrades or enhancements, or educate distributors and sales reps.

One of the best things about direct mail is that you don't need a lot of money to get started. My first mailing of five hundred pieces, in 1982, generated thirty-five leads, a 7 percent response, and fifteen thousand dollars in orders, but cost less than three hundred dollars in typesetting, printing and postage. Even a small amount invested in a limited mailing can generate revenue many times in excess of the cost.

I do have one favor to ask. If you create or come across a particularly effective direct mail piece, please send it to me so I can share it with readers of the next edition of this book. You will receive full credit, of course. Contact:

Bob Bly
Copywriter/Consultant
22 E. Quackenbush Avenue
Dumont, NJ 07628

(201) 385-1220
Fax (201) 385-1138

I also welcome phone calls and letters from readers, and if you have short questions, I will be happy to answer them without charge (my way of saying thanks for spending your hard-earned money and valuable time on my book). If you need more in-depth help, such as a critique of a mailing piece or copywriting for a sales letter or direct mail package, I'll tell you what's involved and what it will cost. No cost or obligation for the quote. Fair enough?

Here's to happy—and profitable—reading. Enjoy!

PART I

PLANNING AND STRATEGY

GETTING STARTED IN DIRECT MAIL

Have you recently started using direct mail, or are you thinking of using direct mail for the first time? Congratulations. You're taking the first step on a road leading to more leads, inquiries, sales, and profits.

If you've already tried direct mail but were disappointed with the results, don't despair. By learning new techniques and avoiding past mistakes, you can make direct mail work for you as never before.

I'm going to give you dozens of rules, hints, tips, strategies, and case histories in this book—techniques that have proven successful in actual mailings. This book is also packed with examples of what works in direct mail . . . and what doesn't.

Of course, you never know if a headline, idea, sales pitch, or mailing format will work until you try it. Testing is an important part of direct mail success, and you'll learn how to test your ideas quickly and inexpensively.

WHAT IS "DIRECT MAIL"?

Direct mail is unsolicited advertising or promotional material (that is, material the recipient has not requested) sent to an individual or company through the mail.

Most direct mail is sent to rented mailing lists containing the names and addresses of people your company has not done business with before. The purpose of such a mailing is *customer acquisition*: You want to turn this person into a customer by designing the mailing to generate an order. Or you can use the mailing to generate a lead, then follow up to convert the prospect into a customer.

Direct mail is one example of a type of marketing called *direct response* or *direct marketing*. Other examples include telemarketing, infomercials and other TV commercials giving a toll-free 800 number, and magazine and newspaper ads containing reply coupons you can use to request information, order a product, or send for a sample.

Direct response is any type of advertising that seeks some sort of reply from the reader. The reply is usually sent via mail, phone, or fax (and more recently, through computer modem via the Internet, E-mail, or other electronic communications).

A direct mail letter that asks you to fill in and return an order form to subscribe to a magazine or join a book club is one type of direct response advertising. And those long late-night TV commercials that sell steak knives, diet products, exercise machines, or get-rich-in-real-estate home-study programs are direct response advertising, too.

"Everything I do is direct response," says Howard Ruff, publisher of *Financial Success Report*. "How can you measure how well you are doing if you don't use direct response?"

HISTORY OF DIRECT MARKETING

Traditionally, direct marketers have sold products directly by mail, eliminating the retailer, distributor, or middleman. But today, direct marketing techniques are also used to support sales reps, agents, and distributors, and in some cases to get products onto the shelves in the stores (or get people to come into the stores to buy the products!).

One of the early direct marketers was Richard Sears of Sears, Roebuck fame. He originally worked in a train station and began in direct marketing using sales letters to sell pocket watches to station masters at other train stations. Eventually he founded one of the nation's leading mail order catalog houses.

Lester Wunderman, chairman of Wunderman, Ricotta & Kline, a New York City advertising agency, came up with the term direct marketing in 1961. Prior to that, it was called *mail order*.

Actually, mail order is a specialized form of direct marketing. Direct marketing is any type of marketing communication that generates a direct, measurable response. In mail order, also called one-step direct marketing, the customer orders the product directly from your ad, letter, catalog, circular, commercial, or whatever. In two-step direct marketing, the initial ad or mailer generates an inquiry or request for more information; the sale is made after follow-up with additional promotional materials or sales pitch.

Junk mail is slang for direct mail. Many professionals who work in direct marketing consider the term a put-down and take great offense when you call their work "junk mail."

According to Gene A. Del Polito, the executive director of the Advertising Mail Marketing Association, the term junk mail was developed by the newspaper industry in the 1950s to disparage direct mail—a rival medium for advertising (mailers and newspapers compete for advertising dollars).

In response to a negative *New York Times* article on advertising mail, Del Polito observed, "The *Times* does not explain why an ad for a fast-food chain or a supermarket supplement carried in a newspaper is OK but the very same ad sent through the mail is 'junk.' "

However, everyone knows and uses this familiar term all the time, and I suspect that the average citizen doesn't have much of an idea of what direct marketing or direct response is—nor do they care.

The book you are reading is about direct mail, and how to use it to boost your sales, no matter what business you are in.

DIRECT MAIL IS BOOMING

Direct mail is a widely used and fast-growing area of marketing. Consider these facts:

- According to the Direct Marketing Association (DMA), direct mail is the third most popular advertising medium (TV commercials and newspaper advertising lead the pack), with 19 percent of all advertising dollars spent on direct mail.
- Pitney Bowes recently surveyed small businesses and found that, of those using direct mail, 85 percent are pleased with the results, citing new customer acquisition as the primary benefit.
- A survey by the Printing Industries of America found the printing of direct mail to be one of the fastest-growing sources of revenue for printers in the 1990s, second only to printing of brochures and other marketing support materials—and ahead of annual reports, inserts, coupons, and wrappers.
- In 1992, direct marketing generated revenue of $350 billion. During that year, 55 percent of adults in the United States ordered one or more products by mail.
- A Simmons Market Research study showed that 68 percent of consumers surveyed said they found direct mail interesting or useful. Only 15 percent of those surveyed throw away direct mail without reading it, while 75 percent open and read their direct mail or set it aside for reference.
- Approximately 13.5 billion catalogs were mailed in 1992 (the majority of them, my wife notes, to our home).
- The direct marketing industry provides more than five million jobs, accounting for 6 percent of U.S. employment.
- More than fifty billion direct mail pieces are mailed annually—more than one every other day for every American.

• Dr. Roger Breslow, a New York internist, saved every piece of direct mail he received in one year and put it in a crate. At the end of the year, the crate weighed 502 pounds.

ADVANTAGES OF USING DIRECT MAIL

Obviously, direct mail is just one of the many weapons available in your advertising arsenal. So you may ask, "Why spend money on direct mail? With that money, I could run an ad or a TV commercial, call prospects on the phone, or hire a salesperson. Why direct mail?"

Direct mail has a number of unique characteristics that make it the medium of choice in many marketing situations:

• *It generates an immediate, tangible response.* Although it can do many things, direct mail is primarily a *response* medium. Few other advertising techniques can match direct mail when it comes to generating immediate replies in volume. If you want people to renew their insurance policies, visit your trade show booth, request a demo diskette of your new software, send for a free brochure, place an order, or subscribe to your publication, direct mail is a good bet for you.

• *Direct mail can pay for itself—quickly.* No other form of advertising can give you such a rapid return on your investment. Especially with lead-generating direct mail, where the size of individual orders is larger than in mail order, a single sale resulting from your direct mail package can often pay back the cost of the entire mailing.

And in mail order selling, a package that is profitable—that is, a package that generates $1.50 to $2.00 or more in revenue for every $1.00 spent on mailing—is literally a money-generating machine. You simply keep mailing to more names on more lists, and collect the profits.

• **The response to direct mail can be measured— scientifically and precisely.** When you run an ad, do you know how successful it will be? If your goal is to build an image, how can you measure whether a particular ad or series of ads has changed the public's image of you (let alone how *much* it has changed or how this translates into greater sales for you)?

If your goal is to create brand awareness, how can you find out how many people are familiar with your brand, what they think about it—and again, whether this change in perception has generated revenue in excess of the cost of the advertising needed to create it?

With advertising, it is difficult to judge performance. Not so with direct mail. By counting the orders or inquiries, you know whether the mailing was profitable.

For example, let's say you mail two thousand direct mail pieces to two thousand prospects. Your cost, including postage, mailing lists, and printing, is seventy cents per package, for a total mailing cost of $1,400.

The mailing generates forty leads. Therefore, your cost per lead is thirty-five dollars and your response rate is 2 percent.

With follow-up, you convince eight of these prospects to buy your product. Your conversion rate is eight out of forty leads—20 percent.

The product sells for a thousand dollars per unit. Eight units sold gives you revenue of eight thousand dollars for the mailing. You would have had to generate $1,400 in sales for the mailing just to break even; at this level, you have earned more than five and a half times breakeven . . . a successful promotion by any standard.

However, some things are not easily measured, even in direct mail. For example, while it's easy to determine whether a mailing succeeded or failed, the results don't tell you *why* it succeeded or failed. Also difficult, if not impossible, to measure is the beneficial effect of putting your message in front of the 98 or 99 percent of recipients who do *not* respond to your piece—a factor more and more direct marketers are attempting to measure and put to advantage.

• **Direct mail can be tested.** When a major automobile manufacturer, airline, or fast-food chain begins a new advertising
campaign, they are already committed, having spent hundreds of
thousands or millions of dollars to create and run newspaper
inserts, magazine ads, and TV and radio commercials—with no
real clue as to whether this campaign will be effective and the
money well spent.

As you will see, you can effectively test a direct mail piece by
mailing only a couple of thousand or even a couple of hundred
pieces, at a cost ranging from a hundred to a thousand dollars. If
the mailing is successful, then you can produce it in mass quantities, secure in the knowledge that it will work and your investment will pay off handsomely.

If the mailing is an utter flop, at least you have not spent much
time, effort, or money. Your losses are minimal. You don't blow
your budget for the year, take out a second mortgage on your
home, or dip into retirement or college funds.

And if the mailing is so-so—neither a clear success nor an
obvious failure? You proceed cautiously, refining the piece and
testing variations until you hit upon a promotion that generates
an acceptable profit in a small test. Once you create and prove
out the piece as a winner, only then do you invest more in its
production and distribution.

• **Direct mail can be rolled out.** Once a direct mail campaign is proven successful in a small test, it can be easily and
rapidly "rolled out," meaning you mail more pieces to more
names and more lists—testing the performance of each list
before renting names in volume.

The initial work is in the creation, testing, and refinement of
the piece. This aspect of direct mail is as labor-intensive as any
other form of marketing—and more so than some (for example,
creating a direct mail piece is more difficult and time-consuming
than creating a newspaper insert or newspaper ad).

But once the piece is developed, rolling out is simply a matter
of printing more mailers, ordering the lists, and tracking the

results. It doesn't require the ongoing efforts that trade show marketing, seminar marketing, telemarketing, in-person selling, and many other forms of promotion do.

If you create a mailing piece that's a big success, you can, for a time, sit back and just collect the cash—sometimes for many years or even decades. Of course, the smart marketer doesn't do this. Instead, she continually refines and tests her mailings to generate even more profitable results.

• ***Direct mail is selective.*** "Effective advertising is that which reaches, at the lowest possible cost, the most people who can and will buy what you have to sell," says Herschell Gordon Lewis, a successful direct mail writer and author of many books on advertising. With direct mail, you have the opportunity to send your message to your best prospects and customers, without wasting money advertising to people who are not potential buyers.

For example, a printer in New Jersey who specializes in restaurant menus wants to target restaurant owners and managers in the New York–New Jersey area. What's the best way to reach them? If he runs ads in one of New Jersey's business magazines, he wastes his ad dollars reaching the 99.9 percent of the subscribers who are not in the restaurant business. If he advertises in restaurant trade journals, such as *Restaurant Business*, he also wastes money, because only a small percentage of the magazine's subscribers are located in New Jersey.

By using direct mail, the printer can selectively send his advertising message to people who own or manage restaurants and are located in New Jersey. Thus, direct mail—not print advertising—is the printer's best bet for reaching the greatest number of qualified prospects at the lowest possible cost.

As a rule of thumb, if you are selling to a mass market containing hundreds of thousands or millions of prospects, space and broadcast advertising is the most cost-effective form of promotion. The cost of contact is just pennies, and since so many of the readers and viewers are potential customers, there is little wasted circulation.

If you are selling to an extremely small and narrow market, with perhaps only a few hundred customers, why bother to spend the money and creativity on advertising or mailing? Just call them up on the phone, visit them in person, or do both. The market is small enough for you to do that.

If you are selling to a midsize market, with thousands or tens of thousands of prospects, and where the market is a subsegment of a larger market (for example, you are selling to radiologists and anesthesiologists as opposed to all medical doctors), direct mail is often the best way to reach them. The market is large enough to justify the time and creativity spent developing and producing the mailing, yet specialized enough that there is no magazine, radio show, or other specialized medium targeting your specific audience.

• ***Direct mail lets you speak directly to your prospect's needs and concerns.*** Because you can be highly selective about who receives your mailer, the mailer can be very specific about how your product or service relates to the prospect's needs. Instead of making general statements about product features, as much general advertising does, you can focus on the specific problems, requirements, and desires of your target market—then show how your product addresses these needs.

For example, a company in Maryland sells filtration equipment used in industry. Although the filters are the same for each application, the benefits the filters deliver are different in each industry. In pharmaceutical manufacturing, the filters contribute to drug purity. In semiconductor manufacturing, they remove contaminants from the manufacturing process to prevent defective chips, which in turn increases yields and profits. Mailings aimed at each industry addressed these specific benefits, generating more interest and response than any generic filter advertising.

• **Direct mail is personal.** Television is a mass medium, with every commercial reaching thousands or millions of viewers at the same instant. Newspapers and magazines are mass media, too, and your ad competes with all other ads in the issue for attention. Direct mail is different. Your sales letter arrives in its own envelope, separated from other advertising messages. Even though the recipient knows it is advertising, its appearance resembles that of a personal letter, which receives a warmer reception. The letter can be written using personal pronouns (I, me, we, you), and it is signed by an individual, not a corporation. It speaks in conversational language, addressing the reader one-on-one. It can even be personalized with the recipient's name and address.

Make your direct mail warm, human, personal, and friendly, and people respond accordingly. Direct mail achieves a level of me-to-you communication not possible in an ad, commercial, or annual report.

• **Direct mail is a flexible format.** Direct mail gives you the greatest degree of flexibility in format, graphics, and copy. Your sales letter, for instance, can be as long or as short as you like: one page, two pages, four pages, six pages, eight pages, or more.

You can include a small pamphlet, a flyer, a jumbo-size brochure, or even a poster in your mailing. You can have two or more letters, multiple brochures, two or more order forms. You can place a microchip in your mailing, so when the reader opens it, she hears a spoken message or music. You can use a nonharmful chemical patch so the mailer smells of steak or flowers or perfume.

You can use color to get attention (try sending your next letter in a bright red or jet black outer envelope!). You can add a third dimension by enclosing a solid object, such as a gift or product sample. The possibilities of direct mail are endless! Compared with a magazine ad, in which you're confined to a seven-by-ten-inch space (or less), direct mail gives you much more freedom,

freedom that can boost your sales, if you learn how to harness and use it creatively.

• *It fits shoestring budgets.* Direct mail can be expensive to write, design, and print, but a simple yet effective mailing can be produced on a small budget. Mailings can be complex packages, with inserts and color brochures and pop-ups and other elaborate gimmicks. Or you can send something much less expensive—a one-page letter in an envelope, or even a simple three-by-five-inch postcard.

Another advantage is that you can mail as many or as few pieces as you wish. When you run an ad in a magazine with a circulation of forty thousand, you are forced to pay for the privilege of reaching all forty thousand people. The magazine doesn't lower the cost of the space simply because only a small fraction of the readers are potential customers for your business.

With direct mail, you can control your quantities precisely, and therefore your budget. For instance, say you've developed a simple sales letter that costs fifty cents apiece to mail (including first-class postage and printing of the letter and envelope). If you can afford to spend only two hundred dollars on marketing, send four hundred letters. Only public relations rivals direct mail for cost-effectiveness and ability to generate results on a limited budget.

NEGATIVE ASPECTS OF DIRECT MAIL IN THE 1990s

Despite these advantages, direct mail, as with every other marketing method, has its drawbacks.

Overall, it has become more difficult to make profit from a single direct mail package, especially when selling products directly from the mailing (mail order). With lead generation, sales potential is usually large enough that even a few sales pay back the cost of the mailing many times over.

But direct mail used to sell mail order products has always had a slim profit margin. A slight shift in response or cost per thousand pieces mailed can quickly transform a losing package into a winner and vice versa.

If quizzed on the effectiveness of direct mail, many experts would say (although not on the record) that direct mail is "still good, but not as good as it once was." Factors contributing to this:

• *Increasing postage rates.* The U.S. Postal Service is a monopoly and therefore raises rates when poor management and inefficient operation create a need for a bigger revenue stream. And even though third-class bulk-rate mail is the most profitable category for the post office, it is the third-class mailers who are often hit with the biggest rate increases.

For example, in a recent four-year period, postage rates for mailing catalogs increased 75 percent. This can easily put smaller and marginally profitable catalogs into the red.

Higher postage rates raise direct mail's cost per thousand, making it increasingly more difficult to break even, let alone make a profit. This has driven mailers to look for alternatives to the standard number ten (business-envelope-size) third-class, bulk-rate direct mail package. These alternatives include double postcards, trifold self-mailers, snap-packs, and postcards.

• *Increased production costs.* The cost of production—paper and printing in particular—has increased significantly over the last decade. Mailing lists are also more expensive, especially highly targeted specialized lists. Add higher postage, and you get a significant increase in the cost per thousand pieces mailed. A higher cost per thousand means the mailing has to generate a higher percentage response to make money.

• *Reduced response rates.* Because there are so many products to choose from and so many being promoted via direct mail, competition for the consumer's direct mail dollars is keen.

As a result, direct mail response rates have declined in recent years. For example, in fundraising direct mail, a 3 percent response rate used to be typical. Today the average is 1 percent or less.

In a recent issue of the *Libey Letter*, direct marketing expert Don Libey observed that while response rates used to be 2 to 4 percent years ago, today response rates of 0.25 to 0.5 percent are common.

In the public seminar business, response rates have declined from 0.5 to 1 percent to 0.25 to 0.5 percent. Similar stories can be told in almost every other area of direct mail.

The conclusion is that while direct mail is still effective and still profitable for many companies, it is harder today, not easier, to create a winning mailing, because of the combined factors of increased cost and decreased response rates.

FEEDBACK, NOT FAILURE

The most common mistake that keeps businesses from enjoying the increased sales and profits direct mail can bring is the perception that if they tried direct mail once and it didn't work, then it does not work for their type of business and will never work for them.

When a direct mail package succeeds, it can be a gold mine, but it can take many tests of a variety of mailings before you hit upon a winner. In launching a new mail order product, the success rate is typically one or two winners out of every ten attempts. In writing direct mail packages to test against existing "controls" (successful packages), the test beats the control maybe 25 percent of the time (and ties it 50 percent of the time, and loses to the control approximately 25 percent of the time).

The biggest mistake you can make is to do a mailing once, have it flop, and conclude, based on that test, that direct mail doesn't work. Yes, I have had direct mailings that were winners the first time out of the gate. But many others were marginals or outright failures—the first time. Still, believing in the idea, I didn't give up. Eventually, many that were initial flops were made to work successfully. Later in the book, we'll talk about testing and how to determine why a mailing didn't work and ways to improve it to create a winner.

SIXTY WAYS TO USE DIRECT MAIL IN YOUR BUSINESS

1. Generate inquiries
2. Follow up sales leads
3. Qualify prospects
4. Sell a product or service directly
5. Generate appointments for salespeople
6. Get prospects to request your brochure or catalog
7. Fulfill inquiries generated by advertising, PR, or other promotions
8. Distribute brochures and catalogs
9. Transmit information
10. Distribute product samples
11. Make an announcement
12. Introduce a new product or service
13. Introduce a product upgrade or enhancement
14. Educate consumers about your product, company, or industry
15. Alert customers about a change in company policy or pricing
16. Thank customers for their business
17. Ask customers for more business
18. Ask customers for referrals
19. Sell accessories and supplies
20. Sell directly to accounts too small for salespeople to call on
21. Invite people to attend a product demonstration, seminar, or sales meeting

22. Get people to visit your trade show booth
23. Renew subscriptions, contracts, insurance policies, and other agreements
24. Upgrade subscriptions, contracts, policies, and agreements
25. Educate customers and prospects about new trends, methods, or technologies
26. Motivate the sales force
27. Recruit new dealers or distributors
28. Make sales to existing dealers and distributors
29. Keep in touch with customers between sales calls
30. Remind prospects of your existence
31. Ask prospects for business
32. Thank customers for recent orders
33. Create goodwill
34. Remind inactive customers of your existence
35. Build a mailing list of qualified prospects
36. Update mailing lists and customer files
37. Conduct surveys, market research, opinion polls
38. Gather information about customer needs, problems, buying habits
39. Announce discounts, price-off specials, and other deals
40. Introduce your company to new area residents
41. Test whether your product has appeal to a specific market
42. Determine which feature or benefit of your product is most important to buyers
43. Stimulate additional sales among current customers
44. Bring prospects into your store or showroom
45. Announce a change of address or new location
46. Distribute promotional newsletters and bulletins
47. Distribute ad reprints and article tear sheets to salespeople and customers
48. Correct and clarify rumors and word of mouth about your company
49. Bring important news to customers first, before it appears in advertisements or is released to the press

50. Revive inactive leads or accounts
51. Reach smaller markets that don't justify a large sales or ad budget
52. Distribute price lists, data sheets, and other ordering information to purchasing agents
53. Screen out people who are not genuine prospects
54. Conduct a sweepstakes or contest
55. Promote special events
56. Sell seasonal merchandise
57. Offer a free analysis, cost estimate, review, or consultation
58. Distribute business gifts and premiums
59. Sell new products and services to old customers
60. Raise funds for charitable events and nonprofit organizations

▾ 2

PLANNING: THE PROFESSIONAL APPROACH

You wouldn't spend $100,000 on a new advertising campaign without carefully setting goals and objectives. Yet, many advertisers will dash off a quick sales letter and mail it to thousands of customers without a second thought.

Planning is the professional approach. It need not be elaborate or complex. But by analyzing your audience, selecting your message, and establishing sales goals, you increase your mailing's chances for success.

This chapter will show you how to plan a direct mail project of any scope and size—from a one-page sales letter to a series of sophisticated mailings sent to thousands . . . or even hundreds of thousands . . . of prospects. We will go through the ten key steps of planning a direct mail campaign, including:

1. Selecting the medium
2. Selecting the product or service to promote
3. Establishing objectives
4. Selecting the market
5. Finding mailing lists
6. Choosing a format, tone, and style
7. Determining your unique selling proposition
8. Identifying supporting features and benefits
9. Creating your offer
10. Scheduling your mailings

STEP 1: SELECTING THE MEDIUM

The first question to ask when planning a direct mail campaign is, "Is direct mail the best medium for accomplishing our objectives? Or should we be using other media—either instead of direct mail or in conjunction with it?"

What other ways are there of promoting your product aside from direct mail? Some of the methods available to you include:

- sales representatives
- space advertising
- directory advertising
- public relations
- exhibitions and trade shows
- catalogs
- brochures
- telemarketing
- case histories
- seminars
- newsletters
- postcard decks
- premiums, incentives, business gifts
- special events
- and many others

The best way to compare direct mail with these other methods and see which works best is by using a tool called the CAST, short for "comparative analysis of sales tools." Figure 2-1 shows a blank CAST worksheet you can copy and use.

How does CAST work? Create a separate CAST worksheet for each effort promoting a specific product to a specific audience. Write in the product and the audience (market) at the top of the sheet.

Next CAST asks you to rate each marketing medium—sales reps, advertising, direct mail, and so on—on its effectiveness in

FIGURE 2-1

"CAST"—Comparative Analysis of Sales Tools*

Product _____

Audience _____

Medium:	Impact or Impression	Size of Audience	Cost Per Contact	Sales Leads	Message Control	Flexi-bility	Timing Control	Repetitive Contact	Reaction Speed	Credi-bility	Closing the Sale
Sales Rep											
Space Advertising											
Directories											
Public Relations/Publicity											
Exhibition/Trade Shows											
Catalogs											
Brochures											
Direct Mail											
Telemarketing											
User Stories											
Seminars											
Newsletters											
Postcard Decks											
Premiums and Incentives											
Other: _____											
Other: _____											

1 = Ineffective   3 = Average   5 = Extremely Effective

* Reprinted from *The Advertising Manager's Handbook* (Prentice Hall), p. 13

eleven categories representing different objectives. You rate each sales tool on a scale of 1 to 5, with 1 being ineffective; 3, average; and 5, extremely effective.

Here are the eleven categories in the CAST worksheet with an explanation of each:

• *Impact or impression.* How memorable is the medium? How much of an impact does it make on the consumer's awareness of the product? A TV commercial broadcast during the Superbowl would rate high for impact, while a coupon insert in the Sunday paper would rate lower.

• *Size of audience.* Is the medium effective in reaching large numbers of people? Direct mail can reach only those people whose names are on a mailing list. A newspaper ad reaches only those who read that newspaper. A billboard reaches only those who drive along that particular road.

• *Cost per contact.* What does it cost to reach a potential prospect with your message? If an ad in a magazine with a circulation of fifty thousand costs five thousand dollars, the cost per contact is ten cents. If a mailing costs five hundred dollars per thousand to mail out, the cost per contact is fifty cents. If it costs $150 to send your salesperson out on the road to visit a prospect, the cost per contact is $150. If your telemarketer makes ten one-dollar phone calls to get through to one person, the cost per contact is ten dollars.

• *Sales leads.* Is the medium effective for generating sales leads? TV commercials may get the consumer to think about your product, but they usually don't generate inquiries. Direct mail, by comparison, is strong in bringing back responses.

• *Message control.* Do you have control of the message in your promotion? When you buy an ad, you do because it appears exactly as you wrote and designed it. With radio advertising, on the other hand, DJs often take liberties with copy, and your commercial might not come across the way you envisioned.

• *Flexibility.* Can you make rapid changes if the promotion isn't working? A telemarketing script can be changed between phone calls. But if you mail five thousand pieces, you can't make a change until you mail the next batch.

• *Timing control.* Do you have precise control over when your message will reach the consumer? When you run an ad in the Sunday paper, you know most of your audience will read it Sunday. When you send out a third-class mailing, on the other hand, it's difficult to know precisely when it will reach your recipients.

• *Repetitive contact.* Can you use the medium to expose your market to the message over and over again? TV and radio commercials can be repeated many times. A speech to the local chapter of a trade association, on the other hand, can be given by you just once.

• *Reaction speed.* How fast can you change, roll out, or pull back on the campaign based on results and feedback?

• *Credibility.* People are skeptical about advertising, but believe what they read about you in a newspaper interview. How believable is your message when delivered in this medium?

• *Closing the sale.* Does the medium merely generate interest or create awareness? Or can it actually help bring in the order?

For your product and audience, you rate the effectiveness of each medium on a 1 to 5 scale, writing the numbers in the appropriate boxes as you go.

Now, when deciding which media to use to deliver your message, you want the ones most effective in achieving those objectives important to you. Let's say you want to generate leads. If only direct mail and directory advertising are rated 5 in lead generation, then these would be the vehicles to consider for your lead-generation program.

STEP 2: WHAT PRODUCT SHOULD BE ADVERTISED?

Now that you have made the decision to use direct mail, what product should be featured? Careful. The answer is not always as easy or transparent as you might think.

Do you feature one product or a product line? Do you sell the deluxe version, the midline model, or the low-cost basic model? Selling the deluxe brings in more money per order, but the higher price might hurt response. Do you sell the product with supplies and accessories as a package, or do you sell the basic product now, then upsell the buyer on supplies and accessories after the initial purchase?

The question you must answer is, "What am I selling?" Finding the answer is not always as simple as you might think.

Let's say you are a bank offering a special low rate on fifteen-year, fixed-rate mortgages. How would you write your mailing? You could talk about the benefits of this particular mortgage— the special low rate, the advantages of fixed versus adjustable rates, the fact that it's paid off in only fifteen years versus thirty for most other mortgages.

But, good as it is, this mortgage is not for everybody. Some people want variable rates. Some want twenty-five- or thirty-year mortgages. Some are willing to pay a slightly higher interest rate if the up-front costs are lower. Maybe, then, your letter should talk about how your bank offers a complete line of home mortgages— "the right mortgage to fit your financial needs"—rather than focus on one specific type. Which approach works best?

Another example: Your company sells a machine that produces boldface lettering on clear tape—lettering for labels, report covers, posters, flyers, overhead transparencies, flip charts, and so on. There are many such machines on the market; yours is medium in quality and capabilities, but very low in price . . . although there are smaller machines that are cheaper but even more limited in function.

What are you selling? If you sell on price, how do you compete with the bottom-of-the-line machines? If you sell on features, what features should you stress? Are your customers at the point where they are shopping around, comparing one machine with another? Or maybe they aren't even thinking about lettering machines, and have to be sold on the idea of buying *any* piece of equipment of this type. Perhaps what you are really selling is better-looking business documents and more professional communications—the end result of using the machine, rather than the machine itself. Which approach would you take? What would you do?

A third case: You sell a complete line of equipment used in chemical plants. You have many different products that perform a variety of functions, but each is purchased by the same customer. Do you highlight individual products, one per mailing? Or should each mailing sell your full product line? Maybe your products are pretty similar to the competition's. In that case, would you be better off stressing service, price, fast delivery, or the reliability and reputation of your firm, rather than trying to convince the customer that the products themselves are superior? What, exactly, are you selling?

Two helpful hints. First, with the exception of catalogs, most successful direct mail sells one thing at a time. Selling two or more items in the same mailer usually doesn't work.

Second, the simpler your offer is, and the easier it is to understand, the better the response. Don't clutter your product offering with too many options, models, colors, and choices. The fewer the choices, the better. If you are going to offer multiple products, or different ordering options, keep everything clear and simple.

STEP 3: ESTABLISH OBJECTIVES

Why are you going to produce and mail a direct mail package? Most people answer, "To increase profits and sales," or "To get leads for new business."

But how many leads? Of what quality? How much profit? How many sales?

The first step in planning a mailing is to set concrete, measurable goals—the more specific the better. Why is this important? Because if you don't have a goal—a specific result you want to get from the mailing—then how do you know whether the mailing has achieved its objective? Only by setting a specific sales objective can you determine whether the mailing is successful.

Many people say, "A two percent response is good." But good for *whom*? For a mailer asking people to pay $495 to attend a seminar, a 2 percent response is excellent . . . and highly profitable. But if you're going for leads, not sales, and you offer a free gift with no strings attached (such as a book, coffee mug, or calendar) to everyone who requests your brochure, it's *easy* to get 2 percent, and 20 percent or more is possible!

Comparing a sales-generating mailing with a lead-generating mailing, or a free gift offer with a straight offer, is like comparing apples and oranges. You have to set objectives that make sense in terms of your audience, your product, your offer, and your sales methods. One manufacturer may want leads for salespeople to pursue; another sells his product direct through a catalog. The type of response you want, and how *much* response you want, is an individual decision that you must make.

Here are some objectives taken from actual direct mail marketing plans (the names, numbers, and products have been changed to ensure privacy, but the excerpts are real):

> There will be a major direct mail campaign to promote the graphics conversion capability of the GENEX graphics software package. Staggered mailings for this

direct mail campaign will begin in late April or early May, and the campaign will total approximately 12,000 pieces when finished. Approximately 2,000 letters will be mailed each month for a total of 6 months. Depending upon the level of response, we can expect approximately 60 inquiries from each mailing of 2,000. Prospects will be invited to see a free demonstration of the GENEX system. The secondary response option is to receive a free brochure on the product.

Program offering: 15% discount on purchase of SM-15 electronic typewriters. Customer to trade in old electric model typewriter EM-10 in exchange.

Audience: Approximately 35,000 office managers. 90% own 10 or more EM-10's.

Goal: Convert 2–3 percent of target audience.

Benefits to customer: Increased capabilities of electronic typewriters. Opportunity to acquire state-of-the-art equipment at significant cost savings.

Problems to overcome: Alienation due to customer dissatisfaction with EM-10 service. Reluctance to spend money. Many customers satisfied with current typewriters. Do not realize the benefits of new electronic technology.

GOALS FOR *SMOOTHFLOW* DIRECT MAIL CAMPAIGN

1. Inform current customers and sales reps that Bruco Membranes and SmoothFlo Filters have joined to offer a complete line of filters under the banner name, SmoothFlow Filtration Systems.
2. Explain to customers the benefits of having a single source for all filter requirements.
3. Ease fears among customers and assure them that the new SmoothFlow is still dedicated to membrane filtration.

4. Generate sales leads. Offer customers new Smooth-Flow filtration catalog.
5. Distribute new corporate brochure (to be enclosed with sales letter).

Sum up your own objectives in a short paragraph or two. Think about the response you want as well as the results you can realistically hope to achieve. The act of writing down objectives will help focus the rest of your efforts.

"Every company must write their own marketing plan," says Ray W. Jutkins of Rockingham Jutkins Marketing. "No one from the outside can tell you what your objectives will be. Consulting on how to do it, using professionals experienced in marketing to aid you with your thinking, planning, and ideas may be good investments. However, when push comes to shove, you and your company must decide your objectives and direction."

STEP 4: DETERMINE YOUR MARKET

The fourth critical step is to determine who you are selling to. In other words: Who is your audience? Who is the prospective buyer? Who will receive, read, and—hopefully—respond to your letter?

The beauty of direct mail is that you can use it to reach *only* those people who are potential buyers for your product or service. This is called *target marketing*. For example, one of my clients, a management consulting firm, finds that they are successful in selling their consulting programs only when they are able to reach the chief executive officer (CEO) of the client company. If they were to advertise in business magazines, they would waste a lot of money, because most of the readers are *not* CEOs. But they can easily rent a mailing list of CEOs and mail their message to those executives only.

"It's still important today for marketers to know their customers and to establish an ongoing means of communication with them," writes Joe Garcia in *Target Marketing* magazine. "The cornerstone of this relationship is targeting—targeting market segments, targeting peculiar, personal messages, whether by mail, phone, broadcast, or some other medium, to those who will be most receptive to the messages."

Think about your customers. Are they male or female? Young or old? Rich or poor? New-wave or grassroots? Corporate or entrepreneurial? City slickers or country folk? Married or single? What do they do for a living? Where do they live? What are their hobbies and interests? If you can accurately describe your typical customer, chances are there's a list of them available.

In some cases, you may be selling one product to many different types of customers, each with different interests and concerns. In such a situation, you can use a standard brochure to describe the product in general, then tailor your cover letter to your different markets. For example, a broker selling investments might stress *low-risk* in a letter to retired couples, but highlight *tax-free* in a letter to doctors, lawyers, and other high-income professionals.

In business-to-business marketing, you often have to reach multiple buying influences within each client company. Let's say you're selling departmental computers to medium-size firms. Mail aimed at top management would talk about service, commitment, and your company's reputation and track record. A letter sent to the company treasurer or vice president of finance could stress the cost savings of a departmental computer versus mainframe-to-micro communications links. Another mailing, aimed at systems programmers, would cover the technical details and explain how the departmental computer integrates easily with existing equipment. And a fourth sales letter, sent to users, would stress the capabilities, features, and improved productivity such a computer could bring to their department.

STEP 5: SELECT YOUR MAILING LISTS

It is not enough to know your market. You must also be able to find a mailing list of such people. Without a mailing list, you can't do a mailing.

Mailing list selection is not as simple as novices think. Old pros know that it is one of the most difficult and time-consuming aspects of direct mail. Mailing list selection is so critical to your success that I devote an entire chapter to it (chapter 4).

STEP 6: FORMAT, STYLE, AND TONE

Next, you want to think about what type of mailing piece you want to send out.

Will it be big or small? Flat or bulky? Expensive or low-budget?

Will it be a full-blown direct mail package with letter, color brochure, inserts, order forms, and reply cards, or just a simple postcard?

Will the copy be hard-sell, or will you go for a low-key, professional approach? Will it be splashy and bright, or quiet and dignified?

Many different formats are available. Selecting the right one is based largely on subjective judgment, knowledge of the audience, the type of offer, and your budget.

Part III of this book describes in detail the many different mailing formats available to you. You'll learn how to put together sales letters, direct mail packages, self-mailers, postcards, and other types of direct mail.

One piece of advice: When in doubt, try a good old-fashioned sales letter in an envelope with a reply card. It's relatively inexpensive and works more often than not.

STEP 7: PICK YOUR SALES APPEAL

Next, decide which sales appeal to stress in your letter.

Your product may have many features that appeal to buyers. And, depending on whether you're after leads or sales, you may decide to mention all of them or just some of them.

But successful advertising copy—in direct mail or any other format—is copy the focuses on *one* key sales appeal.

First, you pick the key sales appeal. This is the benefit that is most important to your customer. If your customers are primarily concerned with cost, the sales appeal would be, "Saves money." If they are more concerned with performance, your key benefit might be "performance guaranteed" or "highest reliability."

Then, you write a mailing piece based on this theme. Sure, you'll talk about other features and benefits. But these will be presented so that they support and reinforce the main message.

Why does successful advertising copy highlight one key benefit rather than many? Copywriter Herschell Gordon Lewis has a saying: "When you emphasize everything, you emphasize nothing." If you stress every point, no point stands out, and the reader doesn't remember your sales pitch. If you highlight one key point, and drive it home over and over, you get your message across, and it sticks in the reader's mind.

How do you know which product benefit is most important to your customer? Experience tells you. For example, you could run two ads, or test two mailings. One says "Easy to Install," while the theme of the other is "Maintenance-Free." By seeing which draws the best response, you know whether the customer is more concerned with easy installation or minimal maintenance.

Your own experience, or that of your sales force, is the best guide for deciding which theme to use. Then you can test it, and see if you were right. If one theme doesn't work so well, you can easily switch to another. That's a major advantage of direct mail—it's easy to test and inexpensive to change.

Another way to find out what customers want is through some type of market research. This can be as informal as speaking to a few customers at a trade show, or as elaborate as a formal survey or focus group. Usually, the informal method of simply getting out there and talking to customers is the best and least expensive way. Formal market research, though helpful, is overrated and probably not necessary. Remember, you can always learn which sales appeal works best through a simple direct mail test. "Direct marketing is research," writes consultant Shell Alpert in *Business Marketing* magazine (June 1986). "Moreover, since direct marketing respondents signal their preferences not with speculative words, but with acquisitive actions—and ultimately, hard-earned dollars—you've got to believe that what they're telling you is 100 percent true."

Companies that use direct mail in volume may do a series of mailings, with each mailing piece highlighting a different sales appeal. One month, I received two mailers from ChemLawn, the lawn specialists. The first envelope had the headline, "CHEM-LAWN HAS A $10 GIFT FOR YOU." The second mailing read, "YOUR DANDELIONS HAVE FINALLY MET THEIR MATCH."

As a homeowner, which has the most appeal to you?

STEP 8: IDENTIFY SUPPORTING SALES POINTS

Now, make a list of all the other sales arguments you might include in your copy.

Remember to talk about benefits, not just features. A *feature* is a descriptive fact about a product or service, such as size, weight, material, form, or function. A *benefit* is what the user of the product gains as a result of the feature.

For example, a feature of my wristwatch is that it is luminescent: the hands and numbers glow in the dark. The benefit is that I can easily read the time, even at night or in a dark room.

How do you uncover benefits? Easy.

Divide a sheet of paper into two columns—*features* on the left and *benefits* on the right.

Look at your product, or study the sales literature written about it. In the left column, list every fact about your product.

Now, in the right-hand column, try to think of how the customer can benefit from each feature. In other words, how does the feature save the buyer time or money, make his job easier, or satisfy his needs in some other way? For instance, a feature of my new car is that it has all-weather tires. The benefit is that I can use these tires all year round. I don't have to switch to snow tires in the winter, so I save money (the cost of buying snow tires) and time (driving to the tire shop to have the tires switched twice a year).

As an example of how to create a features/benefits list, here's one I wrote for a common object—a number two pencil:

▾ Features/Benefits of a Number Two Pencil

Features	Benefits
Pencil is a wooden cylinder surrounding a graphite core	Can be resharpened as often as you like to ensure clean, crisp writing
One end is capped by a rubber eraser	Convenient eraser lets you correct writing errors cleanly and quickly
Eraser attached with a metal band	Tight-fitting band holds eraser snugly in place—won't fall off
Pencil is 7½ inches long	Lasts a long time
¼-inch in diameter	Slender shape makes it easy to hold, comfortable grip
Number 2 hardness	Writes smoothly yet crisply

Yellow exterior	Bright, attractive. Stands out in a pen holder or desk drawer
Sold by the dozen	Convenient 12-pack saves trips to the stationery store
Also available by the gross at a discount	Accommodates the needs of schools and business offices; saves money
Made in the U.S.A.	A quality product. Supports our economy.

This example may seem trivial because of the simplicity of the product. But creating a features/benefits list is immensely helpful in preparing to write copy about unfamiliar or more complex products and services.

STEP 9: DETERMINE YOUR OFFER

Now that you know your main sales theme and your supporting sales arguments, you have to determine the *offer* you want to make. The offer is simply what you send to people who respond to the mailing, combined with what they have to do to get it.

Successful direct mail usually has a free offer, a discount offer, or offers something free along with your paid order. One of the main reasons people respond to mailings is to save money. Another is to get something free.

Also, people are afraid of being hooked by unethical mail order schemes or high-pressure salesmen, so your offer should have no strings attached. Stress that your offer is free, that there is no obligation to buy, that you have a money-back guarantee. Shoppers don't want to commit themselves to a purchase. Buyers want to be assured that they won't be ripped off. Your offer should address these needs.

The action you want your prospect to take is part of the offer.

Use phrases like "Send no money now," "Try it FREE for 15 days," "Mail the no-obligation Trial Request Form today," "Call us toll-free," "Complete and mail the enclosed reply card." These phrases move the reader to action.

Here are some offers made in recent mailings:

"We guarantee complete satisfaction on your subscriptions . . . or your money back for all unserved issues! So be sure to take full advantage of the enclosed Discount Stamp Sheet right now!"

American Family Publishers (magazine subscriptions)

"If this book does not give you all the help you think it will, just return it anytime within 60 days and you will get your money back in full."

Boardroom Reports ($29.95 book sold by mail)

"If you return the enclosed card to us, I will send you the next issue of *Inc.* free. Without cost or obligation to you."

Inc. (magazine subscription)

"To get your free Preview Booklet, just complete and return the postage-free reply card."

Encyclopaedia Britannica

"You need send no money now—and you may cancel at any time. What's more, you are invited to reserve judgment about continuing until after you have had a chance to examine the first Gold Proof for 15 days."

Calhoun's Collectors Society (collectibles)

"For your free copy of all 4 reports, simply detach and mail the above request form in the enclosed postage-paid envelope."

Smith Barney (investments)

"So don't miss this opportunity to apply for EASY MIND. Simply complete the enclosed Application and return it— along with your check for the first month's premium—in the postage paid envelope we've provided."

Mutual of Omaha (insurance)

In your copy, you should sell the *offer* rather than the product itself. If your product is a handbook that sells for fifty-nine dollars, and the customer can return it within fifteen days, then you're not really selling a fifty-nine-dollar book; you are selling the *opportunity* to examine the book, for two weeks, without cost or obligation. Tell the customer he can read the book and use it for fifteen days—free. Then only if he likes the handbook and wants to keep it will you send an invoice for payment.

See the difference? Asking someone to plunk down fifty-nine dollars for an unknown product sold by an unknown company through the mail is scary. And you probably wouldn't get many orders. But offering to let people look at your book for fifteen days, and *then* decide whether they want to buy, is a more attractive deal. Even bookstores don't let you do that!

The same principle works in industrial direct mail. No direct mail letter, no matter how clever, will convince an engineer to order your fifty-thousand-dollar pilot plant system sight unseen. But a good letter *can* get an engineer to ask for a free demonstration of the system—which gets the salesperson in the door and paves the way for that fifty-thousand-dollar sale.

Many different offers are possible. Should you offer a thirty-day trial, a free pamphlet, a pocket calculator, a one-year guarantee, or 20 percent off the price? Choose an offer you feel your prospects would best respond to. Then test it. See which offer works best.

Here is a checklist of common offers. Use it to stimulate your own thinking.

▾ Checklist of Basic Offers

[ ]   free brochure
[ ]   free booklet
[ ]   free catalog
[ ]   free newsletter
[ ]   free information kit
[ ]   invitation to attend a free seminar
[ ]   free information
[ ]   more information
[ ]   free trial
[ ]   free use of product
[ ]   free product sample
[ ]   free gift certificate
[ ]   free coupon
[ ]   use of toll-free hotline
[ ]   free advice
[ ]   free consultation
[ ]   free survey
[ ]   free analysis
[ ]   free estimate
[ ]   free problem evaluation
[ ]   free product demonstration
[ ]   have a technical representative call
[ ]   have a salesman call
[ ]   add me to your mailing list
[ ]   not interested right now—try me again in the future

[ ] not interested—here's why:
[ ] free cassette tape
[ ] free videotape or film
[ ] free gift—for providing names of friends who might be
     interested in the offer
[ ] free special report
[ ] money-back guarantee
[ ] double-your-money-back guarantee
[ ] free sample issue
[ ] send no money now—we will bill you
[ ] cash with order
[ ] order by credit card
[ ] enter our contest and win prizes
[ ] enter our sweepstakes and win prizes
[ ] enter our drawing and win prizes
[ ] discount for new customers
[ ] discount or other special offer for past customers
[ ] your name removed from our mailing list—unless you
     order now
[ ] introductory offer on small trial orders
[ ] free price-off coupon when you request catalog or
     brochure
[ ] extra discounts for large-volume purchases
[ ] free gift with volume orders
[ ] extra discount for payment with order
[ ] seasonal sale
[ ] warehouse inventory reduction sale
[ ] special clearance sale
[ ] remnant sale
[ ] buy at low prices now—before prices go up
[ ] free gift item—in return for your inquiry
[ ] free gift item with your order
[ ] free gift item with your *paid-in-advance* order
[ ] surprise bonus gift with your order
[ ] extra quantity with paid order

[ ] order now—we won't bill you until [specify date]
[ ] order X amount of product/service now—get Y amount free
[ ] order product X—get product Y free
[ ] discount
[ ] discount with paid order
[ ] discount if order placed by a certain date
[ ] discount if certificate or coupon returned with order
[ ] free information if requested on your corporate letterhead
[ ] free information to qualified buyers—others pay X dollars
[ ] call toll-free number
[ ] mail reply card
[ ] complete and mail order form
[ ] complete and mail questionnaire
[ ] complete and mail specification sheet for a prompt price quotation
[ ] send no money now—pay in easy monthly installments
[ ] reply today—while the reply form is still handy
[ ] order today—supplies are limited
[ ] offer good until [specify date]
[ ] this offer is for a limited time only
[ ] subscribe today
[ ] become a member
[ ] discount with trade-in of your old equipment

Offers have a major effect on response rates. Chapter 3 goes into more detail on creating offers that pull in leads and orders.

STEP 10: SCHEDULE, TIMING, BUDGET

Budget and objectives determine the scope of a mailing. For example, if you want to generate 100 orders, and you anticipate a 1 percent response rate, you must mail ten thousand pieces. At five hundred dollars per thousand pieces mailed, your cost is five thousand dollars.

Timing is critical to some mailings, less important in others. Some offers can be mailed year-round with continued strong response. Others are seasonal. For example, for catalog marketers selling gift items, the Christmas season is the most important, and they mail heavily in September, October, and November.

The other concern is whether you need a single mailing or a series of mailings. If your market is large, and your budget limited, you can probably mail one piece for many months or even many years before exhausting all the names available.

On the other hand, if you have a small market, you need a variety of different promotions. If you mail just one piece over and over again, it will soon experience a decline in response rate and wear out.

How many pieces should be in your mailing series, and at what intervals should they be mailed? Dr. Jeffrey Lant, a Cambridge, Massachusetts–based marketing consultant, says you should make contact with your market seven times in an eighteen-month period. Others say to mail more frequently, as often as once a month.

Let's say you decide to do six mailings during the year. You can spread them out, one every other month, to keep your name in front of the prospect throughout the year. Another approach is to do a "blitz" mailing where you hit them with the six mailings in a short period of time, say one a week for six weeks. The first method ensures that the prospect knows about you all year long, while the second method probably makes more of an impression.

Unfortunately, as you will discover, there are no absolute rules or formulas for direct mail. If there were, I could give you a computer program for designing your direct mail campaign. You would enter some information about your product and market, and the computer would come up with the perfect strategy and mailing piece.

Doing direct mail is as much art as science, more trial and error than anything else. You come up with an idea, test it in the mails, and refine your work based on the results. The advantage is that you *can* measure results—an advantage not available with many other types of marketing.

▾3

OFFERS

"*Y*OU *MAY HAVE ALREADY WON $10 million*"
"*The GREATEST SPORTS BLOOPERS VIDEO—yours FREE with your paid subscription to* Sports Illustrated"
"*Affix the token to the reply card for your FREE sample issue*"
"*Buy one—get one free*"
"*FREE tote bag when you become a member*"

Direct marketers rely heavily upon the finding and phrasing of the proper offer to wake up bored consumers, get them to take notice, and persuade them to respond to their ads and mailings.

To get maximum response from *your* direct mail, you must realize the following:

• The offer is of utmost importance to the success of any direct marketing piece or campaign.

• The strategic planning, selection, and testing of offers can make or break a campaign, regardless of how well-designed or well-written the piece is. As a rule, the more valuable and risk-free the offer seems to the reader, the better your response.

• The presentation of the offer—the copy used to describe it, the graphics, the emphasis it receives—is also of critical importance. As a rule, the more you emphasize and stress the offer in copy and graphics, the higher your response rate.

• The clearer and more understandable your offer, the better your response. The lack of a clear, distinct offer can significantly depress response.

This chapter explains what an offer is, different types of offers you can use, and how to construct offers that maximize response.

WHAT IS AN OFFER?

I define the "offer" as:

> What your prospects *get* when they respond to your ad or mailing—combined with what *they* have to do to get it.

Note that the offer has two components:

1. what the prospect gets; and
2. what the prospect has to do to get it.

The simplest, most popular offer in direct marketing is probably the offer of a brochure describing the product or service. In direct mail, this typically reads, "For a free brochure on the Widget 2000, complete and mail the enclosed reply card today." What the prospect gets is a brochure describing your product. What they have to do to get it is fill in and mail a reply card.

This offer can and does work for many, many products and services. However, you can often come up with a much more attractive offer—one that will get many more people to be interested in your proposition and respond to your ad or mailing.

THE FOUR BASIC TYPES OF OFFERS

There are four fundamentally different types of offers: hard, soft, negative, and deferred. In this section, I'll describe them and show you how and when to use each. In the examples, I'll phrase the offers as they might be used in a typical business-to-business direct mail package; however, these can work for radio, print ads, PR, and in many other formats.

- **The soft offer.** My definition of a "soft offer" is as follows:

  An offer in which the prospect requests some type of printed material that is mailed or shipped to him, and makes this request using a reply card or other response mechanism that does not require face-to-face or other personal communication between the prospect and the seller.

The important thing to note about the soft offer is that it's the most painless, risk-free way for the prospect to raise his hand, get in touch with you, and say "I may be interested—tell me more" . . . without the prospect having to subject himself to sales pressure of any kind.

The typical soft offer in a direct mail letter reads as follows: "If you're interested in learning more about what Product X can do for you, just complete and mail the enclosed reply card for a free brochure." Think about what happens: The prospect checks off a box on a reply card and mails it to you. You mail the requested literature back. The prospect has expressed interest, responded, and received information with no personal contact between you.

The soft offer appeals to those prospects who do not have an immediate need and are "just looking" . . . or to those who have an immediate need but want to gather preliminary information without speaking to your agents or sales reps. The soft offer generates a high level of response because there is no sales pressure or risk of being "pitched" by high-pressure sales types. It promises details on the offer, which can be reviewed by the prospects at their leisure.

• **The hard offer.** The opposite of the "soft" offer is the "hard" offer. I define the hard offer as follows:

> An offer that requires or results in face-to-face or other personal contact between buyer and seller in a sales situation or other circumstances where the seller has the prospect "captive" for purposes of doing some selling . . . or an offer that actually requires payment (or promise of payment) in exchange for the product.

In mail order selling, the hard offer is, "Send us payment and we will ship you the product." In lead generation, the hard offer is typically something like: "Call now to schedule an appointment so we can show you how XYZ Product or Service can be of benefit to your company."

In the hard offer, the prospect typically calls or writes the advertiser to arrange a meeting, demonstration, initial consultation, or appointment. There is a direct person-to-person contact between buyer and seller initially over the telephone, and usually later face-to-face. During these contacts, telemarketing representatives or salespeople attempt to persuade the prospects to buy the product or service being offered.

The hard offer is ideal for prospects who have serious interest, an immediate need, are looking to buy something fairly soon, and want to sit down and talk with vendors. The prospect responding to a hard offer, especially if by telephone, typically feels a fairly urgent need to gather more information for an immediate or upcoming purchase.

With a hard offer, the prospect is taking a definite (if tentative or uncommitted) step toward purchase of the product. A soft offer, by comparison, is more of a "let me look you over" or "we'll wait and see" response.

• **Negative and deferred offers.** In addition to hard and soft offers, there are two other basic categories of offers: negative and deferred.

Rather than define them, I will give you the exact wording of these offers as you would use them in a reply card in a lead-generating direct mail package.

The negative offer reads as follows:

[ ] Not interested right now because: _____.
(please give reason—thank you)

Typically, reference to the negative offer is made in the P.S. or elsewhere in the body of the letter, using the following language:

P.S. Even if you are not interested in [name of product or service], please complete and return the enclosed reply card. Thank you.

The negative offer provides a response option for people who are prospects (that is, they have a need or problem your product addresses), but who for some reason do not want to buy from you or get more information on your product.

Normally, a person not interested in your offer will not respond to your mailing. By using a negative offer option, you will get response from a small portion of these people.

The negative offer should be used when you are testing a mailing on a new product, service, or offer you haven't promoted before using direct mail.

The reason you use the negative offer is that without it, if you get a low or no response to your mailing, you don't know whether it's the mailing piece that's ineffective—or whether the product, service, or offer isn't right for the market.

With the negative offer option, people will *tell you* why they are not interested in your offer. Perhaps the price is too high. Or your technology is not compatible with the systems they are already using. Or they don't like your type of product, or don't use it. This information not only helps you readjust your marketing plans; it also demonstrates that the mailing was unsuccessful for reasons other than ineffective copy and design—

something that's good to know if you're the person who wrote or designed it.

A second benefit of the negative option is that it can increase slightly your overall response rate. You might object and say, "But all the people who check the negative option box have told us they are not prospects."

But quite the opposite is true: If someone took the time to tell you why your offer isn't right for them, they *are* a prime prospect—they're telling you they have some sort of need . . . but your product *as described in the mailing* didn't seem quite right . . . and they want you to get back to them with a product, service, or offer that *is* right for them.

Actually, your product or service may be ideal for them, but your ad or mail copy may not have communicated this effectively, or else they misunderstood or didn't read carefully enough. That's OK. By completing the negative offer option box, your prospects have set themselves up in perfect position for follow-up and closing by a skilled salesperson.

If you have ever been a salesperson, then you know the most difficult prospect to sell is the one you can't reach—the one who never responds to your letters or returns your phone calls—or the ones who say they are not interested but won't say why. A prospect who fills in the blank space on your reply card where it says "Please give reason why you are not interested" has framed a specific objection which can be overcome with the proper selling argument. For details on how to do this, see my book *Selling Your Services* (New York: Henry Holt, 1991).

A deferred offer is a variation on the negative offer. Here's how it's phrased:

[ ]Not interested right now. Try us again in _____.
(month/year)

The deferred offer encourages response from prospects who do not have an immediate need but may have a future requirement for your product or service.

Some of these prospects won't check off the soft offer option box—"[ ] Please send me a brochure"—because they think, "If I check off this box they're going to follow up with a phone call and pester me, and I don't have any need right now." The deferred offer option box says to this prospect, "If you have no immediate requirement but may have a future need, you can use this box to let us know that you have a future need, without getting calls and annoying follow-up from salespeople now."

When do you use the negative instead of the deferred offer option? Use the negative offer option when testing a new offer or when you think many prospects might not respond for specific reasons. Use the deferred offer when you think a significant number of prospects are more likely to need your services in the future rather than immediately.

USE OF THE FOUR BASIC OFFER OPTIONS IN LEAD-GENERATING MAILINGS

In most lead-generating mailings you should have two or three options. The best results usually come from having three offers: a hard offer, a soft offer, and either a negative or a deferred offer.

At minimum, you should at least have both a hard and soft offer, with one of the two being the primary offer, the other, the secondary offer.

The primary offer is the one you hope your prospects will respond to, and the one you emphasize in your copy and graphics. For example, if you want a face-to-face meeting with your prospects, you would urge them to call and arrange an appointment. A "free, no-obligation" initial appointment would be your primary offer, and the one you stress in your letter or ad.

The secondary offer is included to give those prospects who will not take you up on your primary offer a second reason to respond. If a prospect is not willing or ready to take you up on your offer of a free initial meeting, introduce the secondary soft offer at the end of your ad or letter copy, for example, "P.S. For a free special report outlining six tax-saving strategies offered by our firm, just complete and mail the enclosed reply card."

Which offer should be your primary offer? Make your soft offer—the offer of free literature or information—the primary offer when:

• the requesting of a brochure or catalog is the typical first step in the buying process in your particular industry or field, and circumventing that step would be counterproductive;

• you feel many prospects would be reluctant to meet or talk with you, so you need some sort of brochure or other literature to create a reason for them to respond to your mailing;

• your product or service is complex and requires a lot of explanation which is best communicated in a standardized written format, such as a brochure or data sheet;

• you have limited staff for telephone contact with the prospect, and your operation lends itself more to the mailing of a standardized inquiry fulfillment brochure or package;

• your prospects are far away and you do not have regional sales reps or branch-office personnel who can call on them in person; or

• you have a great brochure or inquiry fulfillment kit already in place that has proven its ability to (a) screen out nonqualified prospects and (b) sell effectively to qualified prospects.

Industrial equipment manufacturers are a good example of marketers who stress soft offers. Their prospects—engineers and purchasing agents—require a lot of detailed information on technical products before making a buying decision, and this information is communicated more easily in a printed brochure than over the telephone.

Also, having a brochure on your industrial product is standard practice in the industry, and most purchasers won't buy without having a brochure or other technical literature in their purchasing files. So a logical next step in industrial direct mail or ads is the offer of such a brochure or catalog at no charge.

The hard offer should be the primary offer when:

• You would prefer to get a phone inquiry, rather than a written inquiry, because your salespeople are more likely to close when they receive a hot lead via inbound telephone;

• The sending of printed material such as a brochure or catalog is an unnecessary step that only gets in the way and slows down the selling process;

• There is not a lot of information or detail to communicate about your service or product, and you can sum it up quickly and easily in a two-minute phone conversation;

• You have a special free trial offer or other special offer that enables the prospect to try your service or product on a small scale for free or for a nominal fee, and you feel you can get prospects to accept this offer if you can sell them on the phone or face to face;

• Your product or service is unique or unusual and difficult to communicate in printed material, more easily communicated in person or over the phone or via demonstration; or

• Your audience is not print oriented.

An example of an industry that doesn't tend to use brochures is vocational training for adults—offers such as "Learn to be a computer operator in your spare time." One such marketer told me, "We have learned through experience that offering a brochure is a waste. To sell the prospect on taking our program, we have to get them to come to our facility in person for a free introductory class—otherwise it won't work."

Once you have the hard and soft offer options in place, you add either a negative offer option if you want to learn why prospects are not responding as you would have hoped, or a deferred offer option if yours is the type of product or service that is likely to be bought at a future date rather than immediately.

How will the response be split? In a lead-generating mailing for my copywriting services (see Figure 3-1), my letter generated a 10 percent response.

Of the total response, most people—more than 90 percent—check the soft offer ("Please send more information") box on the card.

Fewer than one in ten—less than 10 percent—check the hard offer ("Give me a call") box on the reply card.

I can convert between 10 and 25 percent or more of inquiries to sales within six months of the receipt of the inquiry, if I want that much business. Interestingly, there is no difference in the *quality* of the lead (seriousness of the prospect) between those who check the hard offer box and those who check the soft offer box. Percentage conversion to sales is the same in either category.

Almost all of the response to my mailing is from the reply card. I give my telephone number in my letter, but do not encourage phone calls (I prefer to speak to the prospect only after they have received a complete package of information about my service). I do not give a fax number or encourage fax response.

People check the deferred "Not interested right now" box infrequently, and I mail so few of these letters that I can't give you a statistical result. Qualitatively, however, I can tell you that having the third box for the deferred offer has paid off.

I can recall specific instances where a prospect checked off the "Try us again" option, and when I followed up, I found they did indeed have a specific project in mind to be started at a specific date. Follow-up immediately with literature and later with a phone call at the requested time resulted in a sale in at least two cases.

ENHANCING THE SOFT OFFER

The typical lead-generating mailing uses a fairly standardized soft offer, either "more information" or "free brochure."

While this is adequate in many cases and can work, there is vast room for improvement.

FIGURE 3-1

Bob Bly
Copywriter/Consultant/Seminar Leader

22 East Quackenbush Avenue
3rd floor
Dumont, NJ 07628
Phone: (201) 385-1220
Fax: (201) 385-1138

Dear Marketing Professional:

"It's hard to find a copywriter who can handle industrial and high-tech accounts," a prospect told me over the phone today. "especially for brochures, direct mail, and other long-copy assignments."

Do you have that same problem?

If so, please complete and mail the enclosed reply card, and I'll send you a free information kit describing a service that can help.

As a freelance copywriter specializing in business-to-business marketing, I've written hundreds of successful ads, sales letters, direct mail packages, brochures, data sheets, annual reports, feature articles, press releases, newsletters, and audio-visual scripts for clients all over the country.

But my information kit will give you the full story.

You'll receive a comprehensive "WELCOME" letter that tells all about my copywriting service — who I work for, what I can do for you, how we can work together.

You'll also get my client list (I've written copy for more than 95 corporations and agencies) ... client testimonials ... biographical background ... samples of work I've done in your field ... a fee schedule listing what I charge for ads, brochures, and other assignments ... helpful article reprints on copywriting and advertising ... even an order form you can use to put me to work for you.

Whether you have an immediate project, a future need, or are just curious, I urge you to send for this information kit. It's free ... there's no obligation ... and you'll like having a proven copywriting resource on file — someone you can call on whenever you need him.

From experience, I've learned that the best time to evaluate a copywriter and take a look at his work is <u>before</u> you need him, not when a project deadline comes crashing around the corner. You want to feel comfortable about a writer and his capabilities in advance ... so when a project does come up, you know who to call.

Why not mail back the reply card TODAY, while it is still handy? I'll rush your free information kit as soon as I hear from you.

Regards,

Bob Bly

P.S. Need an immediate quote on a copywriting project? Call me at (201) 385-1220. There is no charge for a cost estimate. And no obligation to buy.

Bob:

☐ Please send more information on your copywriting services.
☐ Give me a call. I have an immediate project in mind.
☐ Not interested right now. Try us again in _____. (month/year)

Name _____ Title _____ Phone _____
Company _____ Address _____
City _____ State _____ Zip _____

My industry is: _____ (Ad agencies — please list types of accounts you handle.)

Type of copy I need: ☐ Ads   ☐ Direct Mail   ☐ Brochures

☐ Press releases   ☐ Feature articles   ☐ Newsletters

☐ Other: _____ (describe)

The key is to use the free offer as a "bait piece" and to maximize requests for the free information you offer by making it seem highly valuable, highly desirable, highly specific, and relevant to the prospect's interests and needs.

There are a number of ways to enhance the soft offer with an attractive bait piece. The most popular, and probably still the most effective, is the offer of a free booklet or special report.

The term *bait piece* refers to free information the advertiser offers in his mailing piece or ad to generate a high number of inquiries. The term is used because the free booklet is offered not for purposes of giving away free information or educating the reader (as the reader is led to believe) but to "hook" the reader by generating a response or inquiry, which can be followed up by telephone and field sales personnel.

Here is a secret many direct marketers do not know and will find difficult to believe:

> The "free booklet" (or "free report" or other free information offer) will *dramatically* increase response to your ads and mailings versus what the response for essentially the same ad or letter copy would be without the free information offer.

Why are free-booklet offers effective? For several reasons. First, today's business prospects, despite being overloaded with reading material, are information seekers, always on the lookout for advice, ideas, and information to help them do their jobs better and more efficiently. Many publishers charge handsomely for such information sold as seminars, audiocassettes, books, newsletters, and manuals. So when people see that they can get similar information from you in the form of a free booklet or special report, they respond. After all, if it's free, they have nothing to lose.

Second, most people are so busy they flip through mail and ads at a frantic rate. The free-booklet offer, with perhaps a cut-out coupon in the ad and a picture of a free booklet, has attention-grabbing power. It forces the reader to slow down, stop, and peruse your copy. The reader thinks, "Oh, this is one of those ads offering something free. Let me take a look for a second and see what I can get." So they call or clip the coupon and request the booklet.

Third, people like getting things for free. In the direct marketing seminars I give nationwide, there is always someone in the audience who says, "Aren't free offers much less effective in business-to-business than consumer marketing? Come on, really, how excited can an executive get about a free booklet or report?"

The fact is, whether they get *excited* is irrelevant; they do get *interested*, and the specific offer of free information dramatically increases ad and direct mail response rates.

The free-booklet offer is so effective, and so important, that for the majority of marketers using direct mail to generate leads, I think it's a mistake not to have such an offer as part of your mailing.

The reason is simple: Unless the prospect has an immediate, urgent need to pick up the phone and call you, your mailing is largely a matter of indifference to them. It's just another sales pitch—one of many they will receive by mail or phone that day.

The prospect feels no need to respond, and doesn't. The free-booklet offer solves that problem. It says to the prospect, "Even if you have no immediate need, don't have time to read our mailing, and don't want to think about our product right now, at least mail back the reply card. You'll receive something of value in return"—and the mailer converts inaction to a response.

Here are some typical titles from successful free booklets offered in actual direct mail and print ads:

"15 ways to improve your collection efforts"	(RMCB)
"14 winning methods to sell any product or service in a down economy"	(Bob Bly Seminars)
"Should I Personalize? A direct marketer's guide to personalized direct mail"	(Fala Direct marketing)
"Choosing business software"	(IBM)
"Aldus guide to desktop design"	(Aldus)
"Family-owned businesses: the 3 most common pitfalls . . . and how to avoid them"	(Consulting Dynamics)
"A special report: Productivity Breakthrough Projects"	(JMW Consultants)
"33 ways to make better displays: What every marketing executive should know about point-of-purchase display marketing"	(Display Masters)
"Steel Log: glossary of metal terms"	(Specialty Steel)
"7 questions to ask *before* you invest in DP training . . . and one good answer to each"	(Chubb Institute)

The title of your bait piece is all important because it determines, in large part, whether you can get prospects interested enough to send for it. So choose the title with care. If you are selling desktop publishing systems and your target market is advertising agencies, how about a booklet titled "What every ad agency executive should know about choosing and using a desktop publishing system to reduce production costs and increase client satisfaction." If you owned an ad agency and were losing clients because you didn't offer desktop publishing capability, would you send for this free report? I should think so!

One way to create additional interest and make your bait piece stand out even more is to produce your information in the form of an audiocassette, videotape, or computer-based presentation.

One advantage of these formats is that they are not widely used and are therefore a bit unusual and likely to get greater notice. Also, audiotapes, videotapes, and floppy disks tend to stand out in an in-basket crowded with paper.

Other advantages? Tapes and floppy disks usually get past secretaries who screen mail and throw away lots of paper. Because a tape or disk has a higher perceived value and is a tangible object, it won't get thrown away.

Experience has shown that prospects will take the time to either listen to or view the tape or disk, or at least make sure it gets passed on to the right prospect within the organization. Printed pieces are not treated with the same degree of importance. Finally, even if the prospects don't immediately listen to or view the tape or disk, they will probably keep it in a desk drawer, rather than throw it away. So every time they open the drawer, they see the tape or disk imprinted with your company name and phone number.

Audiocassettes are the easiest and least costly audiovisual medium to use as information bait pieces. Some marketers using audiocassettes think that briefer is better, and limit the message to ten or twenty minutes. But if the tape contains pure, useful information, it can be much longer. I have been successful promoting both my seminars and my consulting and copywriting services using cassettes on marketing and sales topics that are ninety minutes long.

Audiocassettes don't require the high level of production that videocassettes do. You can record a live presentation or speech at work, a meeting, or an industry event, edit it in a studio, and offer it as an attractive bait piece on audiocassette.

What will all this cost? To hire someone with professional-quality recording equipment to record a presentation costs one hundred dollars to two hundred dollars plus travel expenses. Studio time goes for thirty-five dollars to seventy-five dollars per hour and should take less than half a day. To duplicate my presentations onto C-90 (ninety-minute-long) audiocassettes, including a laser-printed cassette label and soft plastic box, costs less than $1.50 per cassette in quantities of less than fifty.

Videos are another story. You can expect to pay a professional at least one or two thousand dollars to record you live or in a studio. If you want a full-blown production with sets, special effects, and live location shooting, an eight-minute video can cost five to fifteen thousand dollars or more, just for production. Cost to duplicate five hundred copies of an eight-minute video is about seven dollars per cassette with a cardboard box and typed label; plastic boxes and four-color packaging can run much higher.

A relatively new promotional medium is the floppy disk. Sales and informational presentations can be put on floppy disks that the prospect can view using a personal computer. Some direct marketers are reporting success with this medium, though I have no personal experience with it (other than conventional demo disks for software, which are a different thing).

THE HARD OFFER IN MAIL ORDER SELLING, CONSUMER AND BUSINESS

The term "hard offer" has a slightly different meaning in business-to-business direct marketing (especially for lead generation) than it does to the traditional consumer mail order marketer.

In mail order selling, a hard offer is usually thought of as an offer that requires the prospect to pay for the product in advance. The seller ships the product only after payment is received via check, money order, or credit card. Use of a hard offer eliminates credit and collection problems because there is no billing of buyers—everyone pays up front.

By comparison, the soft offer in mail order selling is the classic "bill-me" offer. Here, the prospect can order and receive the product with no money up front. The seller sends a bill and is paid later.

There are many variations on these themes and intermediate ways of phrasing these offers that are neither classically hard nor soft. These may be of interest to you if you are selling business books, forms, gift items, audiocassettes, office products, or other business-to-business products in a traditional mail order or one-step promotion—that is, your prospect orders directly from your ad, direct mail package, or catalog.

SPECIAL CHALLENGES OF
BUSINESS-TO-BUSINESS MAIL ORDER

Business-to-business mail order is a little different from consumer mail order.

In consumer mail order, you can get away with having a hard offer only, and indeed many consumer mail order marketers do not offer a bill-me option. They want to avoid the hassle and headache of collections, and so require payment for the product up front.

Also, with the price tag on many consumer mail order purchases being so low, it often doesn't pay to go after deadbeats who keep your product but don't pay your bill. The deadbeat realizes it's not worth your time and effort taking him to court for a ten-dollar past-due balance, and therefore doesn't feel an urgent need to respond to your dunning letters.

What's more, you don't need to have a bill-me option for consumer mail order marketing. In many cases a bill-me offer will increase gross response, but the question is, how many of those who order on a bill-me basis ultimately pay up?

Many consumer mail order firms, especially smaller operators, do quite nicely without a bill-me option. They know it's easy for the consumer to either write a check, send a money order, or charge it to her American Express, Visa, or MasterCard account. I run a small but profitable part-time mail order business selling books, manuals, and audiocassettes to writers and would-be writers, and we have not had a problem with our payment-with-order policy.

In business-to-business direct marketing, on the other hand, I believe it is a mistake, in most instances, not to include some type of soft bill-me offer to supplement the hard pay-up-front offer. Why? Because the recipient is ordering for his or her company, not for personal use. And most companies are not set up to issue advance checks. Their usual procedure when making a purchase is to issue a purchase order, receive the product, be satisfied with it, get an invoice, then pay you when they are ready—hopefully in thirty days but more often in sixty or ninety days.

If your selling method forces business buyers to go against their company systems, they may decide that buying from you is too difficult or just not worth the extra aggravation and effort, and may take their business to a competitor who is more flexible about payment terms and options.

For instance, if you demand payment up front, the prospect may not even know how to get the accounting department to issue and send you an advance check. Therefore, when selling to businesses, you should offer both a soft bill-me option as well as a hard payment-with-order option.

VARIATIONS ON HARD OFFERS FOR BUSINESS-TO-BUSINESS MAIL ORDER

Fortunately, there are a number of options for using hard offers with soft offers in business-to-business mail order selling that may help you structure an offer that meets your customer's needs as well as your own requirements.

This is done by extending a traditional hard offer (payment up front) with a second one that is conditional, rather than a pure "soft" bill-me offer.

Let's compare the two. The traditional soft offer says, "We'll send you our product and bill you. If you like it, you can keep it and pay the bill. If you don't, you may return it, tear up the invoice, and you will not owe us any money."

Perhaps your product is expensive or easily damaged, and you are afraid of people taking advantage of you by ordering the product, keeping it, and not paying for it.

One solution is to use a modified bill-me offer, in which you agree to send an invoice, but do not ship the product until the invoice is processed and payment is received. This would read as follows:

> [ ] Bill me (NOTE: Product not shipped until payment is received).

The modified bill-me is similar to a soft offer in that it allows the prospect to respond without enclosing any payment and to receive an invoice from you which he can put through the system for payment. At the same time, it is similar to a hard offer in that the product is not shipped until it is paid for.

A variation of the modified bill-me is to agree to ship the product right away but to withhold shipment of any gift item or other premium until payment is received. There is a danger, if your premium is too attractive, that people will send for your product on a bill-me basis just to get the premium, then return the product and keep the free gift.

To prevent this, you use a modified bill-me offer as follows:

> [ ] Bill me (NOTE: Bonus Gift is shipped when payment in full for your order is received by us).

Even if you allow prospects to keep the premium if they return the product, this modified bill-me offer cuts down on freebie seekers. It requires ordering *and payment* for the product in order to get the gift, and few will go to that trouble just to get a free item from you—unless the premium is costly and truly fantastic.

You can even go further and state in your offer that, if they don't want to keep the product and decide to return it for refund, they must return the premium as well as the product. This provides an added degree of protection and is useful when the premium is fairly costly to you.

Another way to modify the bill-me so that you reduce the number of prospects who send for the product and don't buy it is to ask prospects to initial or sign the order card or provide a purchase order number or actual purchase order. For example:

[ ] Bill me. Our purchase order number is: _____.
Signature (required for all bill-me orders): _____.

For phone orders, you can't get a signature, but you can still ask for a purchase order number.

I strongly recommend that you avoid requiring prospects to send you an actual purchase order. The purchase order number itself is sufficient. If you insist on getting an actual purchase order, you will lose sales from prospects who are too busy to generate the paperwork required.

As a rule of thumb, your mailings should never force prospects to read a lot of instructions or fine print or fill out a lot of complicated paperwork. The more work you force your prospect to do to respond to your mailing, the lower your response will be.

HARD OFFERS IN BUSINESS-TO-BUSINESS LEAD GENERATION

A typical hard offer in lead generation is a check-off box on the business reply card or ad coupon that says, "Have a salesperson call me." By choosing this offer option, the prospect is saying, "I have sufficient interest in your product or service that I am willing to have your salesperson make a presentation to me or at least chat with me over the phone a few minutes." This is a more aggressive, active response toward initiating the next step in the selling process than the soft offer, "Send me a brochure."

ENHANCING THE STANDARD "HAVE A SALESPERSON CALL" HARD OFFER

"Have a salesperson call" is probably the most widely used hard offer in business-to-business lead generation. It paves the way for the in-person sales visit that, for many marketers, is a crucial step in getting the prospect to buy their product or service.

In practice, however, very few prospects will choose to ask a salesperson to call or visit. The reason for this is twofold.

First, prospects don't view salespeople as helpful or beneficial. In fact, the word "salesperson" signals to the prospect that sales pressure will be exerted—something most prospects want to avoid.

Second, most prospects don't want to hear your "sales pitch" or "presentation." Again, the word "sales" implies that the prospect will be subject to high-pressure selling tactics aimed at benefiting the seller, not the buyer.

The solution is to "repackage" the "Have a salesperson call me" offer, using skillful copywriting and a change in tactics to convert what is perceived as a "sell job" to what is perceived as a meeting that is beneficial and helpful the prospect.

In a nutshell, this is done by replacing the words "sell" and "sales" with words that are more prospect-oriented.

To start with, do not use the term "salesperson" when referring to the person who will contact or follow up with the prospect. Replace "salesperson" with any of the following (or create your own title, as appropriate):

Account Representative
Senior Consultant
Technical Specialist
Account Manager
Account Supervisor
Industry Specialist
Program Manager
Program Planner
[name of product or service] Specialist

For example, if you are selling financial services, don't say "Have a sales representative call." Say, "Have a Financial Consultant call." Or "Have a Financial Planner call" (if your salespeople are truly financial planners). If you are selling a relational database, say, "Have a Database Specialist call."

Next, do not use the words "sales call," "sales pitch," or "sales presentation" when referring to the initial appointment you are seeking with the prospect. Instead of a sales call or sales presentation, suggest to the prospect that he contact you to arrange a(n):

initial appointment
free, no-obligation consultation
free estimate
free analysis
needs assessment
audit
exploratory meeting
evaluation of their requirements
initial planning session
free demonstration
free executive briefing
free seminar

Therefore, your hard offer might now read:

[ ] Please have a Technical Consultant call to arrange a free analysis of my network requirements. I understand there is no cost for this initial analysis—and no obligation.

If you phrase your offer this way or in a similar fashion, you will get more response than if you simply say "Have a salesperson call."

Why does this technique work so well? If you think about it, you'll realize that any initial contact between buyer and seller is not merely a selling opportunity for the buyer, but also has value to the seller *independent of whether the seller buys your product or service.*

For example, if a printer makes a presentation and gives you a price quotation, that price information is of value even if you do not hire the printer, since it provides a benchmark against which you can judge other quotes to see if they are "in the ballpark." You might also gain some helpful pointers on the print production process, and the printer is not compensated for giving this knowledge to you unless you actually hire her to do the job.

Or say you have an initial meeting with a financial planner during which you ask questions about investment options, your financial situation, and so on. In order to convince you that he or she is knowledgeable, the financial planner will probably answer many of those questions, and you can put that information to work even if you decide not to hire that particular person. Therefore, the initial "sales meeting" has value inherent in the meeting itself and independent of the product or service.

The strategy of offering "free consultations by experts" versus the traditional "sales presentation by our salesperson" simply recognizes this inherent value and increases response by highlighting the value of the initial meeting or contact itself, rather than asking for a "sales opportunity."

Because this is a book on marketing and not on personal selling, a discussion of what takes place in such a meeting is beyond the scope of *Power-Packed Direct Mail*. It is discussed in great detail in my book *Selling Your Services*, available from my Resource Guide listed in the appendix. Basically, while you still use the initial meeting as a sales tool to get the prospect to buy, you make sure to demonstrate your expertise (and further convince the prospect that you are the right vendor for the job) by providing useful information and suggestions during your presentation.

When asking the prospect to request an initial consultation or meeting, two very important rules apply:

1. Make it clear that the meeting or consultation is free.
2. Make it clear that the meeting or consultation is given without obligation of any kind on the part of the prospect to buy from you.

Especially when your offer sounds too good and generous to be true, the prospect becomes suspicious that there is some hidden charge or implicit agreement requiring them to buy something. Always stress in your copy that "This initial consultation is absolutely free, and there is no obligation of any kind." Don't assume that your prospects understand this to be so. State it directly in your offer copy, both in your sales letter and again on the reply card.

THE OFFER IS MORE IMPORTANT THAN YOU THINK

The proper choice and presentation of the offer can make a *tremendous* difference in how successful your ad or mailing is in generating immediate response and sales.

For instance, a company selling business forms decided it could increase sales with the offer of "buy-one, get-one-free."

Conventional wisdom says that FREE is the most powerful word in direct marketing, so this offer should work well.

But the marketing manager had doubts. So he tested "buy-one, get-one-free" against a "two-for-one" offer. And guess what? "Two-for-one" *substantially* outpulled "buy-one, get-one-free," contrary to what all the marketing textbooks and his own consultant had predicted.

Interestingly, the two offers are materially the same. Only the phrasing is different. But as anyone who has ever written advertising copy knows, phrasing is important. The right phrasing can lift response dramatically. And the wrong copy can destroy results for a mailing with a good product or offer.

Another firm had similar results in a mailing selling custom-imprinted executive business gifts. Here they tested "buy X quantity, get Y free" against a straightforward discount of "25 percent off our regular prices." Again, conventional direct marketing wisdom says the free offer is all-powerful. But test results disputed this, because the "25 percent off" significantly outpulled the "buy X, get Y free."

A free offer in lead generation almost always increases response, but I have seen numerous instances in mail order where "free" did not pull as well as a discount, percent-off, or two-for-one deal.

From these case histories we may conclude the following:

Ad agencies, consultants, and other experts or authorities in direct marketing *cannot* predict with any accuracy which offer will pull best. An experienced direct marketer can recommend different offer strategies that may prove profitable and are worth testing, but no one can say for certain which offer will be the winner, nor can anyone guarantee results.

Personally, I am good at coming up with attractive offers and recommending to clients which two or three should be tested. But, while I can pretty easily spot an offer that is destined to be a loser, *I can never predict with certainty which of the better offers will be the winner*. Nor can you.

Therefore, the only way to come up with the best offer for your product or service is through testing.

THE NEED FOR TESTING

Most marketers do not spend enough time and effort experimenting with and testing different offers.

To them, the offer is more of an afterthought, with the description of the product or service as the main thrust of marketing communications.

But in reality, the offer can be the spark that overcomes the indifference barrier. Your prospects are bombarded by ads, mailings, and brochures daily, and respond to very few of them. An enticing offer can make your communication stand out, overcome inertia, and get your prospect to take action.

Because of the small quantities being mailed, many entrepreneurs and smaller firms believe they do not have sufficient quantity to justify testing of offers. But a statistically valid test of offer A versus offer B can be done even with mailings of only four or five thousand pieces, with half offering A and half offering B. Huge volumes are not a prerequisite for testing.

Even if you do not do classic "split" or "A/B" testing (statistically valid testing of two offers with simultaneous mailings of offer "A" versus offer "B"), you should still vary your offer from mailing to mailing and experiment with different variations to see which works best.

DIFFERENT OFFERS WORK IN DIFFERENT MEDIA

The tendency is to assume an offer working in one medium (for example, direct mail) will do equally well in all other media (for example, print advertising, radio, television, electronic bulletin board).

While this is frequently true, it is not always so. As a result, if you are adapting an offer successful in one medium to a different medium, test cautiously before rolling it out.

For instance, a client in the corporate entertainment field came up with a neat offer he thought would work well in a mailing, and I agreed. It involved a special promotion in which the prospect could get a discount on entertainment at his next meeting or event by filling out and returning a simple form.

Response to the mailing was only about 1 percent—less than we had both hoped. Looking back on it, I feel the form may have been too lengthy and time-consuming to fill out.

But when he made this offer in a small print ad, it generated a substantial numer of inquiries—a far greater quantity than the more costly and involved mailing. (In fact, we used extras of the mailing piece as the fulfillment package for the ad.) Based on this, we did no additional mailings but continued to run the offer in small fractional ads in meetings magazines, with good results.

A ONE-WORD CHANGE
INCREASES RESPONSE 15 PERCENT

Here's another case study that demonstrates the importance of proper selection and phrasing of the offer.

A company selling mainframe utility software used simple mailings to generate sales for its products, most of which sold in the range of eight thousand to twelve thousand dollars. The standard offer was for a free thirty-day trial of the product. Prospects would call or mail the reply card to receive a magnetic tape and instructions for running the program. At the end of thirty days, they could return it and owe no money, or keep the software and be invoiced by the software firm for the license fee.

The owner of the company found that he could increase response by 15 percent (that is, go from 1 percent to 1.15 percent) by changing just one word in this offer. Can you guess what it was?

He changed "trial" to "use," so the offer was changed from

"30-day free trial" to "30-day free use." What prompted the change? Explains the owner, "When we talked to data processing people, we found that the word *trial* had a negative connotation. It means coming in on evenings and weekends, interrupting normal DP operations, running tests on files, and a lot of extra work overall—and who wants to do more work?

"Based on this, we decided to try *free use* instead of *free trial*. Our reasoning was that people buy a product to use it, so who wouldn't want to use it for free? Apparently, we were correct, because this one simple change boosted response—and of course, cost us nothing to implement."

Interestingly, the firm achieved a second, similar lift in response by making a second change in the offer—again, by changing one word. Can you guess what it was?

They changed *thirty*-day free use to *sixty*-day free use. As the owner observes, "The typical thirty-day free trial in software is really not enough time for the busy DP professional to evaluate a product. A tape may very well sit for two or three weeks in someone's in-basket before they get around to even opening the package. At that point, they return it because the free-trial-period deadline is approaching and they don't want to be stuck with the product.

"We figured we could eliminate this anxiety by just extending the trial period another thirty days, and it seems to work. Our prospects feel that's a fairer amount of time to do the evaluation, and the offer increases response slightly." The company tested a ninety-day period with no increase in response over the sixty-day period.

MAKE A POWERFUL GUARANTEE PART OF YOUR OFFER

If you are selling directly from your ad or mailing, be sure to back your hard offer with a powerful guarantee. This can be a guarantee of service, support, or return of money.

For a product, the best offer is a strong, long, unconditional money-back guarantee. For example: "If for any reason . . . or for no reason . . . the X-100 Widget is not for you, return it within 60 days and we will refund your money in full—no questions asked."

A longer guarantee period will generally outpull a shorter guarantee period. A ten-day or fifteen-day guarantee period is not long enough for the prospects to comfortably evaluate your product and decide whether it is for them. They will feel rushed and may just return your product without trying it to avoid having the deadline expire and being stuck with it.

A thirty-day guarantee is sufficient for most products, and I think sixty or ninety days is even better. Many books on direct marketing say to offer a one-year guarantee, but this can be a problem with products that are frequently updated, such as software or annual directories—the prospect could just return the old product and ask for the new one after a year.

Make your guarantee as unconditional as possible. The more conditions you put on the guarantee, the less the prospects are likely to trust you—and buy from you.

For instance, one sales training firm marketing a book on selling offers a money-back guarantee if the sales techniques in the book do not help the reader increase income, but adds this condition: "Just return the book along with a record of all your sales calls made using our techniques and the sample scripts you wrote following our outlines." The reader thinks, "Yeah, and you'll just say I wrote a lousy script and not refund my money."

A strong guarantee is an unconditional guarantee. The best offers contain an unconditional money-back guarantee with a long trial period. Prospects are wary of offers that seem conditional or that might obligate them in any way. The offer should be easy to take advantage of, easy to understand, risk-free, and not require any commitment or obligation on the part of the prospect.

DEADLINES AND OTHER ACT-NOW INCENTIVES

Although it is not absolutely necessary, putting in some incentive or reason for the reader to respond now instead of later will generally increase response. Why? Because the prospect is bombarded by direct mail, sales messages, and offers daily. Your best chance of getting a response is to give her sufficient motivation to respond right now, while the piece is still in her hands.

If there is no "respond-now" incentive, the prospect may think, "I'll put this aside and get to it later." Unfortunately, a direct mail package is similar to the Sunday newspaper: If you don't read it within forty-eight hours of getting it, chances are you never will: too many other things surface to compete for attention. In direct mail marketing, a decision deferred usually translates into a decision never made: no response.

How do you get the prospect to act now instead of later? The simplest mechanism is to put a time limit in your copy. This can either be a specific date ("Offer expires March 15, 1995") or a generic time limit ("You must reply within 15 days to take advantage of this special free offer").

Which is better? Both are effective. A specific date is good if you have enough control over the timing of your mailing to ensure that delays in printing and mailing don't make the deadline date obsolete—for instance, you don't want prospects to get a "reply by April 15th" mailing on April 21st. If you do not have precise control over timing, or you print your letters in large quantities and mail them regularly, a generic "respond within the next 15 days" offer may be better from a logistics perspective: no matter when the mailing arrives, it's always accurate.

A client asked me, "How long should the time limit be? Which is better—12 days or 20 days or 25 days or 30 days or two months or something else?"

Obviously, the shorter the time frame, the more pressure there is on the prospect to respond now. On the other hand, too short a time frame may make the prospect feel rushed and uncomfortable. For business-to-business direct mail, a twenty-day time limit seems reasonable: short enough to motivate action, long enough to allow some breathing space. I do not know of any tests of long versus short deadlines and would be interested in hearing from anyone who has data on this.

A variation of the specific date or time frame offer is the limited number offer: "This offer is limited to the first 200 people who respond to this letter." This tactic gets prospects' attention because they have no idea how many pieces you mailed and therefore want to reply right away to ensure that they are one of the first 200 to respond.

Other variations? The limited offer is most effective when you can give a legitimate, credible reason *why* the offer is limited.

For instance, one computer company's offer was free prototyping of the prospect's application. Because prototyping takes time, and the company had a limited staff, they could handle only so many such prototypes at one time.

The sales letter pointed this out, saying, "We urge you to hurry. Based on response to previous mailings, we will get lots of requests for this free prototyping offer, and if you are not one of the first to respond, you may well have to wait longer than we'd both like." This works because it's specific and believable.

If you don't have a real reason to limit the offer, you can always invent one. But, when doing so, always respect the intelligence of your prospects. For instance, one mailing I received told me I had to request a certain report right away "because we have printed only 1,000 copies and supplies are limited." I suspected, though, that if requests exceeded one thousand, they would simply print more—so their act-now incentive lacked a bit of credibility with me.

PREMIUMS FOR MAIL ORDER AND LEAD-GENERATING OFFERS

A premium is a free gift the prospect gets for responding to your mailing. Premiums work well for mail order as well as lead generating business-to-business direct marketing.

A major question business-to-business direct marketers ask is, "Does the premium have to relate to the product or service being sold?" The answer is that it depends whether you are generating leads or sales.

Dick Benson, a successful consultant and entrepreneur, writes in his book *Secrets of Successful Direct Mail* that in mail order selling, it is not necessary for the premium to relate to the product being sold. The most important criteria for premium selection, according to Benson, are the perceived value and desirability of the premium. If the premium relates to the product, fine, but that's of secondary importance.

In mail order, I agree that having a desirable premium is important, and is probably the main selection criteria, but I put more weight on trying to select a premium related to the product. Also, you have to be careful with premiums, because many companies—especially defense contractors and subcontractors—have policies forbidding employees to accept gifts from vendors.

In fact, one of my clients, a firm selling custom-imprinted business gifts by mail, did a test mailing in which they compared a straight 25 percent discount on gift items with a 25 percent discount combined with the offer of a free clock radio. Not only did the premium not increase response; it actually *depressed* it.

When I mentioned this at a seminar, one participant said, "It's probably because the buyers didn't want to be perceived as accepting a gift or bribe for giving the vendor their companies' business." Another said, "Whenever a mail order company attempts to bribe me with an expensive gift, I always assume they are inflating the price of their products to make up for it, and I would rather just not get the gift and instead pay less for the product."

A third participant voiced a similar observation: "In today's economy, the corporate employee increasingly looks good to his or her management by being a good purchaser. That means getting the product at the lowest price possible." His comment suggests that a larger discount would work better than a free gift intended for personal use.

This observation also suggests that if you *do* give a premium for business-to-business mail order offers, make it something related to the product and of value to the buyer's company rather than an item for individual use. For instance, a publisher selling technical journals and information databases on CD-ROM offers a free CD-ROM stacker and reader with the purchase of a group of its expensive CD-ROM-based information products. That's a premium that has high perceived value, is closely related to the product, and makes the prospect look like a smart buyer.

For lead-generating, too, I think the best use of a premium is to offer something directly related to the product or service. My experience shows that unrelated premiums of high value bring in large quantities of freebie seekers and other unqualified leads.

Modest premiums that are directly related to the product or service increase the total number of responses. And, while you will always get some inquiries from those pain-in-the-neck people who seem to send for anything and everything that's free, you will also get a greater volume of qualified leads from good prospects.

FREE DEMONSTRATIONS, SEMINARS, AND WORKSHOPS

Another hard offer commonly used in lead generation is the offer of a free demonstration, seminar, or workshop.

The advantage of a demonstration is that it clearly deals with a specific product, and therefore anyone who accepts qualifies themselves as having a significant degree of interest in that product. Another advantage of a demonstration versus a seminar is that "seminar" implies a scheduled event that the prospect must attend at a certain time and place, whereas a "demonstration" can be given at a time convenient to the prospect.

"Seminar" implies that the event is not a straightforward demonstration of a product but is designed to provide attendees with useful information about a certain topic. For instance, if your product is the W-100 Motionless Mixer, the seminar would not be about the W-100 but might be titled, "How to Specify Motionless Mixers in Chemical Processing Applications." Of course, the manufacturer's agenda is to get process engineers to write their specifications so that the installation requires use of a W-100 rather than a competitor's mixer.

But this agenda must be subtle, and the program must be primarily educational in nature. Otherwise, prospects will feel you have misrepresented the program by calling it a seminar instead of a sales pitch and will not be favorably inclined to do business with you.

Is the free seminar approach right for your firm? It depends on your marketing situation. Free seminars work well when introducing new products or technologies. They are effective for products that require hands-on demonstration, such as software. If your product solves or deals with a problem or issue of interest to the prospect, a seminar is a good place to educate your prospects on the subject—and in doing so, convince them they should deal with you as an expert source of help.

Should you charge for the seminar? No. My feeling about free offers is that they should be free. If your purpose is to use the seminar to generate leads and sell your product or service, make it free. If your purpose is to make money in the seminar business, then put on a more extensive program and charge what other seminar marketers are charging.

Don't take the middle position and charge twenty-five dollars or some other nominal fee to cover costs. What qualifies attendees as prospects is that they took time out to go to the program, not whether they got in free or paid some nominal registration fee. Charging instead of making it free also reduces attendance, defeating your goal of generating the greatest number of qualified sales leads.

Those who have never offered a free seminar as a marketing tool think they'll be flooded with responses because of this free offer. Sadly, that is not the case. The mere fact that the seminar is free is *not* going to get people to come running to your door. Executives, managers, and professionals in business are flooded with invitations to go to free seminars and don't have time for even a small fraction of them.

Will your seminar offer get response? If you're in an industry where free seminars are not commonly used, the uniqueness of your offer may generate a lot of interest and get a lot of response.

On the other hand, if free seminars in your field are common and many of your competitors are offering them, don't expect your audience to get excited about it. The free seminar may work if the topic is attractive or your product is exciting. But don't expect adding a free seminar offer to your reply card to generate a breakthrough for you.

When writing an ad or mailing to get people to attend your free seminar, you should *not* take the approach that all you have to do is say the seminar is free and people will want to attend. Instead, you should write copy that will make the reader say, "This sounds wonderful; I would really love to go. How much does it cost?" Then, tell him or her it's free.

Free seminars need not be as comprehensive as fee-paid seminars and educational programs, nor should they be as long. Most free seminars are a half-day—typically two or three hours of presentation.

When making a free seminar offer to corporate types, have it on a weekday, preferably in the morning, starting with breakfast.

Tuesday, Wednesday, or Thursday are the best days; avoid Monday.

When making free seminar offers to self-employed and entre- preneur types, an evening or weekend is usually best. Saturday morning is better than Sunday.

SAMPLINGS, TRIAL RUNS, EVALUATION

Three additional hard offers you can use in your business-to- business lead-generation programs are sampling, trial runs, and evaluations.

A sampling involves offering to render your service or allow the customer to use your product on a sample basis. This may be for purposes of either demonstrating your product or service or analyzing the customer's needs to determine which of your ser- vices or products is right for him.

For example, a firm selling equipment that turns chemical powders into pellets says in its sales letter, "Send us a 5-pound bag of your compound and tell us what size pellets you want. We will run it through our pelletizer and give it back to you to show you the quality of the pellets it can produce for you."

Another company, a computer firm, sells a software program that businesses can use to quickly create customized applications that work with their databases. One potential buyer was skeptical and asked, "How long would it take to develop a so-and-so application for our database using your product?" The software firm's salesperson, instead of answering, sat at the computer, started pressing keys, and had the application prototyped and working with the database within thirty minutes. The prospect's response? "Decision made! We're buying your product!" While this took place on an individual sales call, it could be the basis of a direct mail offer.

A trial simply allows the prospect to use your product or service for a specified period at no cost and with no obligation to buy. The pelletizer manufacturer's letter went on to say that if the sample pellets were satisfactory, they would ship a pelletizer to the prospect's plant and let them use it for a month with no obligation. Then they would have the option to send it back (at the manufacturer's expense) or buy it.

A trial offer can also work with a service. If you have an on-line database, a long-distance telephone service, or another service where users are billed by the hour, a common offer is "30 minutes' use free."

In the second edition of his book *Profitable Direct Marketing* (Chicago: NTC Business Books), Jim Kobs shows two ads from MCI. The first offers five dollars off the prospect's long-distance phone bill; the second offers thirty free minutes of long-distance calls. The "30 free minutes" pulled roughly twice the response of "$5 off" because customers perceived thirty free minutes of long distance as a greater value than five dollars off. The thirty minutes of free service is, in essence, a free trial of the long-distance phone service.

Similar to the free trial is the evaluation. The tone of this offer is, "Let us send you the product at no cost and you can perform whatever technical evaluation is required to help you decide whether it is the right product for you. If it is not, send it back and owe us nothing. If it is, you can buy it for the list price of X dollars."

One problem with evaluations and free trials is that prospects send for the product to evaluate, and then, because of inertia, laziness, or lack of time, don't do anything with it.

One way to overcome this problem is to combine the free trial or evaluation with an incentive to perform the evaluation or make a buying decision within a specified period of time. For instance: "If you accept our free trial offer and then decide to invest in the So-and-So System within the next 30 days, you will get 10% off the regular purchase price."

Mention of this time-limited offer in your ad or mailing will increase overall response. Periodic reminders to prospects via mail or phone during the evaluation period will help get more of them to try the product and increase the conversion rate of leads to sales.

TO SUM UP ...

1. Do not underestimate the importance of offers.
2. The product or service is key, but a good offer can often mean the difference between a so-so and a super response.
3. Most marketers do not spend nearly enough time on creating and testing offers.
4. You can never tell which offer will pull best and should therefore constantly try and test different offers.
5. When in doubt, the surest way to increase response is to make the offer free and without risk or obligation of any kind.
6. In mail order selling to businesses, have both a hard and soft offer.
7. In lead generation, always include a free booklet or other free information offer in addition to your hard "meet-with-me-now" offer.

FINDING AND USING MAILING LISTS

WHAT IS A MAILING LIST?

A *mailing list* is a list of people—potential customers for your product or service. It contains their names and addresses, so you can address an envelope to a particular individual on the list.

This can be a list of customer and prospect names you've collected over the years. It can be a list of individuals or companies compiled from standard reference books, such as yellow pages, club membership rosters, or industrial directories. Or it can be a list of people who have previously responded to a direct response offer—people who either bought a product or requested further information by mail or phone.

You can rent mailing lists from many different sources. Or you can put together your own lists.

Depending on how you count, there are between thirty thousand and fifty thousand lists available for rental on the market today.

Over a *billion names* are on these lists. Most of the people who have enough money to respond to your offer are on some mailing list somewhere.

Best of all, you can select only those portions of a list that are right for your offer. Selection is available by state, city, zip code, industry, income, job classification, sex, and many other factors.

THE IMPORTANCE OF THE LIST

A mailing list is more than a means of reaching your market. The list *is* the market.

To judge whether your product can be promoted by direct mail, ask yourself, "Is there a mailing list available?" If there is a list, you can use direct mail. If no list is available, it will be very difficult to reach prospects by mail . . . unless you can create or compile your own list.

Most experts agree that selecting the right mailing list is the most important factor in determining whether your mailing will be successful.

"*Whom* you mail to is more important than *what* you mail," says the American List Council, a mailing list firm. "The best performing lists in a given mailing will often out-pull the losers *in the same mailing* by a margin of 10 to 1!"

In other words, proper list selection can increase response *tenfold*, or 1,000 percent. Instead of a hundred replies, you can get a thousand, if you choose the right list of prospects to mail to.

Think about it a moment, and you'll see this makes sense.

For example, let's say the New York Ballet sends out a mailing offering season's tickets to the ballet at a 20 percent discount.

Now, if you dislike ballet, no direct mail writer is going to convince you to subscribe to those tickets, no matter how persuasive the mailing.

On the other hand, if you're a ballet lover, and you've been thinking of going to the ballet more often, the New York Ballet's mailing has great appeal to you. You might very well buy tickets, even if the mailing is not particularly persuasive. The mere announcement of the availability of such tickets by mail might be all that's needed to prompt you to write a check.

You can see that an offer for season tickets to the ballet would do much better when mailed to a list of proven ballet lovers rather than the general public. Thus, proper list selection is critical to a successful response.

This chapter is written to help you select the right lists and put them to good use. Although the information here applies to every mailing, from small to large, I pay extra attention to a much-ignored area—that of getting lists for small mailings ranging from fifty pieces to five thousand. This is a special problem area, since most mailing list firms have a minimum order of five thousand names.

DEFINING LIST REQUIREMENTS

In chapter 2, you learned that one of the ten key steps in planning a mailing is defining your audience. This definition determines which list to use.

When selling to consumers, look for a list of prospects who have responded to past offers similar to yours. If you're selling a diet plan, the best list would be of people who have paid money for diets and other weight-loss programs in the past . . . Weight Watchers members, perhaps.

If such lists are not available, you could mail to lists of people you think are likely to respond to your offer. If you're selling a luxury round-the-world vacation, you might mail to lists of millionaires, corporate executives, and other people who can afford to indulge themselves.

In business-to-business direct mail, lists are chosen according to industry and job title. You could, for example, get a list of process engineers and plant managers at chemical plants in Florida and California that employ one hundred people or more. (Size and location are popular selection factors for industrial mailings.)

Don't neglect secondary markets when selecting lists. A manufacturer of telecommunications equipment was mailing exclusively to telecommunications managers at small and medium-size companies. But the manufacturer soon discovered that independent telecommunications *consultants* have a big say in determining what systems their clients ultimately purchase. So the manufacturer added these consultants to its mailing list. And sales slowly began to rise.

HOW MANY PIECES SHOULD YOU MAIL?

Sometimes quantity may be limited by the actual number of names available. Often, for highly specialized offers, there may be only a few thousand or even a few hundred names on the list.

But for other products, such as personal computers or telephone systems, the potential market is in the hundreds of thousands.

In that case, your budget determines how many names to rent, how many pieces to mail. If you've budgeted five thousand dollars for the mailing, and your mailing costs one dollar apiece (including postage and list rental), then you can afford to mail five thousand pieces.

What if there are more names on the list than you can afford to mail to? Then select the portion that contains the best prospects—the people who most closely fit your profile of the "ideal customer." For example, if location is important, you might select only those prospects in your state. And if the list is still too large? Start breaking it down by zip code, so you get the five thousand prospects closest to you.

MAILING FEWER THAN FIVE THOUSAND

When you rent mailing lists from list brokers, list managers, list compilers, and other resources, the usual minimum order is five thousand. Some may allow a smaller order, such as one thousand or two thousand. But most have a minimum of five thousand names.

What do you do if your mailing plans are less ambitious? There are several options.

First, you can always rent the five thousand names, use only as many mailing labels as you need, and keep the rest for future mailings. Of course, lists get dated quickly, so if you don't do additional mailings within six months or so, the labels will soon be out of date. However, the whole five thousand names will probably cost only two hundred to three hundred dollars, so your investment isn't that tremendous.

If you're mailing to your "house list"—prospect and customer names you've collected through the years—then quantity poses no problem. You simply print as many labels, envelopes, and sales letters as you need.

Don't overlook salespeople's personal files as a source of names. Ask your salespeople to send you copies of their address books, Rolodex files, or business card files. People whom your sales force has personal contact with are usually highly responsive to mail describing new products and services.

A third alternative is to compile your own list of names from directories, magazine articles, yellow pages, or other published sources. This is an excellent way to get good lists in small quantities. For example, *Business Marketing* magazine publishes an annual directory of advertising agencies that specialize in business-to-business advertising. Many trade journals publish similar directories unique to their industries. Often, compiling your own list is the best way to obtain a small, industry-specific list of names. Most mailing list firms are unaware of these specialized lists.

A fourth alternative is to rent mailing lists from organizations that do not require a minimum order of five thousand. These include publishers, trade associations, professional societies, seminar sponsors, and other organizations that have their own lists but are not in the list business full time. For example, the

New Jersey chapter of the Business/Professional Advertising Association rented me its membership list, which contained only 125 names, for a nominal fee. And this list pulled a higher response for me than any other list I had previously mailed to.

THE BEST LIST IN THE WORLD

What is the best list in the world—the list that will pull the most response for you, mailing after mailing?

That question is easy to answer. It's your house list—the list of your current and past customers, and prospects who have already responded to your previous mailings, advertising, and other promotional efforts.

You know that it's usually much easier to get more business from current customers than it is to go out and win *new* customers.

Well, when you mail to your house list, you're trying to get more business from current customers, versus mailing to rented lists, which means going out and trying to win new ones.

Direct mail expert Nick Medici says, "The most important part of a direct mail package is who's sending it." When you do direct mail to your house list, the company sending it is an organization the prospects know and trust—yours. Therefore, more people respond than if the mailing was from a company they don't know.

Direct marketers frequently rent the house lists of other companies that have customers who are good potential prospects for their own products. When renting and mailing to the house list of another company, marketing consultant Jay Abraham advises you to get an endorsement from the list owner for your product and feature it prominently in your mailing piece. That way, the audience sees that the company they know recommends your product, and you get a higher response, closer to that of your own house list than of a rented list.

House lists, if kept up to date, can outpull outside lists by twice as much or more.

Therefore, when doing a mailing, use your house list first. It may not be as much fun or as exciting as going for new lists and new customers. But it is usually much more profitable.

BUILDING THE HOUSE LIST

Despite the tremendous value of house lists, many firms do not keep good records and so have no way of tapping into customer and prospect files for mailing purposes.

If I've just described *your* operation, you should immediately set up a system that allows you to capture customer and prospect names and build a list suitable for mailing. This is a two-step process.

In step one, you make sure that the names of all customers (people who place an order) and prospects (people who respond to advertising, direct mail, publicity, and other promotions) are stored in a central file or database. For mailing purposes, all you need is name, address, and company (if it's a business). But for marketing purposes, you should try to capture additional information: date of purchase, items purchased, and total amount of sale for customers, and the publication date, magazine, and title of the ad generating the inquiry, for prospects. In addition, you'll want to record the telephone number for follow-up by telephone salespeople.

Be sure to instruct the people who take orders and fulfill inquiries to capture and record this information. Create and distribute a standard questionnaire or form to ensure that they get it all down. Below is a form I use in my own business to compile information on people who inquire about my copywriting and consulting services. Adapt it to suit your own needs.

PROSPECT DATA SHEET   Date _____

Source of inquiry _____

Response via (mail/phone) _____

Name _____ Title _____

Company _____ Phone _____

Address _____ Room _____

City _____ State _____ Zip _____

Type of business:

Type of project/services required:

STATUS:

[ ] Sent literature on (date): _____

[ ] Enclosed these additional material: _____

_____

[ ] Next step is to: _____

[ ] Probability of assignment: _____

[ ] COMMENTS: _____

_____

CONTACT RECORD:

Date: Summary:

_____

The second step is to record the names and addresses in such a way that they can be easily reproduced on labels or envelopes for mailings. (It is simply too time-consuming to retype the names on envelopes each time you want to do a mailing.)

The best way is to store the names on disk and use the personal computer to prepare labels, envelopes, and personalized letters with the prospect's name and address. You can use a database or filing program for storing your list, and then link it with a word-processing program to print the mailing. For example, I can produce personalized letters, envelopes, and labels on my Kaypro II using Perfect Filer (file storage) and Perfect Writer (word processing). Consult your computer dealer for which software would work best with your system.

An alternative is to reproduce the names on labels using your office copier. You simply type the names and addresses on special blank forms (called "label matrices"). Then, to reproduce labels, you place sheets of gummed labels in the paper tray, place the label matrix sheet on the copier, and press the copy button. Your office supplies dealer or local stationery store can sell you these labels and sheets and show you how to use them. It's easy once you know how, and I stored my lists this way for many years before I finally bought a computer. But almost no one does this now, because of the widespread use of PCs.

MAINTAINING THE HOUSE LIST

Hundreds of thousands of people move to another address or change jobs every month, so it is important to keep your house list current. Mailing to an old address, where the people you have listed no longer reside, is like sending a door-to-door salesman to make a house call when nobody's home.

Ideally, all the names on your mailing list should be people who have either purchased your product or responded to advertising within the past twelve months.

Go through your list every six months to make sure it contains only current names. Remove names that are over a year old, and place them in a separate "historical file."

You might do a special mailing to the historical file, to see if these people still have an interest in your product (and if they are still at the listed address). Anyone who responds to this mailing is placed back on your active mailing list of prospects.

I've seen companies that have piles of old sales leads that they've never responded to. Rather than waste money mailing expensive literature to these people, or throwing the leads away, send a special mailing asking if they are still interested in receiving the information they requested. Again, anyone who responds can be placed on your mailing list of active prospects. Below is a letter I sent to people whose inquiries had been ignored.

> Dear Friend:
>
> Last week I joined Koch Engineering as advertising manager. And I was shocked to discover that, because of a clerical error, some advertising inquiries had been ignored—including yours.
>
> A few months ago, in response to our advertisement (copy attached), you requested information on the Koch static mixing unit. As the ad explains, this "motionless mixer" saves money, cuts energy costs, and takes less space than conventional "dynamic" mixers.
>
> If you're still interested in receiving a free technical brochure describing the benefits and applications of static mixers, fill out the enclosed reply card, drop it in the mail, and I'll rush you a copy of our bulletin without delay.
>
> Sincerely,
>
> Bob Bly, Advertising Manager

RENTING MAILING LISTS

If you plan to mail five thousand pieces or more, there are many thousands of mailing lists available.

Lists can be rented from many different resources for one-time use. You pay a fee, which is typically thirty-five to seventy-five dollars or more per thousand names, for the right to use the mailing list.

The person renting you the list gives you the names, either on pressure-sensitive labels, "cheshire" (ungummed) labels, floppy disk, computer tape, or in some other form.

You are entitled to use the list once. If you want to use it again, you have to pay to rent it again.

Some people think, "Ah, but I will photocopy the labels or duplicate the floppy disk. That way I can mail to the list again and again, without paying!"

But you can't. First, it is dishonest, and second, illegal. List owners and managers have taken special precautions that allow them to identify cheaters. For example, the list contains several fake names. You won't be able to spot them, but anything you mail to one of these fake names will actually go to the person renting you the list. If he receives two mailings addressed to a fake name, and you've only paid to use the list once, he knows you are cheating. Penalties are stiff, and more and more list managers are going after cheaters. So if you want to use a list more than once, you'll have to pay for it.

(Of course, if someone responds to your mailing, that person's name goes into your prospect or customer file, and you are allowed to mail to him or her as often as you wish, without paying any additional fee to the list company.)

There are basically two types of lists available for rental: response lists and compiled lists.

RESPONSE LISTS

For most consumer offers, response lists are best. These are lists of people who have responded, in some way, to a direct response offer that was made through the mail, in a print ad, or in a television commercial.

Experience shows that people who have responded to direct marketing offers in the past are likely to do so again. Some folks just love to buy through the mail—others hate it. This is why you usually get better results with response lists than with a list of names someone has collected.

But beware. Experience also shows that people who respond to one type of offer may not necessarily respond to a different type. So your best bet is a list of people who have responded to an offer or expressed interest in a product similar to yours.

For example, let's say you are selling a home-study course on how to learn computer programming.

Your first choice might be to use class rosters of students who have taken introductory computer courses at local community schools. But when you mail to this list, you get poor results. Why? Because even though the people on the list have demonstrated an interest in learning about computers, they are not proven mail buyers. Many people who enjoy taking courses with live instructors would never consider doing it by mail. And so results are disappointing.

A second choice might be lists of people who have already responded to offers on home-study courses in computers, electronics, or other similar subjects. These people have demonstrated willingness to study by mail, and have an interest in technology. You mail to this list, and get good results. The response list has worked for you.

You might then do a small test mailing to a third list: people who have responded to home-study courses in subjects not necessarily related to computers. You might find that this type of person just loves to take courses by mail and will respond to course offerings in a wide variety of subjects. This list is worth testing (see chapter 9 for advice on how to do a direct mail test).

Some other factors to consider when selecting response lists:

• How frequently do the people on the list order products by mail? The more often, the better.

• What was the date of their last purchase? The more recent, the better.

• What is the average size of their purchase? People who have responded to ten-dollar offers in the past may not necessarily respond to hundred-dollar offers. One hundred dollars may be too rich for their blood.

• What type of offer did they respond to? A person who subscribed to a magazine to receive a free clock radio may not respond to your subscription mailing unless you also offer a free gift. A person who responds to direct response TV commercials may turn a cold shoulder to direct mail. Look for people who have responded to offers similar to your own.

COMPILED LISTS

As the name implies, a compiled list is a list of names that someone has put together from other sources. The most common source for compiled lists is the phone book—especially the yellow pages for business lists. Other sources include automobile registrations, association memberships, club directories, guest book signatures, and warranty card registrations. For reasons already discussed, compiled lists are usually not as good as response lists for consumer offers.

But there is a limited number of compiled lists of *business* prospects. Therefore, when doing business-to-business direct mail, most of the lists you rent will be compiled. Also, some compiled lists can work well with certain consumer offers, too.

There are many more compiled lists available than there are

response lists. So by using compiled lists, you can reach out to more potential customers. You get the best results when the characteristics of the people on your list match the profile of your "ideal customer."

In business-to-business direct mail, you can specify a list by industry, job function, and title. For a recent mailing, I went to my list broker with the following specifications: "IS managers, systems analysts, and programmers in information systems in banks, insurance companies, and financial services firms." The broker was able to produce such a list.

Often, compiled lists can be broken down according to highly specific categories. Information systems lists, for example, can be selected by size of the company, industry, types of software used, type of mainframe computer, type of operating system. You can say, "I want a list of DP vice presidents at companies with sales of ten million dollars a year or more, and that use IBM mainframes with VM or MVS operating systems."

Take the time to build a profile of your ideal customer, then describe his characteristics to your list dealer. The more the people on the list fit your description, the better your response.

Think about sales opportunities that exist in your industry. If you're a home contractor or handyman, for example, one good market for your services might be lists of people who have just moved to your town. (According to Marketing Assurance, a marketing firm, new residents will spend eight to ten times more than established residents.)

Conversely, mailing to people who do *not* match your specifications can be disastrous. One company selling software did a mailing to medium-size businesses, and the mailing generated zero response. Following up by phone, they discovered their error: the software program ran only on Apple computers, and none of the companies on the list owned Apples. They then did a second mailing to a list of Apple owners, and this time they got some inquiries.

OTHER TYPES OF LISTS

In addition to response lists of buyers of mail order products, and compiled lists, there are several other types of lists direct mailers use. These include:

• *Subscription lists.* Lists of magazine subscribers are excellent for direct mailing, because they are all "response lists" in that the subscriber had to respond to a mailing to order a subscription.

There are two types of magazine subscription lists, paid and controlled. *Paid circulation subscription lists* are lists of subscribers who pay to subscribe to the magazine. Most consumer publications have paid subscriptions.

Controlled circulation subscription lists are lists of subscribers who get the magazine free. Many business, trade, and technical publications have controlled subscriptions. The reader fills out a "qualification card" that has been mailed to her, certifying that she holds a certain position within the industry. This qualifies her to receive the industry publication free of charge.

Those who favor paid circulation lists cite the fact that the subscriber has paid for the magazine, therefore is a mail order buyer and has more interest in the publication. Those who favor controlled circulation lists are looking for more complete coverage of an industry, job title, or demographic—because they are free, controlled circulation publication subscriber lists are generally bigger and contain a larger percentage of the market than paid subscription lists.

• *Donor lists.* Fund raisers rent donor lists, which are lists of people who have donated to charitable and worthy causes by mail. But because donors are mail responsive, mailers use them for a variety of commercial offers as well.

• *Attendee lists.* Many mailers look for lists of people who have attended trade shows and seminars. Seminar attendees are especially attractive to mailers selling via mail order because the seminar attendees registered by mail *and* spent a substantial amount of money to take the seminar.

• *Membership lists.* One way to target business and professional prospects is by renting membership lists of associations and professional societies. If your business is regional, contact local chapters of these groups and see if you can rent their lists of members and prospective members.

• *Credit card lists.* Mail order sales increase when you take credit cards. Therefore, mail order companies seek lists of prospects who hold major credit cards.

• *Sweepstakes.* Many mail order marketers use sweepstakes to increase sales. Dick Benson, a Georgia-based mail order consultant, says sweepstakes can increase response up to 50 percent for some offers. However, some people like sweepstakes, and some (like me) do not. Therefore, mailers planning sweepstakes will look to rent lists of sweepstakes participants.

• *Databases.* A database is a collection of consumer names and addresses from which lists can be selected based on demographics, psychographics, and other lifestyle indicators. For instance, if you were doing a mailing to get people to subscribe to a newsletter on infertility, you could select women, age 30 to 45, who are married, do not have children, have household income of fifty thousand dollars or more, and subscribe to other newsletters or magazines.

• *Hotlines.* A hotline list is a selection from a response list of buyers who have bought something within the last six months. Since the more recently the prospect bought, the more likely he is to buy again, hotline lists can be extremely effective and rent for a premium price.

WHERE TO GET MAILING LISTS

If you rent mailing lists, you can go to one of three different sources: the list owner, the list manager, or a list broker.

The owner is the person or organization who has originally collected, generated, or compiled the list. The owner could be a magazine publisher (for subscriber lists), trade association or professional society (membership lists), trade show or seminar sponsor (attendee lists), mail order company (response lists), or any organization that has a list of customers or prospects.

Some list owners deal directly with list users. Most, however, prefer to turn the management of their list over to professional list managers. These firms actively promote the list, and take care of administrative details such as printing of labels, shipping, billing, and so on.

The advantage of going to a list manager is that these people are experts in using mailing lists. They can take a look at your mailing piece, product, marketing plan, or a rough draft of your letter and recommend lists they know would be good for your offer. List managers don't normally charge for giving advice and recommendations, nor do they mark up the price of lists; instead, they make their money from commissions paid to them by the list owners.

So one way to get started is to contact one of the reputable list managers in the industry. Some of the best are listed below. Call them, explain the nature of the mailing you are planning, and get their advice on which lists you should use. Also, ask for a copy of their list catalog; most list management firms provide them at no cost.

A third source is the list broker, a small firm or self-employed individual who gives you more personalized service than a list manager or owner. Again, there is no charge for using the list broker's service, since he gets his commissions from list owners and managers.

▾ Directory of Mailing List Suppliers

Here are companies that rent mailing lists. For more information, call or write to each firm and request their current catalog.

American Business Lists Inc.
5639 S. 86th Circle
P.O. Box 27347
Ralston, NE 68127
(402) 331-7169
Business lists. Compiled primarily from telephone directories. Free catalog.

American Direct Marketing Services, Inc.
1261 Record Crossing
Dallas, TX 75235
(800) 527-5080
(214) 634-2361
Business and consumer lists. Free catalog.

American List Council, Inc.
88 Orchard Rd. CN-5219
Princeton, NJ 08540-8019
(800) 526-3973
(201) 874-4300
Compiled and response lists. Free catalog.

Chilton Direct Marketing
1 Chilton Way
Radnor, PA 19089-0350
(800) 345-1214
(215) 964-4365
Business, industrial, and engineering lists. All compiled from trade journal subscription lists. Free catalog.

CorpTech
12 Alfred St.
Woburn, MA 01801
(617) 932-3939

Database America
100 Paragon Dr.
Montvale, NJ 07645
(201) 476-2000

Dun & Bradstreet
3 Sylvan Way
Parsippany, NJ 07054
(201) 455-0900

Dependable List Compilation
257 Park Ave. South
New York, NY 10010
(800) 221-7328
(212) 677-6760
Compiled and response lists.
  Catalog available.

Direct Media
200 Pemberwick Rd.
P.O. Box 4565
Greenwich, CT 06830
(203) 532-1000

D.M. Inc.
R.R. 4
Waseca, MN 56093
(507) 835-3204
Specialists in educational,
  church, club, and institutional
  lists. Other lists available.
  Catalog available.

Dunhill International List
  Co., Inc.
2430 W. Oakland Park Blvd.
Fort Lauderdale, FL 33311
(800) 223-1882
(305) 484-8300
Business and consumer lists
  in over 2,000 categories.
  Free catalog.

Ed Burnett Consultants, Inc.
2 Park Ave.
New York, NY 10016
(800) 223-7777
(212) 679-0630
Business, consumer,
  professional, institutional, and
  response lists. Free catalog.

Edith Roman Associates, Inc.
875 Ave. of the Americas
New York, NY 10001
(800) 223-2194
(212) 695-3836
Compiled and response lists.
  Business and consumer.
  Catalog available.

Fred Woolf List Co.
Fortune Building
280 N. Central Ave.
Hartsdale, NY 10530
(800) 431-1557
(914) 946-0336
(212) 679-4311
Consumer and business lists.
  Free catalog.

Fritz S. Hofheimer Inc.
88 Third Ave.
Mineola, NY 11501
(516) 248-4600
Over 24,000 lists. All compiled.
  Free catalog.

Hitchcock Business Lists
25W550 Geneva Rd.
Wheaton, IL 60188
(800) 323-2596
(312) 462-2332
Computer users and retailers,
   manufacturing, engineer, and
   executive lists. Free catalog.

MM Inc.
541 N. Fairbanks Ct.
Suite 1910
Chicago, IL 60611
(800) 621-5073
(312) 467-9500
Medical lists (doctors, dentists,
   hospitals). Free catalog.

PCS Mailing List Company
125 Main St.
Peabody, MA 01960
(617) 532-1600
Business and consumer. U.S.,
   Canada, and international lists.
   Free catalog.

Penton Lists
1111 Chester Ave.
Cleveland, OH 44114
(216) 696-7000
Business, industrial, professional,
   government, and executive
   lists. All compiled from trade
   journals' subscription lists.
   Free catalog.

Qualified Lists Corp.
135 Bedford Rd.
Armonk, NY 10504
(212) 409-6200
(914) 273-6700
Business, consumer, fund-raising
   lists. Free catalog.

Targeted Marketing Inc.
Box 5125
Ridgewood, NJ 07451
(201) 445-7196
Lists of computer users, owners,
   vendors, sites. Free catalog.

Technical Publishing
A company of the Dun &
   Bradstreet Corporation
1301 South Grove Ave.
Barrington, IL 60010
(312) 381-1840
Specialized lists, mostly
   industrial, engineering, and
   business. All compiled from
   trade journal subscription lists.
   Free catalog.

Uni-Mail
One Lincoln Plaza
New York, NY 10023
(800) 223-1033
(212) 580-3000
(312) 998-8990

A wide selection of consumer
   and business lists.
   Free catalog.

TIPS FOR PROFITABLE LIST USE AND SELECTION

1. Your main responsibility is coming up with an accurate, detailed definition of your target market. If you can clearly describe your "ideal customer," a list broker or manager can probably find the right list for you.

2. Be sure that this definition is correct and complete. For example, if you're selling custom hubcaps for Cadillacs by mail, be sure to insist that people on the list own Cadillacs.

3. Don't overlook your own resources. You may have access to directories, attendee lists, subscriber lists, and other sources that list managers don't know about. Compiling and collecting your own list can make sense, especially if your product is highly specialized and your market is small.

4. Most lists range in cost from fifty dollars to $120 per thousand names. Some response lists may be slightly higher. But beware of con artists who offer you "special" lists for five or six hundred, or one thousand dollars per thousand or more.

5. In business-to-business direct mail, I have gotten excellent results from trade journal subscriber lists, trade show attendee lists, and membership lists of professional societies and trade associations.

6. The first step in creating an ongoing, successful direct mail program is to get your own in-house list in order . . . or to start building one if you don't already have one.

7. More and more lists are now available on magnetic media, making it possible to word process your own envelopes and letters on your personal computer.

8. Don't be intimidated by list people or their jargon. Mailing list selection is a highly involved, complex subject. But you really don't need to know much about it—that's the job of the list broker or manager.

9. You can find list brokers and managers in the yellow pages, or through referral. They also advertise their services in such magazines as *Zip*, *DM News*, and *Direct Marketing*. The firms just listed are all reputable.

10. Never rent the whole list at once. Always start with a small portion, and test. Then, if successful, you can rent more names and mail more pieces.

11. Rand McNally and other companies sell maps of the United States by zip code, by mail and in stationery stores. If you do regional or local mailings, get such a map. It will help you in selecting which zip codes to mail to.

12. In consumer mail order, the best list is one that contains people who have bought a product similar to yours, at a similar price, recently. If you sell rose bushes by mail, rent lists of people who have bought seeds and plants by mail.

13. In business mailings, look for lists of prospects who have demonstrated, through some action, interest in your topic. For example, if you are promoting a seminar on Total Quality Management, don't just rent compiled lists of engineers and managers who are in manufacturing. Rent lists of people who have attended quality seminars, subscribe to quality journals, or are members of a quality society or association.

14. Selections from mailing lists (choosing a portion of the list by zip code, sex, age, job title, industry, etc.) cost an extra five dollars per thousand names rented and are almost always worth the extra money. For example, if you sell software designed for small one- or two-person businesses, don't rent a list of all businesses in the United States; rent a list of all businesses in the United States with one or two employees.

PART II

CREATING AND PRODUCING DIRECT MAIL CAMPAIGNS

▾ **5**

HOW TO WRITE DIRECT MAIL COPY THAT SELLS

COPY IS KING

In direct mail, the *word* is king," says Malcolm Decker, creative director of the Stamp Collector's Society of America, writing in *Who's Mailing What!* "Copy is the architect of the sale. Design and art are the strongly supportive interior designers that often set up the sale. Because lookers are shoppers while *readers are buyers* [italics mine], if you can firmly engage your prospect—and *keep* him engaged—through reading, you're on your way to a sale."

There is a long-running debate in direct mail about the importance of copy versus graphic design. Rather than argue about it, let's just say that *both* are important, then do the best job of writing and design on every piece we produce.

However, unlike general advertising, where some advertisements are almost totally visual, direct mail does need words to sell. This chapter will give you some tips that can help you write your own copy or review copy that has been written for you.

GET TO KNOW YOUR PRODUCT

Once you have gone through the planning process outlined in chapter 2 and have a clear definition of your audience and marketing objectives, the next step in writing copy that sells is to immerse yourself in your product.

Dig into the source material with a yellow highlighter. Underline or highlight key information, facts, figures, or phrases that strike your fancy.

Do not be afraid to "steal" sentences, paragraphs, and entire headlines and concepts from previous ads or mailings. As copywriter John Francis Tighe points out: "We are not in the business of being creative. Rather, we are in the business of knowing what works and reusing it."

I cannot overemphasize this point. Many copywriters are afraid to study past materials, because they fear their creative thinking will be tainted and they will be accused of being copycats. But remember, we are after *sales results*, not prizes for originality. John Reed, copywriter for Three Arts Inc. advertising agency, says: "Sometimes it is too easy to forget the obvious: the purpose of all forms of advertising is to *sell something*."

After you complete your study of the background materials, you should be able to answer all the questions presented in the checklist below. If not, get the answers by talking to other people in your company—product managers, salespeople, distributors, engineers, marketing managers. Interviews with users of your product or potential customers can also be revealing.

Is all this research really worthwhile? "Digging pays off," answers copywriter Don Hauptman, in an article in *Direct Marketing*. "Superficial preparation usually generates anemic copy. Do some research. Learn everything you can about your product and your market. 'Brainstorm' ideas with a colleague—or by yourself with a pad and pencil. *Then* start drafting your promotion."

"Facts become the fireworks that light up the prospect's

awareness of his need for the product or service being sold," adds Eugene Colin, a vice president of Lerner Scott Corporation, writing in *Advertising Age*. "They translate into excitement and color and emotion."

FIFTY QUESTIONS TO ASK
BEFORE YOU START TO WRITE COPY

1. What are all the product benefits?
2. What are all the features of the product?
3. How is my product different from—and, hopefully, better than—the competition?
4. What does the buyer expect when he or she plunks down a few dollars for my product? And do we deliver?
5. What methods, approaches, and sales techniques are the competition using?
6. How is the audience for my product different from the general public?
7. How much can my buyer reasonably expect to pay?
8. Does my average buyer have a credit card or a checking account?
9. Will my product be purchased for business or personal use?
10. Can I expect to get multiple sales from my buyer?
11. What is the logical "back end" product to sell someone—after he has purchased my product?
12. Will I need to show my product in color?
13. What's the "universe"—the total number of potential customers?
14. Who will buy my product: teenagers or octogenarians . . . men or women . . . executives or blue-collar workers?
15. Is there a market for overseas sales?
16. Should I offer time payments?
17. Will my product be a good gift item?

18. Should my copy be long or short?
19. Should my copy be breezy or down-to-earth?
20. Should I test the price?
21. Should I test lists?
22. Should I test copy approaches?
23. Should I mail third class or first class?
24. Is there a seasonal market for my product—and am I taking advantage of it?
25. Are there testimonials available from satisfied customers?
26. Can my direct mail efforts be syndicated?
27. Can I use a member-get-a-member approach? (Can I ask buyers to give me the names of other people I can mail to?)
28. Do I need photographs or illustrations?
29. Which appeals have worked in the past for this promotion?
30. What objections might arise from a prospective customer? How can I overcome these objections?
31. Should I use a premium?
32. Should I offer a money-back guarantee?
33. Is this item also sold retail? Are there price advantages I can stress for buying direct?
34. Should I consider a celebrity testimonial?
35. Can I tie in my copy to some news event?
36. Can I tie in my copy to some holiday or seasonal event?
37. Does my product sell better in a particular region or climate?
38. Would a personalized computer approach improve the effectiveness of my message?
39. Should I consider using a sweepstakes?
40. Can my product be sold through billing inserts?
41. Can my product be sold through a two-step advertising campaign?
42. Should I consider using television?
43. What must I do to give the reader a sense of urgency—so he or she will buy my product now?

44. Can I use scientific evidence in my sales approach?
45. Have I allowed enough time to create a direct mail package—or to create a space ad?
46. Can I get my customer to order by telephone?
47. What information will I want to get from my customer to get future sales?
48. What approaches have been used to sell this product without success?
49. Can I get powerful "before" and "after" pictures?
50. Assuming I get a 10 percent return, am I prepared to fill all the orders?

Source: Milt Pierce, Milt Pierce & Associates, 162 West 54th Street, New York, New York 10019

TWENTY-EIGHT TECHNIQUES TO ADD PUNCH AND POWER TO YOUR DIRECT-MAIL COPY

Here, in no particular order, are twenty-eight copywriting techniques that can make your package lively, fascinating, interesting, better read, and more effective in getting leads and sales.

• *Technique 1: Empathize with the reader.* Direct mail professionals use the term "affinity group" to describe a market segment of people with similar interests. Stamp collectors, freelance writers, automobile enthusiasts, pet owners, IBM PC users, and joggers are all examples of affinity groups.

Members of affinity groups often have strong feelings about—and interest in—their particular obsession. Perhaps you have a "hacker" friend who talks endlessly about bits, bytes, boots, and other computer jargon. It may bore you silly. But to him, it's sheer joy. Do you have a special hobby or interest? Then you know how much fun it is to share it with other people.

When writing to affinity groups, empathize with their interests. Show that you are "in sync" with them—that you understand and support their particular cause. Here's an example of "empathy" copy from a letter offering a subscription to *Practical Homeowner*:

> Dear Homeowner,
>
> Do you enjoy your home? I mean *really* enjoy it? Does it still feel good at the end of the day to walk through that door, kick off your shoes, and just be . . . *home*?
>
> By showing the reader that you are "simpatico" with his needs, you are already halfway to winning him over as a friend . . . and a customer.

• *Technique 2: Begin your letter with a provocative quotation.* You can open the reader's eyes by making a statement that is provocative, audacious, outrageous, or controversial. The quotation should be strong enough to arouse interest and prompt people to read further, but not so strong that it insults or angers the reader or turns him off.

Here's a good example. It's the opening of a letter selling a book on advertising.

> "Advertising agencies and other consultants score something on the order of a 9 on my Least-Needed scale of 1-to-10 . . ."
>
> . . . this is what Lewis Kornfeld has to say, based on his extraordinary success as Radio Shack's master marketer for over 30 years.

If you're an ad agency or consultant, you might bristle when you read this. If you're a client, you might find yourself nodding in agreement. But either way, I'm sure you probably want to find out a little more about the author and the book, no?

• *Technique 3: The "Ah-HA" factor.* One way to get the reader on your side is to tell him something he already knows.

The trick is not to tell him something mundane or something blatantly obvious but to bring to the surface a fact, feeling, or emotion the reader may not have openly acknowledged before.

When he hears the fact or feeling stated openly by *you*, his reaction is "ah-ha" or "yes, of course" or "that's right!"

The power of this technique is that we all like to learn more about ourselves and our state of mind. The ah-ha technique builds your credibility with your prospect by reinforcing and dramatizing the reader's own knowledge or beliefs.

Here's an example from a letter selling a home-study program on money management and investing:

> Dear Reader:
>
> My name is Morton Shulman. I am a medical doctor by training, and I still maintain an active practice. I make a good living as a doctor, but I realized long ago that *you can't get rich on a salary alone* [italics mine], not even a doctor's salary. So I turned to investing.

Most of us rely on our salaries for income, not lucrative investments. We know deep down that we can't get rich this way, but through laziness, lack of time, or lack of knowledge, we don't do much about it. That's why Dr. Shulman's letter really hits home. When I read it, I said, "Yes, he's right; I ought to be smarter about handling my money." Which is the exact frame of mind a company selling an investment program would want to create.

• *Technique 4: Turn a potential negative into a positive.* The following story is told by Jim Young in John Caples's classic book *Tested Advertising Methods:*

A few years ago there was a hail storm just before harvest. I had thousands of mail orders and checks, and almost every apple hail-pocked. Problem: Should I send the checks back—or risk dissatisfied customers? Actually these apples were damaged only in appearance. They were better eating than ever. Cold weather, when apples are ripening, improves their flavor. So I filled the orders. In every carton I put a printed card:

Note the hail marks which have caused minor skin blemishes on some of these apples. These are proof of their growth at a high mountain altitude, where the sudden chills from hail storms help firm the flesh and develop the natural fruit sugars which give these apples their incomparable flavor.

Not one customer complained. Next year I received orders which said: "Hail-marked apples, if available; otherwise the ordinary kind."

A brilliant example of a copywriter's using words to alter the customer's perception of reality.

Another example of this technique is the Harry and David mail order catalog advertising their famous Royal Riviera Pears. For years the copy has said of these pears: "So unusual that not one person in a thousand has ever tasted them." Makes you yearn for a bite so much that you never stop to think that this fancy phrase *also* says, "Not too many people buy this product." Another instance of copy turning a negative into a positive.

• *Technique 5: Ask a provocative question.* "Do you want me to give you a surefire way of improving direct mail response?"

That's an example of using a question to grab the reader's attention and heighten his interest.

Question leads can be extremely effective if the question *(a)* arouses the reader's curiosity, or *(b)* deals with a timely, important, or controversial issue, or *(c)* asks a question to which the reader genuinely wants the answer.

Some examples:

WHAT DO JAPANESE MANAGERS HAVE THAT AMERICAN MANAGERS SOMETIMES LACK?	(THE ECONOMICS PRESS)
If you were to find out today that you had only a short time to live, would you feel comfortable with the amount of life insurance that you have provided your family?	(United of Omaha)
IS THERE A ROLL OF FILM IN YOUR CAMERA RIGHT NOW, BOB BLY?	(KODAK)

• *Technique 6: Make a quick transition from your attention-grabbing opening to the sales pitch.* Don't waste too much time with warm-up paragraphs. After grabbing the reader's attention, quickly shift the focus and begin making your sales pitch. People are busy and appreciate letters that get right to the point. In a brilliant fund-raising letter, the American Red Cross makes a fast transition from the reader's concerns to the Red Cross's plight in only two paragraphs:

Dear Friend:

When disaster strikes your home—you may urgently need the Red Cross.
But right now—during the holiday season—the Red Cross urgently needs you. . . .

• **Technique 7: Be specific.** "Platitudes and generalities roll off the human understanding like water from a duck. They leave no impression whatever," wrote Claude Hopkins in his classic book, *Scientific Advertising*. Or, as copywriter Don Hauptman puts it: "Superlatives are often not credible; concretes invariably have the ring of truth."

Be specific. Do not be content to merely claim that a product is better, faster, easier, or cheaper when you can say how much better, how much faster, how much easier, or how much less it costs. Give the specific figures and facts. It makes copy interesting and believable.

In a promotional mailing piece, Click, a New Jersey-based messenger service, makes the specific claim, "We will pick up and deliver to Manhattan, on the same day, for only $9.50." This motivated me to try their service, and I have been a customer ever since.

I received another mailing, this one from a company asking if I wanted to earn part-time income selling their product. The visual showed a picture of the owner holding up a check; the caption read: "I'll send you a check for $4,154.65 for selling just one order." Using a specific number somehow makes the proposition seem much more real and believable than a rounded-off figure or range of figures.

• **Technique 8: Be sincere.** When asked by *Direct Marketing* magazine to name the most important characteristics of a copywriter, direct mail expert Ed McClean included *honesty* in his answer.

And in a recent survey, when the Simmons Market Research Bureau asked people what they disliked most about direct marketing, 41 percent cited *deception* as their answer.

But contrary to the image the general public might have of direct marketing, the majority of direct marketing professionals are honest and strive to tell the truth in their mailings.

This isn't entirely altruistic, of course. Through experience, we have learned that while we might be able to trick the customer with deceptive advertising *once*, a buyer who feels duped will not buy from us a second time. And repeat sales represent the bulk of profits in most business enterprises. So it is more profitable to be honest than to be deceptive or misleading, or to tell outright lies.

People are turned off by direct mail that seems insincere, too high-pressure, or dishonest. But how can you sound sincere in your letters?

To start, be sincere. Tell the truth. If you don't believe what you are saying, it will come through in the copy.

Second, ask other people to read your letters and see if your copy has the "ring of truth." Even an honest salesperson, in his zeal to sell the product, may overstate his case and sound like a phony.

Woodbridge Memorial Gardens sent me a letter that failed to convince me of their concern for my well-being. It begins:

> Dear Neighbor:
>
> It is very disturbing to me to think that you may lose the last opportunity to own your personal, above-ground mausoleum at a price that can save you so much money and heartache.

Maybe I'm a cynic. But I would have found the letter more credible if the writer said he was "concerned." "Disturbed" seemed to be overstating the case.

Another letter which failed to motivate me was this fund-raising solicitation from the American Kidney Fund.

> Dear Friend:
>
> I wouldn't write you like this if it weren't truly urgent.

I thought: "Of course you would. It's your *job* to raise funds. What *else* would you be doing with your time aside from writing to people like me?"

• *Technique 9: Avoid contradictions.* When reviewing your copy, be sure to check for consistency and eliminate any statements that contradict one another.

If you are not consistent with facts and statements, you are automatically wrong at least part of the time.

When people read contradictory statements in a letter or brochure, it destroys your credibility. The reaction is: "These people don't know what they're talking about!"

A factual error is much worse than any grammatical error or typo you can make. In a letter offering a set of gourmet recipe cards, the writer contradicts herself in the first sentence:

> Dear Gourmet,
>
> You may never again have to worry about time for cooking . . .

See the contradiction? Gourmets don't worry about cooking—they enjoy it! They may worry about housework or gardening or shopping. But they'll always make time to prepare a good meal.

Condé Nast recently ran an ad in *Advertising Age*, the purpose of which was to convince companies to run their ads in *Vogue*, *Glamour*, and other Condé Nast women's magazines. The copywriter used Debbi Fields, a successful entrepreneur, as an example of the kind of women who read these publications. "Debbi Fields is the cut-above kind of woman advertisers dream about. There are 26 million women readers a lot like her in the Condé Nast Women's Package."

See the contradiction: How can a woman be a cut above the rest and yet be just like 26 million other women (approximately one-quarter of the entire female population of the United States)? Believability is severely damaged.

• *Technique 10: Narrow the focus.* The narrower your audience, the more specific you can be about meeting their needs.

When people see their specific requirements addressed in an ad or mailer, they are more likely to respond than if the ad is making a broad appeal to all readers.

Let's say you give seminars in business strategy. One possible headline for your seminar mailing is:

BUSINESS STRATEGY

What's unique about your business strategy seminar that could separate it from dozens of other similar seminars being offered? Perhaps you emphasize doing business on an international scale. You could change the title to read:

GLOBAL BUSINESS STRATEGY

Better. Now, if you tailor your seminar to different industries, you can focus the headline even tighter by targeting those industries. For example:

GLOBAL BUSINESS STRATEGY IN THE CHEMICAL INDUSTRY

Chemical Week takes this one step further with a seminar called:

GLOBAL BUSINESS STRATEGY
IN THE LUBRICANT ADDITIVES INDUSTRY

See the improvement? If the lubricant additives industry is a sufficiently big enough market to warrant a separate promotional effort, then *Chemical Week*, offering a seminar geared toward the industry's specific buiness needs, will probably do much better than mailings offering lubricant-additives executives a general business seminar.

• *Technique 11: Make your product sound irresistible.* The master of this technique is the person who writes the mailings and catalog copy for Oregon-based Harry and David's Fruit-of-the-Month Club. Want to get your mouth watering? Listen to how they describe their pound cake:

> Few things are finer on a summer's eve than a slice of this buttery loaf cake, heaped with fresh, naturally sweet Oregold slices. Top with whipped cream, or a little raspberry syrup—makes a deliciously different gift. . . .

Here's how they describe a bunch of grapes:

> Velvety-black, one-to-a-mouthful Belgian hothouse type, these luscious grapes were once reserved exclusively for European royalty.

And peaches:

> Huge, luscious peaches grown right here in the Rogue River Valley, where rich volcanic soil, crisp cool nights and pure mountain water nurture these beauties to juicy, plump perfection. Shipped so fresh you can almost smell the orchards in bloom!

• *Technique 12: Fear.* Fear is one of the most powerful of human motivators. Fear sells us on many things, including alarm systems, life insurance, home medical tests, and child-proof medicine bottles.

A recent mailing from American Family Publishers included a lift letter from (who else?) Ed McMahon. While the central theme of the promotion was, "Enter the contest and win $10 million," the lift letter approached it from a *different* angle: Namely, if you don't enter, you could be *losing* $10 million.

"If you return the winning number in time, I'll be personally handing *you* the first ten million dollars," said the letter. "*But*, if you decide to ignore this letter and throw your exclusive numbers away, I'll *surely* be awarding all the money to *someone else*. PREVIOUS WINNERS HAVE THROWN THEIR NUMBERS RIGHT INTO THE TRASH—THEY LITERALLY THREW AWAY MILLIONS!"

I found this to be tremendously effective. We all have a little nagging voice that tells us, whenever we throw away a sweepstakes mailing, that we could be throwing away a chance at a million dollars. But because we're busy, we go ahead and do it. This letter plays on that fear. It stops the busy person from throwing away the mailing and persuades him to enter the drawing.

- ***Technique 13: Acknowledge the medium.*** Consumers, bombarded by direct mail, print ads, and TV commercials, have become more conscious—and more knowledgeable—about advertising techniques than ever before.

One technique that can get the consumer on your side is to acknowledge his or her perception of your medium.

The best way to show this is with some examples. In a subscription mailing, a publisher began its letter with this sentence: "I know you get a lot of computer-personalized letters in the mail. But this one is different."

See what they're doing? They're not hiding the fact that they are using direct mail to reach you. Rather, they're acknowledging the fact—and your awareness of it. By doing so, they come across as honest and win you over to their side, making it possible to separate themselves from the crowd.

Another example is a classic headline that read, "DO YOU READ SMALL ADS LIKE THESE?" Again, it acknowledged the special nature of small space ads. And allowed the advertiser to then separate himself from the pack.

In a subscription package selling a stock market newsletter, publisher Dick Davis includes a sample issue in his promotional package—something ordinarily not done in this field. And in his cover letter, he turns this tactic into a powerful selling point:

Dear Investor:

The direct mail experts told me that I was crazy to send you the latest issue of the *Dick Davis Digest*. A basic rule of marketing is to "sell the sizzle, not the steak" . . .

On the surface, this Madison Avenue approach sounds logical. But there is one situation in which it does not apply. That's when you have a unique product that is so special it will sell itself. I'm betting that the *Dick Davis Digest* is such a product.

The first paragraph acknowledges something the reader already knows about direct mail. The second paragraph turns Dick Davis's breaking of the rules into an argument that helps sell the newsletter.

Warning: This technique requires a lot of skill to execute effectively. And it only works in certain situations. Only use it when such a situation arises. Don't try to force it into every promotion you write.

• ***Technique 14: Boast.*** Six months ago I received a letter with the following headline plastered across the top:

WORLD'S GREATEST COPYWRITER
FINALLY AGREES TO REVEAL ALL THOSE
SECRETS THAT MADE HIM RICH!

World's greatest copywriter, my foot! I thought. *Who is this guy? I never heard of him. What a braggart!* And yet, before I knew it, I read every word of his eight-page sales letter. The letter copy was fascinating, of course, or it wouldn't have sustained my interest. But what caught my attention—and forced me into the first paragraph—was a boast, pure and simple.

As with the previous technique, using the brag-and-boast method effectively takes a great deal of skill. If you're not a highly skilled copywriter, avoid it. But if you feel confident as a writer, give it a try. The key is, after you make the boastful claim, to quickly make the transition from boasting about yourself to showing how you can help the reader, and back up your boastful claim without appearing to boast further.

• *Technique 15: Address the prospect's most common complaint.* If you can anticipate your prospect's biggest complaint, objection, or problem with your product or service, and answer it right at the start of your letter, you'll have hooked the reader into your sales pitch and created a lot of goodwill in the process.

If you're like me, you've always found public television a little hypocritical. After all, what's the point of eliminating commercial interruption if there's a fund-raising drive on the air every twenty minutes?

Well, I just received a fund-raising letter from Channel Thirteen, our local public-television station. And guess what they said in their letter?

> For years, people like you have commented . . .
>
> "I'll tell you why I don't give to THIRTEEN. It's those pledge drives! If you would just take those drives off the air and give me the intelligent TV I love, then I'd become a member!"
>
> Well, last year we took you up on this challenge by canceling two of our three life-sustaining pledge drives. *And, we're going to take this huge gamble again.*

The hidden agenda here is: "Hey, we listened to your complaints and we did what you asked. Now how about helping *us* out in return?"

• *Technique 16: Make your offer in the first few paragraphs.* If you suspect that people are not likely to read your letter, you can boost the response rate by making your offer right up front. This way, the reader who only glances at the opening of your letter still gets the gist of the sales letter and learns about your offer.

Here's the opening of a letter offering a free booklet on life insurance policies available for children:

> There's no gift
> more meaningful . . .
>
> . . . for the children you love than the one discussed in
> a new free pamphlet. It is yours with my compliments
> if you'll just mail the card enclosed.

And from a mailing offering a free brochure on a new 3M system for creating color slides and overheads:

> Our free brochure
> tells how you can make
> sophisticated slides and
> overhead transparencies . . .
>
> over the *phone*, in *minutes!*

• *Technique 17: Flatter the reader.* As long as you don't overdue it, flattery will get you everywhere. Or, almost everywhere. The American Museum of Natural History sent me a letter that portrayed me as a nicer guy than I really am:

> Dear Reader:
>
> From all indications available to us, you're a rather
> uncommon person.
>
> One who has a special reverence for our natural sur-

roundings . . . an endless and respectful curiosity about the quirks of animal and human nature . . . an unabashed sense of wonder and fascination in the presence of our legacy from the past.

• *Technique 18: Tell a story.* A story, properly told, can engage the reader's attention far longer than mere information or persuasive selling.

However, there is a creative risk in using this technique. For if the story is poorly told, the narrative will turn the reader off. And you will get lower readership—and less response—than if you had written a conventional sales letter.

You should only attempt to write in narrative form if the following two conditions exist:

(1) *You have uncovered a real story worth telling.* Real-life drama is more compelling and convincing than anything you could dream up. "Don't fake it," advises Don Hauptman, writing in the March 1983 issue of *Direct Marketing*. "This kind of credibility can't be fabricated, so don't even try it." If your story is phony, your readers will surely spot it. If your story is true, and well told, readers will respond accordingly.

(2) *You have the ability to tell the tale.* While I make a good living as a professional freelance copywriter, every short story I've ever written was rejected by every magazine I ever sent it to. So I stay away from the story format. However, if you've got the novelist's ability to spin a yarn, or the journalist's skill for weaving the facts into a cohesive tale, try this technique in your next mailing and see what happens.

• *Technique 19: Make it personal.* In some situations, especially those where the product or offer involves the prospect on a personal level, a "human touch" can add drama and impact to your mailing piece. For example, if your business is giving seminars on public speaking, and you had a humiliating childhood experience while giving a presentation to your third-grade classmates, this can form the basis of a very personal letter in which you empathize with similar experiences the prospect may have had.

Here's the opening of a hard-hitting fund-raising appeal received by my wife:

> Dear Ms. Bly:
>
> Do you remember me? I am Don McNeill, and I was privileged to come into the homes of millions of Americans like you during the more than 30 years that I hosted "The Breakfast Club" on ABC radio.
>
> I am now involved in one of the most important battles of my life—the battle to find a cure for Alzheimer's Disease.
>
> *This cruel disease killed my late wife, Kay.* [Italics mine.] My concern now is for the 120,000 people who will die of Alzheimer's Disease this year, next year, and each year thereafter. . . .

Obviously the personal nature of this note strikes a chord. Who cannot help but feel sympathy for the writer and empathy for his cause?

• **Technique 20: Highlight your guarantee.** A strong guarantee is of great reassurance to people who haven't done business with you before. I don't know why so many companies bury their guarantees in fine print instead of shouting about them up front.

A self-mailer from Atlantic Fasteners shows a picture of company president Patrick J. O'Toole holding up a certificate good for a fifty-dollar credit on the purchase of any fasteners sold by his firm. The headline and subhead underneath the photo read:

"YOU GET NEXT-DAY DELIVERY FROM OUR STOCK OF
28,981,000 FASTENERS, OR I SEND YOU A $50 CREDIT!"
ONLY TWO CREDITS ISSUED IN LAST 9,322 ORDERS.

Give your guarantee a greater emphasis than it is now receiving. See what happens. At worst, people will come to think of you as trustworthy. More likely, you'll get more orders out of the deal.

Worried that by stressing your guarantee, you'll get more people taking advantage of it? Stop worrying. The experience of hundreds of mail order companies indicates that people are basically honest. Only an insignificant percentage of people will try to dupe you.

• ***Technique 21: Make it easy to respond.*** The easier you make it to reply to your mailing, the more replies you'll get.

How do you simplify the response process?

• Provide both a write-in and telephone option. Some people prefer to write and others prefer to call.

• Use a loose reply card or order form rather than a reply element that has to be separated from a letter or brochure.

• Don't ask a lot of questions. Just get the minimum amount of information you need to fulfill the reader's order or request.

• Leave plenty of room for the reader to write in the required information on the reply element.

• Better yet, fill in the reply form for the reader, either with computer printing or by affixing a label.

• Pay the postage. Do not ask the reader to supply a stamp.

• When seeking orders, provide a toll-free number and accept major credit cards. According to InfoMat Marketing, a California-based ad agency specializing in direct response, credit card purchases and an "800" number can increase your response by as much as 30 percent.

• When seeking inquiries or orders from business customers, include your fax number and encourage the recipient to fax the completed order form to you. Make sure the reply form is on white paper or other light-colored stock to ensure readability when it is faxed.

• **Technique 22: Use the magic word of direct mail.** What is the magic word of direct mail? Some would say "free." But the word I'm thinking of is "you." Your copy should address the reader directly, as a person. As I have said earlier, the reader is not concerned with your company, your product, or whether you turn a profit. He is only concerned with his problems, his happiness, his security, his wealth. That's what you have to talk about in your copy—the reader, not yourself.

You can achieve this through a liberal use of the word *you* in your copy. When you review your copy, make sure you are using "you"—frequently. A lot of "you's" indicates that you are speaking directly to the reader.

On the other hand, if you see a lot of "I, I, I" or "we, we, we" or "our company," you know your copy is off base. It is too *we*-oriented, when it should be *you*-oriented. Fix it.

Here's a piece of copy that does a good job of speaking directly to the reader:

YOU ASKED FOR THE FULL STORY
OF THE SANDLER SELLING SYSTEM . . .

. . . and here it is. But the real story is about you— about how you can take a giant step up, right now. A step up—in the number of sales you close . . . the quality of those sales . . . the money you make. And just as important, an enormous gain in satisfaction and professional pride.

• **Technique 23: Use the other magic word.** "Free" is surely the runner up in the contest of words that are most important in direct mail. (Although many direct mail writers would choose "free" as the winner.)

On the outer envelope for one of his many successful mail order promotions, copywriter Andrew Linick uses the following teaser copy to highlight his free offer:

Act within *15* days to receive your
FREE Gift worth $10!!!

Here is the FREE Information You Requested

Even a simple teaser such as "Special FREE offer inside" can get people who would otherwise not be tempted by your offer to open the envelope.

• *Technique 24: Give the reader important information.* At the Bly house, we are drowning in paper: direct mail, business correspondence, magazines, books, newspapers, reports. Who can keep up? Many of the magazines I receive go into the trash bin without a second glance.

But if you can give me important information . . . something that can really improve my life, protect my family, help me do my job better, or increase my income . . . I might be more inclined to pay attention to you.

Direct mail has a big advantage over ads and articles. An ad or article competes with all the other ads and articles in the magazine, so it's likely to go unread. But a self-mailer or envelope is separate from all the other mailers and envelopes in my mailbox. So I will at least glance at it before making a "read/no-read" decision.

One very official-looking envelope that caught my attention was from the American Institute for Cancer Research. In big bold type, the teaser shouted at me:

UPDATED SURVEY ON DIET AND CANCER

IMPORTANT: The Enclosed Survey is reserved in your name. You are requested to complete and return your survey.

Since we are concerned about diet and cancer, this got my attention. Any information we can get to help us eat healthier and live longer is welcome in the Bly home. Inside the envelope, unfortunately, was no information but a blatant fund-raising pitch. Had they enclosed a helpful booklet or article reprint or the survey results I expected from reading the outer envelope, I might have been more inclined to contribute.

• *Technique 25: Demonstrate.* If there is any way you can demonstrate your product in your mailing, do it. Few things are as convincing as an actual demonstration.

One of my favorite industrial ads of all time promoted a chemical used in fireproofing. The headline of the ad commanded the reader: "TRY BURNING THIS COUPON." A match would set the page ablaze. But when you removed the match, *the fire went out!* Upon reading the copy, you learned that the page (produced by the manufacturer and bound as an insert into the magazine) was treated with the fireproofing compound being advertised. A brilliant example of a demonstration-in-print.

Difficult with an ad, but easier with direct mail. Remember, a mailing doesn't have to be just a brochure and a letter. You can include a product sample, a demo diskette, a test kit, a material swatch. There are many opportunities to let the customer try your product before ordering.

Seton Name Plate sent me a sample Property Identification Plate along with the following letter of instruction:

> 'Try this simple test. With a ballpoint pen, write your initials next to the numbers on the enclosed sample plate. Now try to erase both. Let me save you the trouble . . . you can't erase them without defacing the tag.

The customer doesn't have to taken Seton's word that the plates are permanent. He can see it for himself. Believability is increased perhaps a hundredfold.

• *Technique 26: Promise to share a secret.* Exclusivity is another powerful direct mail motivator. People like to feel that they are getting inside information, or becoming the first on their block to get a new possession, or getting in on the ground floor of a good deal.

Boardroom Classics, a book publisher, uses a six-page letter to sell its $29.95 *Book of Inside Information*. The headline of the letter reads:

WHAT CREDIT-CARD COMPANIES
DON'T TELL YOU. PAGE 10.
What hospitals don't tell you. Page 421.
What the IRS doesn't tell you. Page 115.
What the airlines don't tell you. Page 367.
What car dealers don't tell you. . . . (etc.)

I know this letter is successful because Boardroom mails it repeatedly. I think I must have received it five times within the last twelve months.

• *Technique 27: Write in a natural, conversational style.* Good direct mail copy sounds like a personal letter written from one friend to another. It is helpful and friendly, not stuffy or formal.

"Write like you talk," suggests Cynthia Smith, president of C/D Smith Advertising, of Rye, New York, writing in *Micro Marketworld* (December 1, 1986). "Use conversational language. Do not feel you must make your statements in formal, stiff English just because they are being put down on paper."

I recently received a brochure I had requested. Attached to the brochure was a card with the company logo, address, and the phrase, "As per your request." That's it.

What a cold, informal, reply—a real turn-off. Why use such stuffy corporatese? Why not just say, "Thanks for your request.

Here's the brochure you asked for. If you have any questions, or want to place an order, give us a call. We'll be happy to help."

Here are some other examples of how you can convert business language to people language:

Business language	*People language*
as per your requested	as you requested
enclosed please find	here is; I've enclosed
kindly advise	please let us know
utilize	use
at this point in time	now
in the event that	if
optimum	best
it is our considered opinion	we think

• **Technique 28: Be precise in your use of language.** "The difference between the right word and almost the right word," wrote Mark Twain, "is the difference between the lightning and the lightning bug."

In direct mail, words are the salespeople, the product demonstrators, the customer service representatives, and the order takers. If you use them improperly, you steer your customer in the wrong direction.

For instance, do you know the difference between *beside* and *besides*? *Beside* means by the side of. *Besides* means in addition to.

How about *affect* and *effect*? *Affect* is a verb meaning to change or influence. *Effect* is a noun meaning result or outcome. *Effect* is also a verb meaning to bring about.

Fewer vs. *less*? *Fewer* is used when units or individuals can be counted (*fewer* cavities). *Less* is used with quantities of mass, bulk, or volume (*less* weight).

SEVEN RULES FOR REVIEWING COPY

If you do not write your own copy, your job will be to review and approve copy written by someone else—a staff writer, an ad agency, or a freelance copywriter. Copywriter Richard Armstrong, writing in *Target Marketing*, suggests these seven rules for reviewing copy:

• ***Don't insist that the writer be present at your first reading.*** Spend the first few hours with your new copy alone. This way you won't feel obligated to make snap judgments about it.

• ***Read the copy once without a pencil.*** People do not read advertisements with pencils in their hands. Yet whenever clients review copy, the first thing they do is reach for a pencil.

Customers won't be reading the copy with an eye toward correcting grammar, improving the phrasing, or critiquing the style. If it's interesting they'll read it; if it's not, they won't. In other words, readers will make an overall, gut-level judgment about the copy—not a detailed cerebral one. So why don't you do the same?

• ***Check the facts.*** Do a decent job with making sure all the facts are correct. It's your product, isn't it?

• ***Forget you ever heard the word "grammar."*** Ninety-nine times out of a hundred, when a professional copywriter makes a grammatical error, it's because she felt it sounded stronger, more natural, or more persuasive than doing it the "right" way.

• ***Be specific.*** Specific criticism is like surgery that cuts out the malignancy and spares the rest of the body. Vague criticism is like chemotherapy; it causes the copy's hair to fall out and makes the whole thing look sicker than it really is.

Don't say, "This ad is too negative." Instead, find four or five sentences that you think are phrased in a negative way, and write in the margin, "Can we express this more positively?"

• *Be kind.* As hard as we all try to be professional about it, writing is a very personal thing. To a copywriter, the words "I don't like your copy" sound an awful lot like "I don't like you." So always try to say something nice about the copy before you begin to rip it apart.

• *Don't walk away from the task of revising the copy just because it isn't easy.* If you spend the time required to go over the copy, the writer can take care of your reservations and give you a very effective direct mail piece.

If you're ever not happy with some copy, put it on a shelf and let it cool for a day or two. Then come back to it later and ask yourself if it isn't better than you first thought.

HOW TO DESIGN AND PRODUCE
EFFECTIVE DIRECT MAIL PACKAGES

SUCCESS BY DESIGN

The slickest writing, the finest paper, printing, and artwork can't make a good idea out of a bad one or an attractive offer out of a poor one," said Maxwell Sackheim, who created the classic ad "DO YOU MAKE THESE MISTAKES IN ENGLISH?" for the Sherwin Cody School.

Maybe so. But a well-conceived design and quality printing job *can* get people to read an important message they might otherwise put aside. How many times have you stopped to look at a brochure or ad because the color stood out or the artwork was attractive? Design and production do make a difference.

This chapter deals with the design, production, and mailing of your letters, self-mailers, and packages.

SETTING YOUR PRODUCTION SCHEDULE

Your production schedule depends largely on the complexity of the format you have selected for your mailing. A one-page form letter can be printed, inserted, and mailed within a week. An elaborate four-color package, with multiple inserts and computer personalization, may take a couple of months to produce. With desktop publishing, a small mailing may be written, designed, printed, and mailed within a day!

The *Januz Direct Marketing Letter* offers the following schedule as a guide for how much time to allow in planning direct mail campaigns from concept through delivery to the post office. Note that it is intended as a rough guideline only. You must ask your own suppliers if they can meet these deadlines; do not assume they can.

▾ Direct Mail Promotion Planning Time Table

Concepts and development of strategy with consultant	2 days to 1 week
Copywriting and copywriters rough layouts	2 weeks
Artist's semicomprehensive layouts	1–2 weeks
Photography or obtaining stock photos	2–5 weeks
Finished artwork, typesetting, keylining, mechanicals	2–3 weeks
Artwork corrections, revisions of boards	1 week
Color separations	1–2 weeks
Revisions in color separations, new proofs	1–2 weeks

Production services
All of the following items can be done simultaneously:

Ordering of mailing lists	2 weeks
Merge-purge computer work, carrier routing	2–3 weeks
Envelope manufacturing and printing	3–5 weeks

Printing of other components	2–3 weeks
Manufacturing of computer forms (if needed)	3–5 weeks
Computer running (programming done in advance)	1–2 weeks
Ordering of special fix-ons, special items, etc.	1–10 weeks
TOTAL TIME NEEDED FOR PRODUCTION SERVICES: (if no special items are required)	3–5 weeks
Mailing services (affix labels, insertions, stuff and seal envelopes)	2 weeks
Time for post office to give you nationwide delivery on the mailing from drop date (day mailing is delivered to post office)	2–3 weeks (maybe)

Source: *Januz Direct Marketing Letter*, Report no. 13-0001

Cutting corners on your schedule can result in substantial overtime charges. It may also force vendors to sacrifice quality in order to yield to your deadline pressures. It is better to allow too much time rather than too little when setting the schedule for the production of a direct mail package or any other form of advertising or promotion.

DETERMINING THE COST

Cost depends on many factors including:

• Format of the package. The more inserts, the greater the cost.
• Use of color. Four-color is more costly.

• Computer personalization. Personalized packages are much more expensive than printed form letters.

• Size. Odd-size packages are more expensive because they require the manufacture of customized envelopes.

• Method of mailing. First class is much more expensive than bulk-rate third class.

• Using outside vendors is usually more expensive than creating your mailing in-house, when measured on a pure cost basis. But using outside vendors may be a better choice if you are unable to do it in-house, or if outside vendors produce a better-quality package that pulls in more response.

• Choice of outside vendors. As copywriter Sig Rosenblum observes, "Fees are all over the lot." One copywriter might charge ten times as much as another to write the same amount of copy selling the same offer.

• Brochures. You might test a letter versus a brochure and letter package. If the brochure doesn't increase response, drop it. The brochure is one of the costlier elements of producing a direct mail package.

• Size. A number-ten package is less expensive than a six-by-nine-inch package. The six-by-nine-inch package generally costs less than a jumbo or oversize package.

• Package versus self-mailer. When mailing in large volume, a self-mailer may cost a few pennies, as opposed to twenty to forty cents or more per full-scale package.

• Package versus direct-action postcard. A postcard mailing, including production and media costs, costs about one-tenth as much as creating and mailing a full package to the same number of prospects.

• Photography and illustrations can double or triple the creative costs. I have created many successful mailing packages that were all copy or used only very simple sketches or photographs. Try to avoid designs that require new or elaborate drawings or photographs. Original artwork adds to cost and can delay production many weeks.

• Number of pieces produced. As with sales brochures, the

more mailing packages you produce, the lower the cost per package.

• Specialty items. Premiums, product samples, or other three-dimensional inserts can cause an astronomical increase in cost per thousand and are usually affordable only in small-volume business-to-business mailings.

"For many companies who use direct mail, rising costs are making it more and more difficult to use the traditional direct mail package to profitably make a sale," notes Vivian Sudhalter, director of marketing for Macmillian Software. "In particular, paper and printing costs have risen enormously." Postal rates are also expected to increase over the next several years. She notes that Macmillan Software has virtually abandoned the traditional package in favor of less costly self-mailer formats.

If you have a manuscript you want to turn into a package, get cost estimates from your vendors before proceeding. If you're not sure how many copies you need, it's perfectly OK to get estimates for several different quantities. On a small mailing, I will often ask for an estimate for five thousand and ten thousand pieces.

The number of vendors you must go to for estimates depends on who you hire. An ad agency will handle the whole job for you and present a single bill. So will many consultants. Another alternative is to manage the project yourself, in which case you'll be dealing with many different vendors: writers, artists, photographers, printers. Some artists use their own typographers and include type in their package price. Others ask you to pay the typographer directly.

As a rule, I suggest you get three different bids on creative costs and printing. With three bids, you can more easily spot an estimate that is suspiciously high (or suspiciously low). Once you have established an ongoing relationship with a vendor, you may not feel a need to get bids on every job. That's perfectly OK.

The following Direct Mail Cost Estimator Worksheet may be helpful in organizing your estimates.

DIRECT MAIL COST ESTIMATOR WORKSHEET

Type of vendor	Estimates		
	Name of vendor	Quantity A	Quantity B
Consultant	_____	_____	_____
Copywriter	_____	_____	_____
Artist (design)	_____	_____	_____
Artist (mechanical)	_____	_____	_____
Typesetter	_____	_____	_____
Photographer (or stock photography house)	_____	_____	_____
Illustrator	_____	_____	_____
List broker	_____	_____	_____
Printer	_____	_____	_____
Lettershop (if separate from printer)	_____	_____	_____
Color separator	_____	_____	_____
Specialty item supplier (if insert or premium is used)	_____	_____	_____
Computer time (for merge/purge of list)	_____	_____	_____
ADD postage to all estimates	_____	_____	_____
TOTAL COSTS:	_____	_____	_____

GETTING HELP

Where can you find printers, letter shops (printers specializing in direct mail production, insertion, and preparation), and artists who can help you?

One good source is *Who's Charging What!: Design*, a roster of freelance direct mail graphic artists. The roster lists artists specializing in direct mail along with their fees for designing a standard mailing package. This roster is published annually by the newsletter *Who's Mailing What!* For details, call or write *Who's Mailing What!*, P.O. Box 8180, Stamford, CT 06905, (203) 329-1996.

Prices for designing a package range from seven hundred dollars to five thousand dollars, with two thousand to three thousand dollars being mid range. Most artists charge an hourly fee for producing mechanicals, with typesetting, illustrations, photography, and separations billed extra—usually at a markup. Hourly rates for mechanical work range from seventeen to fifty dollars, with thirty-five to forty dollars being about average.

Another good source of direct mail suppliers is the current "Who's Who" issue of *Target Marketing* magazine. For details, call or write: North American Publishing Company, 401 N. Broad St., Philadelphia, PA 19108, phone (215) 238-5300.

A third resource is *The Creative Black Book*, published by Friendly Publications, Inc., 401 Park Ave. South, New York, NY 10016. It lists thousands of photographers, illustrators, graphic designers, printers, ad agencies, and other vendors grouped according to geographic region. It is available by mail order through the publisher, and in some major bookstores. The *Black Book* does not distinguish between general and direct response suppliers.

A fourth directory is *Direct Mail Market Place*, which is perhaps the most comprehensive directory of suppliers in the direct mail industry. A copy may be ordered from Hoke Communications in Garden City, New York, phone (516) 767-7470.

The best way to find a supplier is to ask your colleagues to recommend someone. This is what I do whenever I need the name of a good artist, printer, consultant, or what have you.

Selecting the right vendor for direct mail or any other task is largely a matter of good business sense. When evaluating a vendor you may want to:

- interview the vendor to discuss his or her capabilities and your specific assignment
- review samples of work the vendor has produced for other clients
- talk to some of the vendor's clients
- tour the vendor's facilities

PRODUCING THE PERSONALIZED LETTER PACKAGE

One of the simplest and most effective direct mail packages is a well-written personalized letter mailed with reply card in a number-ten envelope. This format is so effective because it comes the closest in appearance to a personal communication.

Today any company with an inexpensive microcomputer and the right software can produce a computer-personalized letter in-house. All you need is a word processing program to print the letter, a database program to store your mailing list, and a "mail-merge" type of software that allows the computer to personalize the letter with the recipient's name and address.

If you have a laser printer, your computer can even print letters that include a signature. A laser-printed signature or other simulated handwritten note, generated with today's improved technology, is nearly indistinguishable from real handwriting. Although laser printers used to be out of the price range of most smaller companies, the price has dropped dramatically in recent years and continues to do so.

You don't have a computer? Don't worry. Today there are many outside service companies that specialize in generating laser-printed letters for direct mail purposes.

Arnie Begler is president of High Technology Associates, a Pittsburgh-based firm specializing in database marketing. He has had great success using one-page personalized letters aimed at a highly targeted database of potential prospects. Here are Arnie's ten key parameters for producing a sales letter:

1. Address envelopes—no labels.
2. Sign the letter in blue ink.
3. Do not right-justify the letter.
4. Use stamps on envelopes, not a postage meter.
5. Merge the company name, location, line of business, or person's name into the body of the letter where it logically makes sense to do so.
6. Mail on Monday morning, if possible.
7. Return calls from customers the same day, if possible. (Arnie's letters do not usually include a reply card; instead they ask for a telephone response.)
8. Fold the letter twice to fit into a standard number-ten envelope.
9. Check to make sure letters and envelopes match, that the right letter is sent to the right prospect.
10. Use a letter-quality printer—not dot-matrix.

Remember, Arnie's tips apply only to small-volume, highly targeted mailings aimed at high-level executives in medium-size and large corporations. They do not apply to high-volume consumer mailings.

HOW TO DESIGN A WINNING
DIRECT MAIL PACKAGE

The following tips are written to help you design a more effective direct mail package.

Keep in mind that these are suggestions and ideas only.

The key question to ask when planning a direct mail design is, "Is it appropriate for the audience and the selling proposition? Will it create the proper environment for my sales pitch and get people to open, read, and respond to the package?"

• ***Outer envelope.*** In business mail—especially mail aimed at high-level executives—we often strive to make the outer envelope look like a personal communication rather than an advertising message.

To do this, use a number-ten business envelope—nothing bigger.

Print the envelope on heavy, high-quality stock. A paper with an elegant weave or pattern through it implies importance, dignity, and value.

Do not use teaser copy or illustrations on the outer envelope.

Computer-print the recipient's name and address directly on the envelope. Do not use a window envelope or a label.

Do not put the company's name or logo in the address block in the upper left corner of the envelope. Instead, use only the sender's name and address: "Lee Iacocca, P.O. Box XXX, Detroit, Michigan."

If you do not have the budget for personalized letters, or you are mailing to a broader audience (middle management, technical people, and staff personnel rather than upper executives), it's OK to give your mail a more promotional look.

Use of teaser copy is effective for creating a favorable expectation for what's inside the envelope. I am generally not in favor of cluttered envelope designs, vivid artwork, and long teaser copy when mailing to business and professional audiences. I prefer a short, punchy, powerful teaser, printed in large, bold type on the front of the envelope.

In consumer mail, the envelope design should be appropriate for the product and the audience.

For instance, when doing a mailing from a bank to its customer list, I avoid teaser copy and use the bank's regular number-ten stationery. The reasoning is that practically everyone will open an envelope from their bank.

A sweepstakes mailing, on the other hand, should probably be plastered with loud, colorful advertising messages to create excitement for the promotion.

A mailing for a children's book club should have lots of colorful drawings and photos to attract interest and show that the material is geared to a young audience.

The most popular envelope sizes are monarch, number-ten, six-by-nine-inch, and nine-by-twelve-inch.

If you use a nonstandard envelope, you will probably pay extra to have it custom manufactured for you. But before you do so, take a "dummy" (mock-up) to the post office to be sure they will accept your format.

Some mailers create envelopes that look like official notices, such as bills, invoices, or a letter from the Internal Revenue Service. The theory is that such an envelope is always opened. But I am against such scare tactics, because they invariably anger and upset the reader and do not create a positive environment for selling your offer.

Envelopes do not have to be all paper. A paper envelope can have plastic windows which reveal the recipient's address label (affixed to the reply card or order form to make it easier to respond) or some other portion of the mail package (perhaps the cover of the brochure). Or, you can use an all-plastic ("poly") envelope that lets everything show through.

If you are enclosing a premium, product sample, or other three-dimensional object, use a paper envelope without windows. The bulging envelope creates curiosity, and you want the reader to have to open the envelope to find out what's inside.

I have never seen any test results that positively demonstrate whether it's better to use a brightly colored envelope or a plain white, brown, or gray envelope. I usually use white or off-white. But maybe you should try color.

• *Reply element.* Do not disguise the reply element or make it hard to find.

The reply element should literally fall onto the table when the reader opens the envelope or unfolds the letter. It should not be attached to the letter or brochure.

Some direct marketing experts say that a "busy" reply element—one that is crammed with copy and visuals—will outpull a simple reply element. The theory is that the busy element looks important, while the simple one does not. Others report that in recent tests, less cluttered reply elements (for example, those with copy and graphics on one side only) are doing better than cluttered reply elements with printing on both sides.

My opinion is that you have to strike a balance. The reply element must be designed so that it is easy to find, easy to understand, easy to complete.

At the same time, the reply element should not be bare of information. It should repeat the offer, restate the guarantee, and explain what the consumer is getting for her money.

People think of the reply element almost as a contract. If you graphically highlight the phrase "Money-Back Guarantee," they feel confident that the offer is risk-free. If you fail to repeat the guarantee on your reply element, they are afraid to sign because your "contract" is not complete—even though you discussed the guarantee in your letter. Remember, you are asking them to mail back a reply element, not the letter. So the reply element must be complete.

A reply element should have a bold headline that identifies it as an order form or reply card. Of course, you may give it a fancier name. But there should be no mistaking the purpose of the reply element. One copywriter, in his own self-promotional mailing package, prints his order form with the headline, "USE THIS FORM TO ORDER YOUR COPY TODAY!" What could be more direct?

I prefer to print the reply element on a different color and texture of stock than the letter and brochure. If, for example, the letter and flyer are printed on off-white paper, I will print the reply element on light blue or yellow or hot pink . . . and on heavy stock. My theory is that this makes the reply element immediately stand out from the rest of the package. However, I've never confirmed the theory in an actual direct mail test.

The reply element should be typeset, not typed. If you want to put a certificate-type border around it to make it look more official, fine. Anything that draws attention to the reply element is good.

A texture change is another way of separating the reply element from the rest of the package. If you print your letter and brochure on rag stock, for example, print the reply element on glossy, smooth stock. People separate things by feel as well as by sight.

• **The sales letter.** If the letter is personalized, use a fresh piece of paper for each page. Do not print on both sides of the page.

One way to save money is to computer-personalize the first page, then print the second page by offset. This makes it possible to print page two in two colors, so the text of the letter can be black, the signature blue. The personalized letter should be typed in black ink, but if you can afford a second color, put the signature in blue.

In a form letter, don't hesitate to print on both sides of the page. It will not hurt response. Printing on one side only is a waste of money here.

In a two-page form letter, print the letter on both sides of an 8½-by-11-inch sheet of paper.

In a four-page letter, print on an eleven-by-seventeen-inch sheet and fold once to form four pages.

I usually use a one-color printing job to save money. But a second color is useful for printing the signature in blue as well as highlighting certain segments of the copy in color. Blue is the usual choice for the second color because most people sign letters with blue pen.

Computer letters should be produced on a letter-quality or laser printer, not dot matrix. It should look as if it was typed on a typewriter—not on a computer.

Printed form letters should be produced from a typewritten original. Do not typeset your letter. The main goal in producing a direct mail letter is to make it resemble a personal letter as closely as possible.

I prefer the smaller IBM Prestige Elite typeface for sales letters. Because it is twelve-pitch, it lets you get about 10 to 20 percent more words on the page. But some people prefer a larger typeface. My recommendation for larger type is the ten-pitch IBM Courier typeface. It is very attractive, clean, and readable. These are the two standard styles of type for sales letters.

Avoid computer printers or typewriter typefaces that make the letter look as if it was typeset or produced on a computer. In particular, some desktop publishing systems and laser printers produce printouts that seem typeset, not typewritten. This may be fine for brochure work, but it is a drawback in direct mail letters.

The graphic appearance of the letter is very important. You want a letter that is easy to read and easy to scan. How do you achieve this?

- Use short paragraphs and sentences.
- Use arrows, bullets, asterisks, and other typewriter symbols to set off key paragraph or phrases.

- Use underlining and boldface (available on many computer printers) for highlighting.
- If you are laser-printing, you can easily add marginal notes that look handwritten. This always gets attention.
- Use subheads to break the letter up into sections and make it easy to scan.
- Indented paragraphs also help readability.
- Use dashes (—) and ellipses (. . .) to separate phrases and paragraphs . . . like this—because it breaks long sentences into short sections . . . and adds a welcome change of pace.
- Collect sample sales letters and adapt any techniques they use to make the letter more readable.
- Letters are generally typed single space. But you can double-space an occasional paragraph to make it stand out.
- Avoid long paragraphs and pages where all paragraphs are of uniform length and design. Variety makes the page more appealing to the eye.
- Use the typewriter or computer keyboard as a design device. Experiment with symbols, indentations, and spacing to find new ways to breathe life into your sales letters.
- Always end a page in the middle of a sentence rather than cleanly at the end of a sentence or paragraph. This forces the reader to turn to the next page.
- In a form letter, use a headline to grab attention.
- An alternative to the headline is to type a short summary of your offer or key sales theme at the top of the letter, and surround it with a border. This is known as a Johnson Box.
- Do not place your letterhead at the top of page one, as it appears on your office stationery. The only thing at the top of the letter should be your headline, salutation, and opening paragraph. You do not want your logo to compete with your letter opening. In a direct mail letter, put your logo and address at the bottom of the last page of the letter, after the signature and P.S.

• ***Brochure.*** The brochure should always be made from a single piece of paper folded to form pages and panels. Do not use a stapled or bound brochure in your direct mail package. The reader's tendency is to view a folded piece as something of temporary value which is to be read immediately and then acted upon or trashed; a stapled brochure is viewed as something to be filed for permanent reference or later reading. But you want immediate action, so use a folded design.

There is no limit to the number of different sizes, shapes, and formats you can use in your literature. Choose a format appropriate for your message and the amount of copy and visuals you have.

However, if your design gets too complicated, you can confuse yourself as well as your reader. For this reason, you might want to stick to a simple, standard format.

For a number-ten mailing, I usually take a piece of 8½-by-11-inch paper (a letter-size sheet) and fold it twice to form six panels. If my message is brief, I cut off one-third of the brochure to form a four-panel booklet. If I need more room, I'll fold an 8½-by-14-inch paper (a legal-size sheet) three times to form eight panels.

For a six-by-nine-inch mailing, I'll take an 8½-by-11-inch sheet and fold once, horizontally, to form a four-panel brochure (each panel measuring 8½-by-5½ inches). Or I can start with a larger sheet if I need more room.

For a nine-by-twelve-inch mailing, I like to fold an eleven-by-seventeen-inch sheet once vertically to form a four-panel brochure (each panel measuring 8½-by-11 inches).

Brochures should be typeset to set them apart from the letter. They should also be printed on a different stock. They need not be elaborate. Format depends on what you're selling.

If the brochure is informational in nature, I will often set it all in type to make it look like important information, rather than a sales pitch.

If copy carries the burden of selling, as it does in most direct mail brochures, I use a one- or two-color printing job. The design is mostly copy, augmented by some simple visuals. In a brochure selling a reference directory, for instance, I might show a picture of the directory, a photo of the book open (with call-outs highlighting the information and ease of use), and a picture of the author (to establish credibility). This type of illustration doesn't require an expensive printing job or expensive photography.

In another package, this one selling high-priced laboratory equipment and computers, I used top-quality photos of the equipment in actual laboratory operation, along with close-ups of the screens, printouts, and chemical operations being performed. The brochure was printed on glossy stock in full color. This was done for two reasons: the equipment and chemical operations were in themselves very colorful, so it would be a shame not to highlight this visually; and I wanted to "prove" to the reader that such sophisticated equipment did indeed exist, had already been manufactured, and was in use in actual laboratory operations. Color photographs offered this proof.

The outer panels of your brochure—the ones that show before the brochure is unfolded—should highlight, in large bold lettering, a provocative headline that lures the reader into the body of the piece.

Once you unfold the brochure, the inside spread is where you do your real selling and product demonstrating. Use plenty of subheads to break your story up into logical units. Many readers prefer to skim brochures, so they should be able to get the gist of the story just by reading the subheads. Use typography to make the subheads and headlines stand out on the page.

Typography should be inviting to the eye and easy to read. Avoid a design that is fancy, treats words as "design elements," or draws attention to its own beauty rather than to the discussion in the copy.

• ***Checking your work.*** Before you print your mailing, use the following "Design Aid Checklist" to check your designs for common direct mail mistakes that can cost you money.

▾ **Design Aid Checklist**

THE ENVELOPE:

[ ] Does the prospect's address show clearly?

[ ] Is there a return address and indicia?

[ ] Is the carrier route or presorted first-class mark preprinted, if necessary?

[ ] Are the windows positioned to show the portions of enclosures you want to show?

[ ] Show folded enclosures to your lettershop. Ask if what you've done is machine-insertable.

[ ] On the largest insert, is there a ¾-inch tolerance side to side and a ⅜-inch tolerance at the top to allow easy insertion?

[ ] Is the envelope within the post office's proportional tolerances?

[ ] Are perforations, tabs, window edges at least ¼ inch away from the envelope edge?

[ ] Check your color break.

[ ] Request samples of stock from your printer—make sure they are correct.

[ ] Demand a color-press proof to assure even inking.

THE ORDER FORM:

[ ] Does the order form fit in the reply envelope cleanly?

[ ] Does the name and address show through the outer envelope correctly?

[ ] Are tokens or three-dimensional items affixed to the order form machine-insertable?

[ ] Are perforations in the correct place? Be sure and check with your printer which perforations are easiest to tear.

[ ] Can the token be produced in the time allowed between now and the mail date?

[ ] On personalized order forms, are account codes and scan line positionings acceptable to the fulfillment operation?

[ ] Check for key codes and return address.

[ ] Look at overlays of tests to see that they make sense and are positioned correctly.
[ ] Are the folds correct?
[ ] Check for missing headlines.

THE LETTER:
[ ] Is it folded correctly?
[ ] Are fold marks indicated?
[ ] Are there any pieces of copy that could be enhanced by a type adjustment?
[ ] Are all test versions correctly overlayed?
[ ] Are the pages in sequence?
[ ] Are the prices correct?
[ ] Do the instructions in the letter match instructions on the order form?
[ ] Is the naming of the package elements consistent?
[ ] Are capitalization and style consistent?
[ ] Check the color break. See how you might enhance it.
[ ] Does the letter have a good strong P.S.?
[ ] Does the headline of the letter face out when it is folded?

PERSONALIZED LETTERS:
[ ] Check to see where the personalization falls, to see if it is positioned correctly. Use a transparent computer grid sheet.
[ ] Count characters of the longest fill-in to see if allowed spacing is correct.
[ ] Line up scan lines and automatic order entry account numbers to be sure they are correctly positioned.
[ ] Demand a sample printout and put it on your blueprint or mechanical to make sure the positioning is correct.
[ ] Are letters positioned properly to accommodate the width of the printer?

THE BROCHURE:
[ ] Are folds correct?
[ ] Is the color break correct?

[ ] Are photographs positioned and cropped properly?
[ ] Is all the copy there?
[ ] Are overlays done correctly?
[ ] Does it have a closed edge for machine-gripping on insertion?
[ ] Does it come out of the package in a sequence that makes the best promotional impact?
[ ] Check for even inking and color reproduction at the color-proof stage.
[ ] Have you checked the color proof against all original photos?
[ ] Are you approving the color proof on the paper the job is to be printed on?

PERIPHERALS:
[ ] Are all folds correct?
[ ] Does the peripheral insert in its correct sequence?
[ ] Does it belong in the package?
[ ] Is it the right version?

BUSINESS REPLY INFORMATION:
[ ] Are facing identification marks in the right position?
[ ] If the outgoing or return piece is a postcard, does it conform to postal requirement size:
   [ ] minimum: 3½ by 5 inches
   [ ] maximum: 6 by 4¼ inches
[ ] Is the address area no closer to the left-hand edge than one inch and at least ⅝ inch up from the bottom edge?
[ ] Have I checked my package against this list at all important stages of production?
   [ ] mechanicals
   [ ] blueprint
   [ ] color approval

Source: "It's Not Creative Unless It Sells!—The Basic Guide for Designing Winning Direct Mail," published by Direct Marketing Graphics Inc., 18-20 Purdy Avenue, Rye, NY 10580. Reprinted with permission.

PRODUCING THE MAILING PIECE

Once you have approved the artist's mechanicals using the "DM Design Aid Checklist," you must get the mailing piece printed, collated, stuffed, sealed, stamped, addressed, and mailed.

If you are using a direct mail advertising agency, they can handle the whole job for you and free you from worrying about the details. A consultant may also serve as project manager, eliminating the need to coordinate the work of many vendors.

If you are doing a small volume of direct mail, a local printer might be ideal for producing your package. You can then assemble the pieces yourself or pay the printer to do it for you. It is usually more convenient to have the printer do it, especially if he has special machines for the job.

If you are doing a small volume of *personalized* direct mail, you will probably have to print and hand-insert it on your premises. However, many word processing services and computer service bureaus are now offering personalized direct mail computer printing, stuffing, and mailing services to local clients. Why not see if you can farm out your computer letters to a word processing service? This way you don't tie up your own computer systems and staff.

If you do repeated large-volume mailings, a letter shop may be your best bet. A letter shop is a firm that handles all the mechanics of direct mail, from printing and insertion to addressing, metering, and taking the mailing to the post office. They are more familiar with direct mail production than most general printers and can save you from numerous headaches and costly mistakes.

ADDRESSING YOUR ENVELOPES

The best-looking method is to use a letter-quality daisy wheel or laser printer to print the recipient's name and address directly on the envelope. This technique can produce outer envelopes virtually identical to individually typed mail. A drawback is that computer-personalized envelope-and-letter packages usually have to be inserted by hand—to ensure that the right letter goes in the right envelope.

Unfortunately, while computer addressing gives you the highest quality, it also costs a lot. And it can't be done unless you can get the list in computer-readable form, either on floppy disk, magnetic tape, or via direct transmission.

The second-best method is to print the recipient's name and address on a reply card and let it show through a clear window on the front of the envelope. You can personalize the reply card either with computer-printing or by affixing a mailing label. If you use this method, check your mechanicals to make sure the prospect's name is aligned so that it does indeed show through the window.

If you are mailing a large volume, an inexpensive method is to use cheshire labels. The mailing list house supplies your labels on plain paper sheets, perforated for easy separation by machine or by hand. Most letter shops are equipped with machines that can apply cheshire labels to envelopes at extremely high speeds.

If you are doing a small mailing—say, only a few hundred a week—you might want to order your mailing list on pressure-sensitive (gummed) labels. A secretary or assistant can just peel the label off the sheet and affix it to the envelope by hand.

Avoid the temptation to address envelopes in script, by hand. It looks amateurish, takes a tremendous amount of time, and often serves to hurt response rather than increase it.

Naturally, I always recommend that you use a mailing list of recipients *by name*, whenever possible. But in some cases, business lists contain only the company name and address. In such a case, use an envelope teaser that identifies the title of the intended recipient, eg, "ATTENTION: ELECTRONIC COMPONENT BUYER."

POST OFFICE OPTIONS

Postage can be applied in one of three ways:

- An "indicia"—a postage permit printed directly on the envelope. This indicia design is reproduced on an offset press when the envelopes are printed, eliminating the need to apply a stamp or meter to each envelope individually.
- Postage meter.
- Stamp.

There is no definitive answer as to which method is best. Some mailers swear that using a stamp increases response. But Ray W. Jutkins of Rockingham/Jutkins Marketing says that mail from a business using a postage meter usually outpulls the same package sent with a real stamp—and that a printed postage indicia usually does as well as a postage meter. And at a recent meeting of a local ad club, an advertising director confided in me that he had extensively tested all three and found absolutely zero difference in response rate.

Based on what clients tell me, I'd say in most cases there is no great variation either way, and therefore you should use either a postage meter or printed indicia—whichever is most convenient. Lee Epstein, an expert in letter shop operations and direct mail mechanics, advises companies to use an indicia when mailing from two or more locations, because it permits you to use the same outer envelope for all your shops.

The one exception is when mailing to high-level executives at Fortune 500 companies. Recent experience has proven that mail-room personnel and secretaries at these firms routinely screen and destroy third-class bulk-rate metered and indicia mail. Secretaries do it to save the boss from "wasting his time" reading advertising material. Mail rooms do it to save themselves the time and expense of circulating your ads for you. In this environment, first-class computer-personalized envelopes mailed with a 29-cent stamp are your best bet for getting past the mail-room and secretarial barrier.

• ***Third class versus first class.*** Because of the high price of postage, third class is really the only economical choice for the majority of mailings. First-class postage adds so much to the cost that you simply cannot afford to use it.

Third class is slower, taking an average of two weeks or longer to reach its destination, rather than just a few days for first class. And if you have a very large third-class mailing that needs to get out, it might take two or three weeks before it all arrives at its destination.

Fortunately, although it is slower, most tests have shown that there is no significant difference in response when the identical package is tested in a third-class versus a first-class mailing. So by cutting costs dramatically, third class is an important means of lowering cost per thousand and increasing overall direct mail profits.

Currently it costs twenty-nine cents to send a letter first class, in contrast with 19.8 cents for third-class bulk rate. The difference is ninety-two dollars per thousand pieces mailed.

You should learn the ins and outs of third-class bulk mail, because you'll be using it for most of your mailings. Your local post office can provide you with publications and assistance explaining all about third class—what it costs, how it works, what you have to do to use it. Your consultant, letter shop, or ad agency can also guide you.

• ***Business reply mail.*** The post office can also provide you with a booklet explaining business reply mail. The booklet provides a drawing and specifications that you can follow to create the proper business reply imprint for use on your reply envelopes and postcards.

Before you can use business reply mail, you need to get a permit number from your local post office. This number will appear on all your business reply cards and envelopes. The annual fee is approximately fifty dollars for the permit, plus an additional optional $160 "accounting fee."

If you elect to pay the accounting fee, you can leave money on deposit with the post office. They will subtract the cost of postage for incoming reply mail from the deposit, rather than require you to pay cash every time the mail carrier delivers a fresh batch of reply cards and envelopes to your door. You should pay this accounting fee and give the post office a small deposit (the exact amount depending on how much reply mail you expect to receive). This saves money and is much more convenient than paying the mail carrier from your pocket every day.

How does business reply mail work? Simple. You do not pay postage for any business reply cards or envelopes not returned to you. For every card or envelope mailed back to you, you pay the appropriate first-class postage (twenty-nine cents for a letter, nineteen cents for a postcard) plus an additional fee of seven cents—assuming you have paid the accounting fee and made a deposit. If you do not leave money on deposit and pay the fee, the additional cost is twenty-three cents per envelope or card.

Is business reply mail worth the extra time and trouble? Absolutely. Direct mail tests prove that in consumer mail, postage-free business reply cards generally bring in more response than those to which the respondent must affix postage. One reason for this may be that many people simply do not keep stamps handy, especially the nineteen-cent stamps needed for postcard mail.

In business mailings, the jury is still out. In small mailings of my own, I have personally tested the same package using a business reply card and a postcard requiring a stamp. There was *zero* difference in response. My friend from the ad club did the same test, only he tested *three* variations: (a) business reply card, (b) reply card with stamp affixed, and (c) reply card requiring the recipient to affix a stamp. He also found no difference in response.

Yet I still recommend business reply mail for business-to-business mailings. Why? Two reasons. First, people expect it, and to omit it may create a feeling of annoyance at your company's perceived stinginess. Second, we are trained to think "response device" whenever we see that well-known business reply format on a card or envelope. The business reply permit, in a sense, functions as another design element which contributes to the overall response-oriented feel and look that you are trying to achieve in your design. So I say use it. What can it hurt?

Whatever you do, don't *you* put stamps on reply cards or envelopes. Either let the customer pay the postage or use business reply mail. But don't put stamps on cards or envelopes you enclose with your package. It's an absolutely foolish waste of money.

▾7

USING DIRECT MAIL
TO GENERATE SALES LEADS

THE IMPORTANCE OF SALES LEADS

For many organizations, a prime objective of advertising and promotion is to generate inquiries. And one of the best ways to do this is with direct mail.

In a comparative evaluation of sales tools, published in *Chemical Engineering Progress*, George Black of the Bozell & Jacobs ad agency rated the effectiveness of various forms of marketing communications in selling industrial equipment. When it came to effectiveness in generating sales leads, direct mail received a 4 out of a possible 5. Only publicity was rated higher.

American business spends billions of dollars each year to generate, track, and follow up sales leads. For some companies, the sales lead program represents a tremendous investment in time and money. For instance, in *Business Marketing* magazine, Don Mallisons, marketing communications manager of Digital Equipment, reported that his company processed 120,000 inquiries in a recent year.

But, regardless of whether you receive 1,200 inquiries this year or 120,000, you naturally want the best-quality leads—inquiries from genuine prospects with real interest in your product or service. My experience shows that direct mail is often the most effective tool for generating *high-quality* leads. Publicity may generate more leads at less cost, but the quality is frequently not as good.

More and more companies are using direct mail to generate leads. One survey, reported by *DM News*, revealed that presidents, general managers, and division heads receive more than seventy-five pieces of business mail each week. Some executives receive as many as two hundred pieces per week. With all that competition, it pays to develop the strongest, most effective mailing possible. Otherwise, your letter will just be lost in the crowd.

QUALITY OR QUANTITY?

The overwhelming majority of companies I've encountered measure the success of a lead-generation program strictly by the number of leads produced or the percentage of responses.

But all leads are not created equal. Some inquiries represent impulse responses from people who are curious but not really interested. Other inquiries are from people who want your free brochure or slide rule or booklet but have no need for your product. Yet some leads, the best leads, are urgent inquiries from genuine prospects who have a real need, are actively looking for a solution, and want to buy—*now*.

A successful lead-generation program looks at both quality and quantity. The goal should not be to gather great numbers but to generate the highest quantity of "hot" inquiries: phone calls and reply cards from genuine prospects who say, "I'm interested in this—really. What's the next step?"

One advertising executive, who handles the inquiry-generating advertising and direct mail campaigns of a number of schools offering computer training, said to me recently, "We rarely offer a brochure. The response we want is for someone to pick up the phone or come into the school for an interview. We want inquiries from people who are motivated enough to call or visit, not just from people who want to get free brochures in the mail."

Why has the quality aspect of lead generation been ignored for so long? For the simple reason that it is difficult to measure. Anyone can count reply cards. But how do you determine what is a "good" lead from what is a mediocre one?

In theory, it's not so hard. You determine what information you need to know about each lead, set up a system for tracking the lead and collecting the information, and report on the results. For instance, for each mailing, you might want to know:

- number of leads generated
- percentage of leads that result in a sale
- dollar value of total sales generated

Every person has different standards by which he or she judges a mailing's effectiveness. Some say, "A maximum quantity of leads is what we look for. Whether the sale is made depends on the follow-up, not the sales letter itself." Others say, "We judge a mailing by how many dollars in sales each mailing piece brings in. What good are reply cards that don't turn into customers?" Ultimately, only you can determine the yardstick by which you will judge your direct mail efforts.

In practice, gathering this type of information is not always easy. It depends on cooperation from the sales force and administrative personnel; gathering data and keeping records involves a lot of counting and paperwork. Today, much of this work has been simplified by computer systems and software packages designed specifically to track and monitor lead-generation programs.

With a computer, files are quickly and easily updated, and up-to-the-minute reports can be printed in a flash. For each mailing, you can track the leads, sales, and profits produced. The computer gives you fast access to better data for more informed decision making. Often the inquiries recorded in the lead-generation database double as the source of your in-house mailing list.

A discussion of how to create and manage a lead-generation system (computerized or manual) is beyond the scope of this book. If you need to know more, you might start by talking with a direct marketing consultant, computer programmer, or one of the consultants specializing in lead management. You can have a staff or independent computer programmer create a system for you. Or you can buy one of a number of packaged systems that come complete and ready to go. Some of these consist of hardware and software installed in your office; others are computerized inquiry-fulfillment services that are performed for you off-premises. A partial list of vendors is presented below.

▾ Lead Management and Tracking Systems

Automated Sales Support System
Epsilon Data Management, Inc.
24 New England Executive Park
Burlington, MA 01803
(617) 273-0250, (800) 225-1919

DCS
Dynatron Computer Systems, Inc.
127 W. 30th St.
New York, NY 10001
(212) 947-1212

ISA
Inquiry Systems Analysis
35 Morrissey Blvd.
Boston, MA 02125
(617) 482-6256

LCS Lead Conversion System
LCS Industries
120 Brighton Rd.
Clifton, NJ 07012
(201) 778-5588

The Order Prospector
Marketing Applications Software Company
5963 Tulane St.
San Diego, CA 92122
(619) 453-8758

Pending Business Reporting System
SMS Sales Management Systems
50 Church St.
Cambridge, MA 02138
(617) 492-1571

Prospecting
Key Systems, Inc.
512 Executive Park
Louisville, KY 40207
(502) 897-3332

Qualified Lead System
McGraw-Hill
1221 Ave. of the Americas
New York, NY 10020
(212) 997-3413

Quantum
Computer Marketing Services
1895 Mt. Hope Ave.
P.O. Box 1011
Rochester, NY 14603
(716) 271-2500

The Sales Manager
Market Power Computer
  Innovations
11780 Rough & Ready Rd.
Rough & Ready, CA 95975
(916) 432-1200

SEVEN WAYS TO GET BETTER LEADS

In some situations, you may be after the best leads possible. If, for example, each lead is to be followed up by a salesperson, you don't want salespeople wasting their valuable travel or telephone time chasing after nonprospects. Thus, you would be willing to sacrifice quantity to improve quality. In his book *Direct Marketing: Strategy, Planning, Execution*, Ed Nash gives seven ways to get better sales leads:

1. Mention the price.
2. Say that a salesperson will call.
3. Give a lot of information about the product, including any potential negatives.
4. Ask the prospect to give you a lot of information on the reply card, such as phone number, best time to call, number of employees.
5. Charge something. Even a small amount for a booklet or sample will eliminate the freeloaders.
6. Require a stamp. Don't use a business reply card or business reply envelope.

7. Make the offer specific and relevant to the product or service you are selling.

All of these rules are really common sense. Take rule 7 as an example. Imagine how many replies you would get if you offered a free clock radio to everyone who responded to your mailing! But how many of these people, do you think, would respond just to get the clock radio, without having any real interest in your company or your product?

On the other hand, if you changed your offer to a free booklet entitled, "Seven Ways to Protect Your Computer Equipment Against Power Surges," only people interested in protecting their computers against power surges would be inclined to send for the booklet. Thus, you would be attracting the right type of prospect for a surge protection device.

AND SEVEN WAYS TO GET MORE LEADS

In other situations, you might want to increase the number of leads your mailing generates. For instance, I had a client tell me, "We have a new product, no prospects, and three new salespeople sitting around twiddling their thumbs. I need leads and lots of them—FAST!"

As a rule, the more leads you get, the lower the overall quality of the leads. In his book, Ed Nash also gives seven ways to get more leads:

1. Tell less. Leave something to curiosity.
2. Use your computer printer to personalize the response device so the prospect doesn't have to write in his or her name and address.
3. Add convenience. Supply the stamp, the envelope, maybe even a pencil.
4. Give a gift or a premium—one that is valuable and not

necessarily related to your product. The more valuable, the more leads you'll get.

5. Make the entire offer FREE.
6. Ask less on the reply card—the fewer questions, the better.
7. Add a prize. Sweepstakes can really boost response.

▾ Checklist of Lead-Getting Offers

Key: 1 = low   5 = average   10 = high

Offer	Quantity of Leads Produced	Quality of Leads Produced
Free gift by mail	10	2
Free information report by mail	9	3–6
Free brochure	8	5
More information	7	5
Demonstration	5–6	5–6
Sales presentation/ consultation	4	7
Salesperson will call	3	7–8
Write on your letterhead to request information	1	8
Complete questionnaire or spec sheet	2	9

THE LEAD-GETTING LETTER: HOW MUCH TO TELL?

In mail order there is an old saying that goes: "The more you tell, the more you sell."

But in lead generation, things are different. The lead-generating direct mail package does not have to do the whole job of selling the customer and bringing back the order. Rather, the goal of the lead-generating package is to get a prospect to raise his hand and say, "Yes, your product sounds like something that might be able to help me. Tell me more!"

However, if you tell your whole story in the mailing, there is nothing left for the reader to inquire about. The prospect may feel that he or she knows everything there is to know about your product or service, and that there is no reason to respond—unless he or she is ready to buy now.

For this reason, lead-generating packages do not tell the whole story. Rather, they provide enough information to whet the reader's appetite for further details. The interested reader is invited to send for more details—which might be a brochure, a presentation, or a demonstration of the product.

Exactly how much information should your package include? Enough to give the prospect a good idea of (a) what you are selling; (b) the problem it solves or the key advantage of your product over similar products; and (c) how the reader can personally benefit from the product. You should also specify, in detail, the action you expect on the part of the reader—and provide an incentive for immediate response, if possible.

PHONE OR MAIL RESPONSE?

Not all prospects are ready to buy your product today, of course. A few might be. But there are plenty of others who may be ideal buyers for your product—except that they don't have (or don't think they have) an immediate need for what you offer.

Your lead-generating mailing should accommodate both the hot prospect and people with a more casual interest in your offer. For this reason, I recommend you give readers the following options:

• In your sales letter, tell the reader he can contact you either by mailing an enclosed reply card or picking up the telephone and calling you directly. You will get more phone calls if your phone number is toll-free. And you will get more reply cards if you pay the postage.

• On your reply card, have at least two options the reader can select by checking the appropriate box. The first option says, "Have a salesperson get in touch with me. The best time to call is————." The second option says, "Send me your free brochure."

In this way, you can get qualified responses from all levels of prospects—both those who are inclined to pick up the phone and speak with you now, and those who prefer to review sales literature in the privacy of their own homes, without being bothered by a salesperson.

Some direct marketers frown on free-brochure offers, arguing that it is a waste of money to mail expensive literature to consumers who are just "brochure collectors." I disagree. There are many people—and I'm one of them—who want to see a brochure first and read it before making a buying decision . . . *without* being badgered by telephone salespeople. We are not cranks and we may buy your product, but we will do it on our terms—not yours. If you want our business, you must give us the option of getting a brochure in the mail without being grilled on the phone, pestered by salespeople, or having a company representative insist on visiting us to deliver your literature in person. I personally know many people who say they have a policy of never buying *anything* sold over the telephone.

SAMPLE LETTER: FREE INFORMATION KIT

I recently wrote a new sales letter to generate sales leads for my own services as a freelance writer.

Rather than focus on my background and credentials, as previous letters had done, I stressed the offer of a free information kit. The new letter pulled a 10 percent response versus 7 percent for my old letter.

Here is the text of my new letter:

Dear Marketing Professional:

"It's hard to find a copywriter who can handle industrial and high-tech accounts," a prospect told me over the phone today, "especially for brochures, direct mail, and other long-copy assignments."

Do you have that same problem?

If so, please complete and mail the enclosed reply card, and I'll send you a free information kit describing a service that can help.

As a freelance copywriter specializing in business-to-business advertising, I've written hundreds of successful ads, sales letters, direct mail packages, brochures, annual reports, feature articles, press releases, newsletters, and scripts for clients all over the country.

But my information kit will give you the full story. You'll receive a comprehensive "WELCOME" letter that tells all about my service—who I work for, what I can do for you, how we can work together.

You'll also get my client list (I've written copy for over 65 advertisers and agencies), complete with client comments . . . biographical background . . . samples of work I've done for others in your field . . . a fee schedule listing what I charge for ads, brochures, and other assignments . . . helpful article reprints on copywriting and advertising . . . even an order form you can use to put me to work for you.

Whether you have an immediate project, a future need, or are just curious, I urge you to send for this information kit. It's free . . . there's no obligation . . . and you'll like having a proven copywriting resource on file—someone you can call on whenever you need him.

From experience, I've learned that the best time to evaluate a copywriter and take a look at his work is *before* you need him, not when a project deadline comes crashing around the corner. You want to feel comfortable about a writer and his capabilities in advance . . . so when a project does come up, you know who to call.

Why not mail back the reply card TODAY, while it is still handy? I'll rush your free information kit as soon as I hear from you.

Regards,

Bob Bly

I think this letter has been successful for me for a number of reasons:

• The first two paragraphs immediately identify and empathize with the reader's problem.
• The rest of the letter positions my free information kit as offering a solution to this problem.

• The reader can get this solution with no cost, no obligation, no sales pressure—just by mailing a reply card.

• I invite response from people of varying degrees of interest—from those with an immediate project to those who are just curious.

• By describing the package in detail, I persuade the reader that it is something worth having.

• The second to last paragraph gives the reader some free helpful advice about selecting copywriters ... which demonstrates that I have his or her best interest in mind.

• The letter closes with a strong call to action.

SAMPLE LETTER: FREE SEMINAR

My friend Gary Blake wrote an even more successful lead-getting letter which he has generously agreed to share with us. Gary's company, The Communication Workshop, offers writing seminars to corporations.

The problem is that managers are bombarded by sales pitches from such firms. So Gary decided to do something different. Instead of using his letter to pressure people to hire him, he offered a free seminar—no cost, no obligation—to people who responded.

Approximately one out of ten people receiving Gary's letter registered for the free seminar, and so he had no trouble filling the session.

Offering a free seminar makes sense for Gary, because it allows prospects to sample his service directly. Oh yes, at least one of the people attending the free seminar hired Gary to give a full-length seminar, so the mailing has already paid for itself many times over.

Here is Gary's letter—simple yet effective:

Mr. Joe Smith
Manager of Development
Big Company
Anywhere, USA

Dear Mr. Smith:

No, this is *not* another pitch for your business. Not yet, anyway. This is an opportunity for you to attend a FREE three-hour overview of The Communication Workshop's popular seminar in effective business writing.

You may have heard about The Communication Workshop. We've been featured in *Crain's New York Business*, *Training & Development Journal*, *Training News*, and *Across the Board* (enclosed).

You are among a select group of training professionals being invited to see the writing workshop in action. Here's your chance to pick up some valuable writing tips, socialize with your colleagues, and find out why so many people turn to The Communication Workshop for writing seminars.

The attached sheet gives you all the specifics. As a participant, you'll be invited to submit a writing sample to me two weeks before the seminar. I'll personally review it, and give you clear, consistent feedback on your writing.

Please join me for an enjoyable, information-packed three hours.

Sincerely,

Gary Blake, Ph.D.
Director

Along with the personalized letter Gary enclosed an article reprint (from *Across the Board*) and a descriptive flyer with a registration coupon attached.

Why does this letter work so well?

• The opening ("No, this is *not* another pitch for your business") is a shocker—not what the reader is expecting. It also empathizes with the fact that the reader is deluged with sales pitches.

• It offers something of incredible value (a three-hour business writing workshop) for free.

• It flatters the reader ("You are among a select group of training professionals").

• It builds credibility by mentioning all the publications that have written about The Communication Workshop and by enclosing a reprint for the reader.

A THREE-DIMENSIONAL MAILING

Lewis Advertising, a Baltimore ad agency, decided to use a three-dimensional mailing to invite customers and prospects to its fifty-fifth anniversary celebration.

The package was a box with a teaser on the lid: "You're in for a real treat!" Inside was a realistic photograph of a slice of cherry cheesecake on a plate. Next to the "cake" was a stainless steel fork engraved with the company's logo.

Out of 250 customers and prospects who received the mailing, two hundred people attended the celebration—a 72 percent response rate. Some of those who were unable to attend asked for a tour of the agency's facilities later on.

The moral? Expensive mailings can be a costly waste if not done properly. But well executed, a high-cost mailing piece can dramatically outpull a plain-jane mailing in certain cases. (Source: *Imprint* magazine, Summer 1985, p. 14.)

BUDGETING THE LEAD-GENERATING PACKAGE

In mail order, it is easy to determine how much to spend on direct mail. You know approximately what range of response you will receive, based on past experience. You know how much your product sells for, and you know your profit per sale. You can calculate, based on profit per sale and anticipated sales per thousand pieces mailed, how much you can afford to spend if you want to break even on the mailing.

In lead generation, such precise formulas fall apart, because we don't know how much profit we can make from each lead. Also, when a lead is converted to a customer, the dollar volume of sales can be hundreds of times greater than in mail order.

For example, if you are writing a package selling subscriptions to a $19.95 magazine, you know that each order will bring in exactly $19.95. But if you are writing a lead-generating mailing for a law firm, a person who responds may spend anywhere from fifty dollars for an initial consultation to $100,000 or more for major litigation. Especially in industrial marketing, one sale can often be a yearly contract worth up to several million dollars.

Therefore, I can't really give you a formula for determining how simple—or how elaborate—to make your mailing package. In the truest sense, it is *up to you*.

My recommendation, of course, is that you start with the least expensive package and work your way up from there. I prefer a simple, inexpensive package consisting of a business reply card (BRC) and a one- or two-page sales letter ... with a booklet added, if appropriate.

But other companies use more elaborate packages, often with great success. One engineering firm, promoting a new type of joint, sent out a mailing that included an audiocassette tape of the inventor of the product explaining how the joint worked, its importance, and the ways engineers could use it in their designs.

The tape was sent to about five hundred prospects. In addition to these, the engineering firm sent a separate, more expensive mailing to their fifty top prospects—large corporations representing potential contracts of millions of dollars. These fifty prospects received a box containing not only the audio-cassette but a free Sony Walkman on which to play it. Expensive? Yes. But certainly bound to get attention. And well worth the price if it brought in just one of those fifty people as a customer.

Again, though, my advice is to start with a simple package. If it works, think about upgrading to something fancier. "Bells and whistles" *can* increase response, but they are no substitute for a strong offer or sales proposition. Concentrate on making a strong offer that people will respond to. *Then* dress it up to make it pull even better.

ANALYZING YOUR NEEDS

Unfortunately, there is no formula I can give you that tells you which package format or sales approach to use in your particular situation. Each mailing is different; what works in one situation may not be right for yours. However, by asking the right questions, you can quickly get your strategy on track.

Here are some of the questions to ask when planning a lead-generating mailing.

• *Do people know my product?* Let's say you want to get people to come into your store and look over a new computer.

If the computer is an IBM PC or other well-known brand, people are probably somewhat familiar with your product and your company. Your letter does not have to "sell" them on your machine; your TV commercials and ad campaign have already done it.

Instead, your letter should focus on giving people a *reason* to go to the store, such as a free demonstration, free software with purchase, or $250 rebate.

• *Is my prospect familiar with my product category?* In some cases, not only has the person receiving your letter never heard of your product, but he or she may be totally unfamiliar with the entire product category.

This was surely the case when Apple began advertising its first personal computers in the late 1970s. People had never heard of a personal computer and could not conceive of having such a device in their homes. Early Apple ads had to educate people about computers before they could begin selling the Apple brand.

I recently did a mailing package promoting a new service that produces color slides from computer graphics created on PCs and stored on floppy disks. Since this was something new, we included with our sales letter a rather lengthy brochure illustrating what the system was and how it works.

Most people believe it is easier to sell and promote new and different products. In fact, the opposite is true. With a new product, you must *educate* the public as well as sell them. And educating people takes time—and money.

• *Does my prospect understand the problem my product solves?* Can you would imagine how hard it would be to sell a product that reduces high blood pressure if people didn't understand what high blood pressure is and that it can harm their health?

If your prospects do not understand the problem your product solves . . . or if they have the problem but are not aware of it . . . you must educate them about the problem before you can effectively sell your product as a solution.

A company called KnowledgeWare sells software packages that automate part of the work usually done by programmers, systems analysts, and other people who design new software. Specifically, the software automates a particular set of techniques known as information engineering.

Many IS professionals don't know or don't use these techniques, so part of KnowledgeWare's challenge was to educate them and sell them on these techniques. The solution was to write a forty-page white paper on Information Engineering and offer it through direct mail.

The mailing consisted of a letter and reply card stressing the offer of the free white paper. A small booklet was also enclosed. The title of the booklet was, "Can you answer these ten questions about Information Engineering?" The purpose of the booklet was to tease the prospect by asking ten important questions that would be answered in the free white paper. Response to this mailing was 10 percent.

• **What is the next step in the buying process?** This is the most important question you can ask in lead generation. The primary purpose of your mailing is to get the prospect to take this next step—and not to sell the product itself.

Do you want prospects to come to your store or showroom? Give them compelling reasons for making the trip, such as a free test drive, free gift, or discount.

Do you want prospects to send for a catalog, brochure, or other free literature? Stress the offer of the literature. Tell them that it is given free and without obligation. Describe it in attractive terms that will compel readers to send for a copy.

Do you have to visit with the prospect to describe your services in more detail? Don't think of this visit as a sales call; in your mailing, promote it as a "free consultation." Your copy should stress the value of this free consultation and describe how it benefits the reader. For example, tell the prospects you will analyze their particular problem and make suggestions on how they can solve it (if this is indeed what you do).

Do you offer a free gift, such as a poster or wall calendar or pen-and-pencil set? Stress this free offer in your letter.

Naturally, you don't want to give away too much for free. But the more valuable your free offer, the more leads you'll get.

• ***Who is the logical prospect for my product or service?*** I know you don't want to give away free service, free information, or free gifts to people who are not prospects for your product or service. So it's important to identify and find mailing lists of logical prospects for your order.

For example, let's say you have an office-cleaning service. Who at a company would be the person to hire your type of service? The office manager? The company president? The owner of the building? You will get a higher-quality sales lead by mailing to the right prospect: someone with the authority, money, and desire to own your product or take care of the problem it solves.

• ***But what if I don't know who my best prospect is?*** Take a guess and do a mailing to people you think are likely to buy. Then, in the P.S. of your letter say, "If you would like us to send information about our product to other people in your organization, please fill in their names and titles on the enclosed reply card and mail it back to us." In a mailing to consumers, you can say, "Please give us the names and addresses of friends who might also be interested in our product." On the reply card, leave space for the recipient to write in the names of two or three other people.

In this way, you get the recipient to *tell* you who you should be mailing to . . . and provide the names, titles, and addresses for you. This technique is known as *member-get-a-member*, probably because it has frequently been used to get current members of an organization to provide the names of other people the organization could solicit for membership.

• ***Do I need a brochure?*** Should you include a booklet in your mailing, or should you just send a letter and reply card?

You should consider including a flyer or booklet if:

- your product is unfamiliar to the reader and needs to be explained
- it's important to tell the reader *how* the product works
- you need to show a picture of the product
- your firm is unknown and you want to build credibility with your market
- your prospect needs some background education in the technology or subject matter your product addresses.

• *What will I send to people who respond to my mailing?* If you have a great sales brochure or a helpful, informative pamphlet, great! You can increase response to your mailing by emphasizing the value of your free information.

However, if your brochure isn't really very good, or you don't have any literature, you may want to talk more about your product and your company, and downplay the free-literature offer. There isn't much point to getting people to request literature if the brochure you send does a poor selling job.

Have any articles been published about your company or product? Often you can turn an article into an informative booklet which can be offered in your mailing. For example, I reprinted one of my articles as a report, "23 Ways to Create Business-to-Business Mailings That Work." A one-paragraph mention of the free report in a business magazine generated sixty-five inquiries.

Take a look at existing brochures, booklets, speeches, article reprints, press releases, and other sales and technical literature. Is there any material there that can be repackaged into free information to form the basis of a direct mail offer?

• *Must I include a reply card?* Yes. You will always get more responses when you include a business reply card or order form with a return envelope. I think it is a mistake not to include a reply element with your mailing. Even when your primary goal is to generate a telephone response, you should still include a reply card to capture those prospects who don't want to call.

• *Is a toll-free number available for inquiries?* Although having people call you toll-free costs you money, you generally get a better response with a toll-free number than if you force the prospect to make a toll call. Don't forget to tell the reader that the call is free.

• *How many people am I mailing to?* If you are mailing to many thousands of people, you may be limited by budget constraints to a standard package consisting of a one-page sales letter, business reply card, and simple pamphlet in a number-ten envelope.

If you can segment a small portion of these people—say, 10 percent or so—as prime prospects, you may want to send them a more elaborate version of your package. Since these people represent a greater potential dollar volume of sales, you might spend five or even ten dollars per package instead of just fifty cents.

On the other hand, if you are mailing to a small market— several hundred people or less—producing an elaborate brochure for such a limited mailing cannot be done cost-effectively because of the development costs. For small mailings, you are better off sending a sales letter and reply card with an inexpensive enclosure, such as an article reprint or inexpensive black-and-white folded pamphlet.

• *Where am I getting my mailing list?* If the mailing list is available on floppy disk or tape, you can personalize the mailing on your in-house word processing system or at an outside letter shop.

The problem with personalization is that it consumes either a lot of your time or a lot of your money.

If you do it in-house, you tie up a person and a computer until the mailing is done. Even with a fast letter-quality printer, you might only be able to produce fifty or sixty personalized letters and envelopes an hour. Thus, most companies only go this route if the mailing list is a few hundred names or less.

If you use an outside letter shop, personalization is rarely cost-effective for mailings of less than five thousand to ten thousand. For smaller quantities, use a printed form letter.

In many cases, small mailing lists are available on labels only, not in computer-readable form, which makes it extremely difficult to personalize your letters unless you have someone key all the names on the list into your computer.

• *What special action do I take if someone has an immediate need for my product?* Some people who receive your mailing may be ready to buy right now. Your letter should tell them how to get immediate service from your firm. For example: "If you have an immediate project in mind, call us toll-free at 800-XXX-XXXX for a prompt survey and price quotation. Response within 24 hours." You should be able to accommodate the urgent prospect as well as people who are just shopping around.

• *Will my mailing be screened by a secretary?* One of the big problems in using direct mail to reach business executives is getting past the secretary. As a rule, the higher up you go in the corporate ladder—especially at Fortune 1000 companies—the more likely the secretary is to screen incoming mail.

How do you get around this?

• A popular technique has been to mark the outer envelope PERSONAL AND CONFIDENTIAL. But it doesn't work anymore because everyone is doing it and secretaries are wise to the trick.

• Secretaries look for clues that your envelope contains advertising material rather than important correspondence. A sure sign of this is teaser copy or graphics on the outer envelope. So don't use a teaser when mailing to high-level executives.

• Make your mailing look like a personal communication from one business executive to another. Use a high-quality paper stock. Personalize the letter on your word processor. Run the envelope through your printer; don't affix labels. Use postage stamps instead of an indicia or postage meter. Mail first class instead of bulk third class.

• Xerox Corporation used a unique format in which a smaller number-ten envelope was glued to a larger six-by-nine-inch envelope. Teaser copy on the small envelope reads:

> Dear Secretary,
>
> Your company needs your expert opinion, And so do we.
>
> We also have a free gift for you.
>
> P.S. Please peel off this envelope and keep it for yourself. Then just pass along the larger one.

This clever approach openly asks the secretary for help, turning a potential enemy into an ally.

• Personalize any gifts, premiums, or other enclosures. For example, if you send a typed report, add a title page which says, "Prepared exclusively for T. C. Smith." Smith's secretary, thinking that the report may be important, will not throw it away.

• *Is there a time limit on my offer?* You can increase response by stressing the urgency of your offer. When running a special promotion, for example, be sure to let the reader know that (a) the promotion is special, (b) it is being offered only through direct mail to a select group of customers and prospects, of which he or she is a member, and (c) the offer is for a limited time only, and once it expires it may never be repeated again. If there is a specific date by which the offer will expire, state this in your letter.

• *How many leads do I want to generate?* According to The Computer Studio, a Tuckahoe, New York, firm specializing in lead-generation programs, you should limit your mailings so you don't produce more leads than your sales staff can properly handle. For instance, if your response rate is 2 percent, you might generate twenty leads per month from one thousand pieces per month. This may be enough to keep a full-time salesperson busy if selling your product requires a lot of customer contact and up-front effort.

• *What information do I need to collect about the prospects and their needs?* A reply card that restates the offer and asks for a response is doing only half the job. Reply elements should also be used to gather information that helps qualify prospects.

For instance, if you're selling accounts-receivable software, the reply card should ask: What type of computer do you have? What is your operating system? How many invoices do you write a month?

Remember that mailing from KnowledgeWare . . . the one offering a free white paper on "Information Engineering"? The reply card asked the readers to tell what type of mainframe computer, database management system, and programming tools they used in their data center. It also asked how many systems analysts worked at their company.

If gathering detailed information is your primary goal, you might consider doing a mailing in the form of a survey or mail questionnaire. Response rates of 20 to 30 percent or more are not uncommon. Try to keep your survey short: two sides of a single 8½-by-11-inch sheet is the maximum. Use yes/no or multiple-choice questions rather than a fill-in-the-blank or essay format. And always include a business reply envelope.

8

USING DIRECT MAIL TO GENERATE MAIL ORDER SALES

MONEY IN YOUR MAILBOX

This chapter is written for companies that already sell products by mail as well as those that want to or are just thinking about it.

Even if you are not primarily in the direct marketing business, mail order can be a great way to generate additional sales and profits for your firm. Mail order is ideal for selling secondary products . . . or reaching customers that are too distant to travel to your store . . . or servicing accounts that are too small to warrant personal attention from a sales rep.

WHAT SELLS BY MAIL?

According to a recent study published by the Maxwell Scroge Company, the leading mail order products include:

- insurance
- general merchandising
- home furnishings
- housewares

- gifts
- magazine subscriptions
- books
- ready-to-wear clothing
- collectibles
- sporting goods
- crafts
- foods
- records and tapes

Your product may not be on this list, but that doesn't mean you can't offer it through the mails. Every day, clever marketers all over the country are finding new ways to profit from mail order sales. But first you need to know why people will buy something through the mail instead of at a store or through a sales representative.

EIGHT REASONS WHY PEOPLE ORDER PRODUCTS THROUGH THE MAIL

• *Price.* According to a survey in *Family Computing*, 50 percent of mail order software buyers cited lower prices as the reason they buy through the mail. A common theme in mail order copy is, "Because we eliminate the middleman, we can offer you our products at prices significantly below retail."

• *Convenience.* Whenever I need paper for my photocopier, I pick up the phone, call Nancy at Minolta, and place an order. It takes less than a minute. The supplies I need come to my doorstep a few days later. And they send me a bill I have thirty days to pay. Why on earth would I want to get in my car, drive to a stationery store, pay cash out of my pocket, and lug a heavy box all the way home?

• **Time.** Every time I go to the mall it takes ten minutes just to find a parking space. Then I have to fight the crowds, deal with rude salespeople, and waste time selecting merchandise only to learn that it's out of stock. Many people don't have the time to go shopping and prefer to save time by ordering through the mail.

• **Fun.** Mail order buying is a lot of fun. It's exciting to get colorful mailings and catalogs, read through all the interesting offers, and look at the beautiful pictures. My wife and I especially enjoy the food catalogs from Harry and David in Oregon; reading a Harry and David catalog is like walking through the finest gourmet store and sampling the goodies. And when your merchandise does arrive, it's like getting an unexpected gift from a friend. There's a pleasure in opening the box not unlike unwrapping your presents at holiday time.

• **Availability.** A big appeal of mail order is that it offers people an opportunity to buy many interesting, unusual, or odd products they cannot get locally. Each year, for example, we order bulbs of beautiful, exotic flowers that local greenhouses don't carry. Take a look at mail order advertising—both print and TV. They frequently use the phrase "not available in stores." This tells the customers that if they don't order from you, they won't be able to get the product at all.

• **Free trial.** If I buy a book from a bookstore, I'm stuck with the book even if I discover after reading the first ten pages that it's boring. But when I order books by mail, I can keep them for fifteen or thirty days, read them, and then decide whether to keep the book and pay for it—or return it without cost or obligation of any kind. Although we have had our share of problems with getting the wrong merchandise and dealing with incompetent telephone representatives from some mail order houses, returning mail order merchandise is generally easier—and less costly—than going back to the store.

• ***Service.*** To get your business, mail order companies often offer a lot of extras that retailers don't provide. Such as free delivery . . . free gift-wrapping . . . free gifts . . . discounts for being a good customer . . . discounts for prompt payment . . . buy now, pay later privileges . . . help with ordering and merchandise selection . . . toll-free telephone numbers to call . . . computer printouts that remind you what you ordered last year. Is your local department store as generous?

• ***No sales pressure.*** If you've ever set foot in an automobile dealership or time-sharing resort, you know what sales pressure is. In direct mail selling, you can examine the product, read the brochure, and ponder the offer in the privacy of your own home . . . without being pressured by a salesperson. Yes, it's true that some direct marketing companies exert undue pressure with telephone follow-ups. But it's a lot easier to hang up the phone than it is to get out from under the thumb of a live salesperson.

TEN QUESTIONS TO ASK WHEN EVALUATING WHETHER MAIL ORDER IS FOR YOU

• ***Does it fit in with my current product line?*** Real profit in mail order is not in one-shot sales but in selling a series of related product to the same group of customers over and over again. If you have already sold your customers a product through the mail, and you find a related product that's right for them, you might want to offer it in a mailing. For example, the person who has bought business cards through the mail is also a good prospect for letterheads, envelopes, labels, and other such items.

• *Can I sell my customers accessories, supplies, and add-ons through the mail?* If you sell your customers personal computers, you might be able to sell them peripherals, software, printer ribbons, and computer paper. Even if they bought the computer from you in person, they might find it more convenient to order supplies by phone or mail. Try it!

• *Do I have any "marginal accounts" that are not profitable for salespeople to handle?* Many customers order so little and so infrequently that is doesn't pay to keep servicing them in person. However, these small accounts can be handled quite profitably by mail and phone. Direct mail can allow you to profit from a large number of small accounts that you might otherwise have to drop.

• *Can I make this product or buy it from a supplier?* You may have a great idea for a mail order product. But if the product cannot be made in sufficient quantity to fill orders, your effort to generate orders will have been wasted.

• *Does anyone else sell the same product by mail?* If *nobody* else sells the product, it may be a bad sign. No competition tells you that others have probably tried selling the same type of product by mail—and failed (unless you are so brilliantly innovative that no one ever thought of selling your type of product by mail before).

If there are a few people out there selling the product by mail, great! It proves that the idea has worked for others and can work for you, too. All you need to do is differentiate yourself from the competition in some way. Perhaps your price is lower . . . or your product has a feature the competition does not . . . or you sell your product for a different application . . . or to a different group of buyers.

If there are many people selling the same products, watch

out! Some fields get so crowded that it becomes very difficult to compete successfully and make a profit. I would be cautious, for example, about going into the computer supply business because I get six or seven look-alike computer-supply catalogs in the mail each week, and I throw all of them away without a second glance.

• ***Does the product need to be replenished?*** There are greater profits in products that run out and must be replenished than in products that last forever. For example: Vitamins run out and must be reordered. A magazine subscription expires and must be renewed. An insurance premium provides coverage for only a year and must be paid again at the end of the first year. Shoes wear out. Clothing goes out of fashion. An annual directory quickly becomes dated. Does your product have this kind of repeat-order potential?

• ***Is the price right?*** To sell by mail, you have to offer the product at a price that will generate a lot of orders yet still allow you to make a profit. If people can get the product cheaply through other sources, or if the profit margins are small, the product is probably not a good mail order item.

• ***Do a lot of my customers and prospects need this product?*** If only a few people can use your product, you won't generate enough sales to pay the cost of doing a direct mail package. Minimum potential market should be at least in the thousands . . . preferably higher.

• ***Can the item withstand shipping?*** Some products are too big, too heavy, too fragile, too dangerous, or too perishable to be shipped through the mails.

• ***Am I set up to handle a mail order business?*** Do you have the time? the space? the administrative personnel? the computer systems? Even a small mail order operation needs two or three people to handle and process the orders. If there's no one available in your company to take on this task, no place to store your inventory, and no budget for setting up a mail order operation, you may not be able to get started.

HOW TO SET MAIL ORDER PRICES

Basically there are two kinds of items sold by mail:

- merchandise available only through your mail order offer
- merchandise sold by other firms and through other means, such as in stores or from sales reps.

If you have a unique product you are selling by mail, such as a one-of-a-kind newsletter, a special report, or a software program, how much will you charge for it? The answer, really, depends on what the market is willing to pay.

One of the major factors you might test in your direct mail is price. For instance, let's say you publish a forty-page booklet on "How to be Successful in Business." What is it worth? Three dollars? Ten dollars? Fifteen dollars? You could mail three versions of your direct mail package, the only variation being the price.

The results may surprise you. In many instances, I've seen the higher price pull the most orders. You'd think it would be the lowest price. Apparently, many people equate high price with value. They are wary of buying something that seem too "cheap."

In the second mail order situation, you are selling an existing product available from other sources. One of my clients is a mail order house selling software by mail. They do not sell their own products, but rather, they offer packages published by other firms and available in retail stores. Obviously, they cannot charge more than the computer stores; no one would buy. Their big selling advantage, then, is the ability to offer the software at prices *below* retail.

In the same way, if I'm going to order envelopes from a mail catalog, I expect to get a bargain compared with buying them at the corner stationery store. I'm certainly not going to pay more than the store charges. In such a situation, the mail order company's prices are determined, in large part, by what others are selling the same merchandise for.

Some people sell very low-priced products successfully through the mail, but they are the exception, not the rule. Because of the high cost of doing direct mail today, it is difficult to sell products that cost less than fifty dollars through direct mail profitably.

Advertisers that have lower-priced products often use a combination of small space and classified ads, and direct mail to sell their products. The ad is used to generate an inquiry, which is fulfilled with a mailing package consisting of a sales letter, brochure, order form, and reply envelope. An effective mailer will convert at least 10 to 15 percent of the inquiries to orders; an exceptionally successful mailer can convert 20 to 30 percent or more.

If the ad is effective at generating leads, you should not be paying more than one dollar or so per lead. So an ad that costs you $150 should generate at least 150 leads.

HOW TO DETERMINE YOUR PROFIT POTENTIAL

A little simple math can show you how much money your direct mail sales can bring you.

Let's say we are sending out a direct mail package offering an automotive tool kit that sells for $29.95. For this price the customer gets a variety of hand tools (which we buy wholesale) and a free tool chest. The tools and tool chest combined cost us $8.00.

For each sale we collect $29.95 from the customer plus $1.50 shipping and handling. In reality, shipping and handling—including packaging—costs us $2.00. Our profit per sale is:

$29.95 in sales
+ $1.50 shipping and handling
= $31.45 net income
− $8.00 material costs
− $2.00 freight, packaging, and handling
TOTAL PROFIT
PER SALE: $21.45

Now, we have to print and mail a direct mail package to get orders. Let's say our cost for promotion—including production, printing, and postage—is fifty cents per mailing piece or five hundred dollars per thousand (a very typical figure for volume direct mail).

To break even on a mailing of one thousand pieces we need

$$\frac{\$500 \text{ promotional expense}}{\$21.45 \text{ income per order}} = \frac{23.4 \text{ orders per thousand}}{\text{pieces mailed}}$$

In terms of percentage response, this comes to

$$\frac{23.4 \text{ orders} \times 100}{1,000 \text{ mailings}} = 2.34\%$$

Thus, to break even on this mailing, your package would have to pull a 2.34 percent response. Anything below that would lose money. Anything above it would bring you pure profit.

SETTING YOUR MAIL ORDER GOALS

Everyone has a different goal in mail order.

Some people expect to make money with every mailing, every product. A direct mail piece that breaks even without generating profit is a disappointment to them. A piece that loses money is a disaster.

In his book *Mail Order* (New York: Boardroom Books), mail order guru Eugene Schwartz says he considers any mail piece a success that generates revenue that is 1.3 times breakeven or greater. So if a mailing costs five hundred dollars per thousand, he would want revenue of at least $650 per thousand.

In addition, success is defined differently in different industries and for different products. Howard Shenson, author of *Shenson on Consulting* (John Wiley & Sons), says that in promoting seminars, your mailing must generate at least double the cost of the mailing for the seminar to be profitable.

But others are more than willing to break even or take a small loss on the first mailing. Why? Because they know that most mail order enterprises make their money on repeat business, not on the first sale. They view the initial mailing as an expense which they will recover in future mailings. The purpose of that first mailing is not just to sell a product, but to gain a mail order customer.

A person who buys in response to your direct mail package represents a great value to you. Once people buy your product through the mail, they identify themselves as proven mail order buyers. That's important, because many people don't buy through the mail. Even better, they have proven that they will buy your type or category of product by mail . . . and will spend at least the amount of money you charged.

By building a list of proven mail order customers, you build your mail order business. Such a list is a gold mine for you; typically, the response you get to your own "house list" of customers will be anywhere from two to ten times greater than you can generate with the same mailing piece sent to a rented or compiled list. The real profits in mail order are repeated mailings to your customers, offering more products like the one they already bought.

What's more, if your list gets large enough, you may be able to generate additional profits by renting it to other firms. A professional "list management" company can act as your agent, actively marketing the list for you in return for a percentage of the profits. You generally need a minimum of twenty-five thousand names (and preferably fifty thousand) to interest professional list managers in handling the list. However, if your list is highly specialized, and you know your market, you may be able to rent it to other firms directly, without an intermediary.

THE IMPORTANCE OF THE OFFER

Of equal importance to the product and the mailing list is the offer. Your offer, as we've discussed, is what the customer gets when he or she responds to your mailing. In mail order, the offer consists of:

- the product being purchased
- any extras that come with the product (carrying case, attachments, instruction booklet, accessories)
- any free gifts offered with the product (such as a free booklet or secondary, smaller item)
- the price
- the discount
- the guarantee
- the method and promptness of delivery
- the service and support offered by the company
- the method of ordering
- the method of payment or billing

Most beginning direct marketers concentrate on the product and don't worry too much about the offer, believing the items mentioned above are trivial details. But that's a mistake. The offer is of critical importance and can make or break your mailing. Sometimes, a good offer can lure many people into placing an order for a product they otherwise might not buy. Have you ever, for example, bought a box of cereal because you or your children wanted the free prize inside? Or have you ever donated money to public television or another worthy cause because of the free tote bag or other gift they offered you? If you have, you know how tempting a good offer can be.

Let's take a look at some common direct mail offers and see how they work.

TEN POPULAR DIRECT MAIL OFFERS

• *Product for cash.* The most basic business transaction: "Send us money and we will send you our product." Rarely works in mail order unless accompanied by a firm money-back guarantee.

• *Satisfaction guaranteed or your money back.* Here we are still getting cash, check, money order, or a signed credit card order in advance. But now we add the all-important phrase, "If you're not fully satisfied—for any reason—send back the product and we'll refund your money, in full, promptly and without question." It is of vital importance to include a firm money-back guarantee in every mail order package, ad, or TV commercial you produce. Would you buy merchandise you have never seen, from a company you don't know, located thousands of miles away, without a money-back guarantee? Of course not. Yet hundreds of direct mail pieces ask consumers to do this, every day of the year.

You will generally get more orders if your guarantee is unconditional ("you'll get a refund no matter what") than conditional ("you must return the product in good condition or we won't give you a refund"). Also, a long guarantee offer ("refund if returned within 90 days") is better than a short refund offer ("must be returned within 10 days").

• *"Bill me" option.* You give the customer a choice of paying in advance or checking a box on the order form that says, "Send the product and then bill me."

This is a trade-off situation. A bill-me option generally increases the number of orders. But it costs money to send out and keep track of bills, and a certain percentage of customers won't pay you. Try both methods and see which works best.

• *Incentive for cash with order.* You can offer a bill-me option but then offer a bonus to people who pay cash up front. This might be a discount, free shipping and handling, or a free gift. A free gift given for payment with order is called a *keeper*. Copy tells the prospect that, even if he returns the product, he gets to keep the free gift (which is why it's called a keeper). For example: "If you act now, we will also include a free 'SAVE THE WHALES' bumper sticker. Even if you decide that *Whale-Ho* magazine isn't for you, the bumper sticker is yours to keep—our way of saying 'thank you' for sampling our publication."

• *The kicker.* A "kicker" is a free gift you offer as an incentive for fast action.

We know, from experience, that the majority of customers who buy through the mail do so almost immediately after receiving your mailing. Rarely do they put your mailing aside for leisure reading or philosophical pondering. Which means if you don't get someone to order immediately, you've probably lost the sale.

For this reason, many companies offer a bonus gift for prompt response. For example: "Send in your order by March 15th and you'll receive a free copy of our CORPORATE GUIDE TO DESKTOP PUBLISHING." You can allow them to keep the kicker regardless of whether they buy, or say that they can keep it only if they buy your product.

• *Sample it free.* If you offer a bill-me option and a money-back guarantee, you are in essence allowing the customer to sample the product, for free, before he decides whether to buy.

I have had great success making "free 30-day trial" the main theme of my mailings—especially selling publications and software by mail. For a product that prevents computer errors, for example, my headline might be: "NOW YOU CAN PREVENT COMPUTER FAILURES IN YOUR DATA CENTER FOR THE NEXT 30 DAYS—FREE." Copy tells the reader: "Let us send you our product without cost or obligation. Don't send us any money. Just try the product. If you like it, then buy it. If you don't like it, return it—and you won't owe us a penny. What could be fairer or easier?" This works well because the reader perceives that he is being allowed to use a product free, rather than being sold the product.

• *Free issue.* Popular with newsletters, magazines, other subscription services. Instead of appearing to sell a magazine subscription, the copy says, "Send back the reply card and we'll send you an issue of our publication—absolutely free. We'll also start your subscription. But if you don't like our magazine, just write 'CANCEL' across the bill and you won't owe us anything. And you get to keep the free issue as our gift to you."

This works. After all, which would you rather do: pay money to subscribe to a magazine you don't know . . . or get a free magazine in the mail? However, some publishers report that this kind of offer is unprofitable because it results in a high volume of people sending for the free issue and then canceling the subscription. The key would seem to be finding a balance between selling the magazine on its virtues and pushing the free offer.

• ***Order the product, get a premium.*** Here we tell the customer, "Order our product and we will also send you a free gift." The headline and opening paragraphs of the sales letter stress the product, and the free gift offer is downplayed. It may not be mentioned until the closing paragraphs or P.S. of the letter. Or, there might be a small slip of paper enclosed that highlights the free gift. But the main brochure and sales letter would stress the product. This way, you know people understand the offer and have a real interest in the product. The gift takes on secondary importance and is only there to provide an extra little push to get people to take out their checkbooks.

• ***Free gift, free gift, free gift (and our product, too).*** This is the same offer as above, except the priorities are reversed.

The outer envelope teaser, headline, main body of the letter, and enclosed brochure all stress the offer of the free gift. They repeat many times that the gift is free, and highlight the value of the gift. Buried in the middle of the letter is copy that says, "To get this gift, order our product." Here the gift is the key theme, the product secondary.

I've seen this tactic used with varying degrees of success in both mail order and lead generation. *Money* magazine recently sent me an elaborate mailing offering a free three-part "Financial Advisor Investment Portfolio." The free portfolio was stressed in the envelope teaser, computer-personalized letter, a circular, a certificate, and the order form.

As it turns out, this magnificent "portfolio" is, in reality, reprints of articles that were published in past issues of *Money* magazine. But they were good articles. And I suspect that the package was successful, because *Money* has repeated the free portfolio offer in other mailings.

The danger, of course, is in getting orders from people who

want the free gift but are not interested in the product. You may generate a higher volume of orders initially, but get more returns, cancellations, and nonpayment.

The debate about whether to use "premiums" (free gifts) to get orders has been going on for decades and is still unresolved. "The quality of subscribers is difficult to measure," said Jon Swallen, director of media research for Ogilvy & Mather, in a recent interview with *Incentive Marketing* magazine. "We won't know if a subscriber with a premium is any different than a regular subscriber."

• **Trial order.** Instead of forcing the prospect to order a regular shipment, we allow him to "sample" a smaller order. For example, we may normally sell typewriter ribbons in boxes of six, but as a special offer, we tell the customer he can buy one and try it. In publishing, a mailing might offer a short-run subscription (three months, for example) to those prospects who may be hesitant about committing to a full year's subscription.

ELEMENTS OF THE MAIL ORDER PACKAGE

Although format varies widely, the standard direct mail package selling a product consists of the following elements:

- outer envelope
- the main letter
- lift letter or other secondary letter (optional)
- brochure or circular
- second brochure, hot sheet, or buck slip (optional)
- order form
- reply envelope

Let's take a look at each of these elements in more detail.

OUTER ENVELOPE

Physically, the job of the outer envelope is to carry all the components inside it from your mail room to the customer's in-basket.

But it can do more than just hold papers. A well-designed envelope, with the right teaser copy, can create a positive expectation, an interest and excitement for what's inside the envelope.

The Moneypaper, a financial publication for women, lures you with this message on the outside of a number-ten envelope:

> How much do you know about your money?
> *Take the Quick Test Inside*
>
> More Successful Women Read THE MONEYPAPER
> Than Any Other Financial Newsletter
>
> OPEN THIS LETTER NOW AND FIND OUT WHY.

Publisher Vita Nelson says that no one has been able to beat this mailing package.

Teasers that arouse curiosity or offer a hint of mystery are also generally successful, because readers are forced to open the envelope to satisfy their curiosity or find the answer to the mystery.

The envelope teaser for a package selling a book on self-defense reads:

> Act within two weeks to receive your
> SURPRISE GIFT!

Naturally you want to find out what the surprise gift is.

THE MAIN SALES LETTER

"The letter itself is the paper-and-ink embodiment of a sales-person who is speaking personally and directly to the prospect on a one-to-one basis," explains Malcolm Decker, director of the Stamp Collector's Society, writing in *Who's Mailing What!*

A letter selling subscriptions to *Writer's Digest* magazine speaks directly to the reader on a writer-to-writer level:

> Dear Writer:
>
> I don't have the Great American Novel in me. I flunked Poetry 102 in college. My first, last and only short story was rejected by 14 magazines.
>
> Talent or not, just ten years ago, I had to support myself somehow. It wasn't easy at first, but this year I may make as much as $75,000 writing brochures, booklets, ads, press releases, TV scripts, cartoon captions and sales materials for clients all across the country. . . .

The letter, according to Decker, "is the most powerful and persuasive selling force in direct marketing once the product, price, and offer are set." Your letter must capture readers' attention. It must hold their interest long enough to make the sales pitch. It must show the readers what your product is, why they need it, and why they should buy from you instead of from the competition. It must overcome objections, anticipating any questions or problems the readers might have with your offer. And it must delicately bring up the subject of money and get readers to place an order.

SECONDARY LETTER

Some mail order packages use two letters.

Typically, there is a long, central letter, doing most of the selling, and a smaller second letter, known as the lift letter or publisher's letter. The theme of the lift letter is usually along these lines: "If you're not sure about ordering, read this letter." The copy then restates a key benefit or repeats the offer, pointing out how great the product is or how much money the offer will save the reader.

In one package I wrote, the main letter asked the reader to become a distributor for a product aimed at the food industry. In the P.S. of this letter, we offered a free cassette of a seminar on how to make money in the food industry. I wrote a short second letter that talked solely about the free cassette and how the reader would profit from the information it contained.

Another strategy I like is to print the second letter on a brightly colored stock, such as yellow or pink. Then, in your main letter, you can refer to the "pink bulletin enclosed" to steer the prospect toward reading the lift letter.

BROCHURE OR CIRCULAR

The brochure is included to convince the reader that the claims made in the letter are true. It can do this by:

- demonstrating the product
- showing a picture of the product
- showing people enjoying the product or the results of using the product
- proving product performance through graphs, charts, photos, diagrams, and tables
- explaining how the product works, how it is made, how it can be used

The brochure is also the ideal place for client lists, testimonials, corporate background, and descriptions of related products, accessories, or services you offer.

SECOND BROCHURE

Should you talk about everything in one brochure or have many different enclosures in your package, each highlighting a different facet of your product and your offer?

Opinions—and test results—show that there's no right answer to the question. In some situations, a single brochure works best. In others, it pays to have multiple enclosures.

The subscription package for *Telecommunications Alert*, a newsletter covering the telecommunications industry, contains a brief letter accompanied by a lengthy brochure designed to look like an important informational prospectus. The "prospectus" is eight pages long—much longer than most experts would advise for a mailing brochure. Yet the package is successful.

Copywriter Milt Pierce, on the other hand, tells the following tale:

> A few years ago, I was asked to write a test package for the Newsweek School Program. Harry Sears, who was then director of the program, told me there was no change in the offer from the previous mailing, and no change in premium.
>
> In the previous mailing package, the total message was contained in only one element—a handsome letter-brochure. "Let's try something different," I suggested. "Use a different piece of paper for each element. One page would feature the free subscription that the teacher got. Another page would feature the free maps the teacher received for classroom use.

Another piece of paper would feature the filmstrip that *Newsweek* gave to the teacher."

Newsweek agreed—and the resulting package had nearly a dozen different pieces of paper instead of only one. Several months later, Harry Sears told me that my package had outpulled the previous mailing by nearly double.

Since then, I have retested this theory many times—with similar results.

One brochure or several? It depends on your product and your offer. Do you want to tell a coherent story? Or are there many key sales points that are strong enough to stand on their own?

OTHER INSERTS

Other popular inserts include:

- *Buck slip*. Small slip of paper, generally four by nine inches. Used to highlight some additional key sales point or last-minute news.
- *Premium slip*. Buck slip emphasizing and describing the free gift that goes with the offer.
- *Testimonial slip*. Buck slip presenting testimonials from satisfied customers.
- *Hot-sheet*. Buck slip printed on inexpensive stock and designed to have the look and feel of a last-minute insert. Hot-sheets typically emphasize a last-minute development or stress a discount, time-limited deadline, or something else to convince the reader that ordering *now* is urgent.

ORDER FORM

Many writers use the order form not only as an ordering device but to restate the guarantee, reprint testimonials, or highlight key sales points. "The busier the order form, the better," I've heard some say. But there are differences of opinion on this issue, as with nearly everything else in direct mail. Tony Arau, of the A&R Group, reports that to-the-point, one-sided order cards generally pull more orders than "confusing" devices that put copy on both sides.

Do not neglect the little details when writing order form copy. If you accept credit cards, for example, you must get readers to indicate which card they want to use, the card number, and the expiration date. You also want their signature on the form.

REPLY ENVELOPE

The reply envelope is a physical device for carrying the order form back from the customer to your order-handling department.

You need a reply envelope, not just a reply card, when you want the reader to send you a check or give you confidential information, such as a credit card number.

Some mailers print the words RUSH, PRIORITY HANDLING, or similar teaser copy on the front of the reply envelope to stress the urgency and importance of replying. I have never bothered with this and usually use a plain, unadorned reply envelope.

In most direct mail packages, the reply envelope is a business reply envelope. Be sure to follow the format provided by the post office in their manual for creating the business reply card. If you're not sure you've done it correctly, take your mechanical or laser proof to the postmaster and have him inspect and approve it before printing your business reply envelopes.

TEN MORE TIPS FOR SELLING YOUR PRODUCT OR SERVICE VIA MAIL ORDER

1. Rent response lists of proven mail order buyers who have bought products similar to yours. Do not use compiled lists when selling products directly from the mailing.

2. According to Don Libey, publisher of the *Libey Letter*, recency, frequency, and monetary are three important factors in mailing list selection. You want lists of buyers who have bought recently, and often, and have purchased products in the same price range as yours (or higher).

3. Good lists to test include mail order buyers, catalog buyers, magazine subscribers, and seminar attendees.

4. Sell only one item per direct mailing. Do not confuse the reader by offering multiple items in a single mailing piece. (Catalogs are the major exception, of course.)

5. Accepting major credit cards and offering a toll-free 800 number for ordering will increase response 10 to 30 percent.

6. It is difficult to make a profit using direct mail to sell a product costing less than fifty dollars. It is nearly impossible to break even selling a product costing under thirty dollars.

7. Unless you have a back end (other products to sell your buyers), you probably should not go into direct mail. Very few mail order sellers get rich selling a single product.

8. Because of the small profit margins in direct mail selling, it is usually best to use third-class bulk mail and mail as cheaply as possible.

9. The best format for mail order selling is still a letter, brochure, order form, and reply envelope in an outer envelope. The most cost-effective size is a number-ten package.

10. The most important things to test in mail order selling via direct mail are lists and price. You do not know which price is most profitable until you test.

9

TESTING

WHAT IS "TESTING"?

In direct mail, *testing* is the process of putting a letter or package in the mail, counting the replies, and coming to some conclusion based on the results.

In traditional direct mail tests, two or more mailings or mailing factors are tested against one another simultaneously.

For instance, you might test letter A against letter B to see which pulls more orders.

Or, you might take letter A and mail it to two different lists, to see which list produces the better response.

But testing doesn't have to be an A versus B proposition, even though that's the way it's traditionally viewed.

Even if you only mail one package or one letter or use only one list at a time, you can still learn something from the mailing—as long as you keep track of the results.

Learning is the real purpose of direct mail testing. By counting replies and monitoring results, we learn what works for us in direct mail—and what doesn't.

This chapter is written to give you some basic guidance in tracking results and doing direct mail tests.

KEEP IT SIMPLE

Although discussions of testing can get elaborate and complex, I have deliberately kept things simple, so you can immediately apply the information to your ongoing direct mail activities.

If you already have a sophisticated testing program in place, I agree that you probably won't get much new help here.

But I suspect that you are like many marketers, in that you do minimal testing . . . or at least not as much as you could.

If that's the case, I hope this chapter does two things for you:

(a) gives you the motivation to begin testing and tracking all your mailings from now on;

(b) provides some helpful yet easy-to-follow hints and techniques for conducting simple tests on low budgets and in limited quantities.

TEST EVERY TIME YOU MAIL

"Every time you do a mailing you should test something," writes James E. A. Lumley in his book, *Sell It by Mail*. "If you don't you've wasted an opportunity to learn something about the prospects who respond to your offer."

I agree with Lumley and urge you to measure leads and sales on every mailing you do.

Some say, "You can only test one thing versus another, such as package A versus package B."

I disagree. If you mail five thousand letters and get two responses, you have learned something about how that particular audience of five thousand people responded to the particular product and offer you featured in that particular mailing.

Many industrial firms, for instance, can quickly and inexpensively discover whether a new product or service has appeal to a given market by doing a small test-mailing. Using direct mail to test the waters in a new market can actually be much less expensive than hiring a market research firm or creating a new ad campaign.

Many direct mail experts also say, "There is no sense testing a mailing list unless it is large enough to allow for a full-scale mailing if the test mailing should be successful." In other words, don't test ten thousand names unless there are another ninety thousand people on the list you can mail to after you learn the test results.

Again, I disagree. Even if your list is only ten thousand or even five thousand names, why not split it in two sections and test something—an offer, a product, a price? Why settle for just selling when you can also learn in the process?

TRACKING RESPONSE IS THE KEY

To test, you must be able to track response. That is, when you receive a reply, you must be able to identify that reply as coming from a specific mailing or from a reader whose name was on a specific mailing list.

There are several ways to do this.

The simplest is to put a key number or code on the reply element. The code can be a series of numbers and letters in fine print tucked away in the corner of the reply card. Or, it can be worked into the address.

For example, you might use the return address, "USA ENGI-NEERING ASSOCIATES, DEPT. DM-2, YORKTOWN, USA." The code "Dept. DM-2" tells us this reply card came from package 2 as opposed to package 1.

The same thing can be done for telephone response using either an extension ("call Ext. 123") or a person's name ("ask for Jennifer Smith"). If the person asks specifically for extension 123 or Jennifer Smith, the operator knows the call is in response to a specific mailing package.

(This coding technique is also used in print ads. Try calling the toll-free numbers used in print ads; ask for the specific extension listed in the ad. Often, you are not switched and the operator who answers handles your call. This is because there is no such extension; the number is solely a tracking device.)

If you are affixing labels to your reply card or order form, the mailing list owner can use his computer to put a key code directly on the label. The charge for this service is nominal—usually about one dollar per thousand names. "Let your mailing house key the order cards or reply envelopes while labeling," advises Lee Epstein. "This will save you many on-press keying and inventory control headaches."

TRAIN YOUR PEOPLE

All the keying and coding in the world is useless if you don't train your people to keep track of response.

Obviously it's very important to track all responses if you're going to have accurate test results. In particular, you must keep track of five types of responses:

1. People who respond by mailing or faxing the reply card or order form you have provided.

2. People who write on their own letterhead or send a company purchase order or a personal check *without* your order form.

3. People who phone in and ask for the person or extension you have specified.

4. People who call and don't specify the extension or person.

5. People who don't reply to you directly but are motivated by the mailing to contact their local sales representative or distributor.

Keeping track of responses 2, 4, and 5 is admittedly a difficult task. You will always get some leads and sales for which you can't pinpoint the source. But be diligent about tracking those responses you *can* identify. The more accurate your counts, the more meaningful the conclusions you draw from your tests.

ANY RESPONSE IS A GOOD RESPONSE

If you become a student and practitioner of direct mail, you will read a great deal about tables and formulas for calculating whether a response is statistically valid.

A "statistically valid response" means that, based on the results from your test mailing, you can pretty accurately predict that an identical mailing to other portions of the same mailing list will give you similar results.

Generally you need to mail several thousand pieces to get a statistically valid response. (I'll get more specific about this in a minute.) So does this mean the results of a smaller test should be ignored because they are not statistically valid?

The experts will tell you: yes. I say: no. In my opinion, all results tell you *something*. Just be sure to let common sense be your guide.

Recently I wrote a sales letter for a local print shop. The client called me the other day and said, "I am very excited. I tested your letter and got a 10 percent response!"

I replied: "I'm delighted. But I didn't know the list had even been delivered yet. Tell me . . . how did you arrive at this test result?"

"Oh," said the client. "That's easy. I mailed ten letters to people whose names I had on file and got one call back!"

Obviously, you see the danger of this thinking. With a mailing of only ten pieces, you cannot get a statistically valid result in terms of percentage response. For example, if that one person who responded had been too busy to read his mail that day, our rate would have plummeted from 10 percent to zero!

But even a small test is meaningful if the information it reveals is good enough for your purposes. For instance, a good friend of mine runs a management consulting firm. They mail low volumes to local corporations; one thousand is a big mailing for them. I asked him how he tested.

"We do a letter and mail out five hundred copies to a portion of our house list, which has about ten thousand names on it. Or we may use a rented list," he replied. "If we get back twenty-five replies, we call that 5 percent and assume it's a good mailing (5 percent is good for us). I know that in some circles that isn't exactly scientific. But it satisfies our needs, and based on a result like that, we might mail out another five hundred to two thousand copies of that letter—depending on how many new-business leads we needed to generate."

SCIENTIFIC TESTING

OK. Let's say you want to be more sophisticated. How many test pieces do you have to mail?

Actually, test results are based on number of responses—not pieces mailed. So the real question is, "How many *replies* do we have to get back in order for the test to be considered statistically valid?"

Different authorities quote different numbers. James Lumley says twenty responses. Ed Burnett, writing in *The Handbook of Circulation Management*, says between thirty and forty responses. Milt Pierce, who teaches the direct response copywriting workshop at New York University, says you need one hundred replies to get a statistically meaningful result.

In my experience, the most accurate measure of how many replies you must receive (and therefore, of how many pieces you must mail) to get a statistically valid response is shown in figure 9-1, reprinted from *The Basics of Testing*, written by Ed McLeon (and now out of print).

On the top line, you find the deviation percentage (or decline

FIGURE 9-1

Percent of Decline

		(The difference between your estimated return and your break-even point—or the decline percentage you wish to protect yourself against)			
		50%	25%	12.5%	6.25%
Here is your confidence level	75%	1.8	7.3	29.2	116.8
	85%	3.5	14.0	56.0	
	90%	6.6	26.2	104.8	
	95%	11.0	42.8		
	99%	21.7	86.9		

Take a look at the chart above. Go along the top line until you find 25 percent, the deviation percentage—I prefer to call it the *decline* percentage—you want to protect yourself against. Then go down the 25 percent column until you reach the 85 percent confidence level you want. The number in the box will be the number of returns you must set up your test sample to get. To find the correct sample size, divide the number of returns in the box (14 in this example) by the percent return you expect (1.5 percent in this case): 14 divided by 0.015 equals 933. So try a test of 933, or around 1,000.

From: *The Basics of Testing* by Ed McLean (reprinted with permission) percentage) you want to protect yourself against. Decline percentage tells you the maximum amount by which your roll-out—subsequent mailings to additional names on the same list following a successful test—will vary from the test.

Let's say you select a 25 percent decline. That means if you get a 1 percent response from the test, the roll-out will generate no less than 0.75 percent response and no more than 1.25 percent response . . . a plus or minus 25 percent variation from 1 percent.

The Degree of Confidence tells you how certain you can be of staying within the decline percentage you selected. If you choose an 85 percent level of confidence and a 25 percent decline percentage, you are saying, "I want there to be an 85 percent certainty that my roll-out will stay within plus or minus 25 percent of the response rate my test generates."

Look at figure 9-1 again. Read down the vertical column under "25 percent decline" and across the horizontal row at "85 percent confidence." They intersect at 14.

This means you need fourteen responses to get this level of statistical validity from your test. If you anticipate a 1 percent response, then you need to mail 1,400 pieces per mailing list in your test (fourteen is 1 percent of 1,400). To be on the safe side, I'd make it an even two thousand. Therefore, when people ask me, "How many pieces do I need to mail to get a statistically valid test result?" my recommendation is two thousand names per list, based on the above analysis.

Is this accurate? The above formula was introduced to me not by Ed McLean (who is now a good friend and valued colleague) but by a large mailing list brokerage that has been involved in thousands of mailings. "We have been using this formula for more than thirty years, and we find over and over that you can get a statistically valid test result mailing two thousand names, not five thousand," says the president of the firm. I have since used it numerous times with clients doing smaller mailings, and have found it to be valid.

ROLL-OUT

Can the results of a small test mailing remain statistically valid regardless of how many additional names we mail to?

The answer is no. The rule of thumb for roll-outs is that the total quantity you mail to should be no more than *ten times* the number of names you tested.

Therefore, if you got a 5 percent response in a test of five thousand names, you can mail to as many as fifty thousand additional names on the list with the confidence that test results are repeatable in the roll-out.

No matter how sorely you may be tempted, never do a roll-out to more than ten times the test quantity. Results may not hold valid in these large numbers.

Let's say you have a list of eighty thousand names. If you tested two thousand, you can roll out to up to twenty thousand names and expect the decline percentage not to exceed the percentage you selected when using figure 9-1 to conduct your test. Should results prove profitable on the twenty thousand names, you can then safely mail to the remainder of the list.

The booklet *444 Begged, Borrowed, Stolen & Even a Few Original Direct Response Marketing Ideas*, published by Rockingham/Jutkins Marketing, 147 Richmond Street, El Segundo, CA 90245, presents a table showing you the probability that response from the rest of your mailing list will be similar to the test results.

Response Probabilities

Size of test mailing	Response of test mailing	Anticipated response° (95% accurate)
2,000	1%	0.55 to 1.45%
2,000	2%	1.37 to 2.63%
2,000	3%	2.24 to 3.76%
2,000	4%	3.12 to 4.88%
2,000	5%	4.03 to 5.97%
2,000	10%	8.66 to 11.34%
2,000	20%	18.21 to 21.70%
10,000	1%	0.80 to 1.20%
10,000	2%	1.72 to 2.28%
10,000	3%	2.66 to 3.34%
10,000	4%	3.61 to 4.39%
10,000	5%	4.56 to 5.44%
10,000	10%	9.40 to 10.60%
10,000	20%	19.20 to 20.80%

° When mailing to remainder of mailing list.

How to read the table: Let's say you do a test mailing of two thousand pieces and get back one hundred replies—a 5 percent response. The chances are ninety-five out of one hundred that when you mail to the rest of the list, your response rate will be between 4.03 and 5.97 percent. Mailing to another two thousand prospects will therefore generate anywhere from eighty-one to 119 additional replies.

THE THREE MOST IMPORTANT THINGS TO TEST

What are the three most significant factors you can test?

Number one is the mailing list. As discussed in chapter 3, there may be half a dozen mailing lists that might be right for your offer . . . maybe more. You cannot assume you know which one is best, based on your personal prejudices. The only way to know for certain which list will pull best with your package is through a test mailing.

The second most important factor to test is the price. This applies mainly to mail order selling.

For instance, let's say you've published a one-thousand-page report on the telecommunications industry. How much will people pay for it? $195? $495? $1,200? You simply do not know until you test. And frequently, you will be amazed at how many people place orders at prices you thought were sky-high.

The third most important factor to test is the offer. For example, should you try for mail orders or leads? Should you offer a premium—a free gift? Will you get better response offering a gift item, such as a clock radio, or free information, such as a booklet or special report? You won't know which works best unless you test.

Make your mailing list broker your partner in testing. For instance, when you want to test a small portion of the list, ask your broker to supply you with what is called an nth name selection.

How does this work? Let's say the list has seventy thousand names, and you are going to test-mail to seven thousand. In this example, seventy thousand divided by seven thousand equals an n of ten. That means the computer will select (for your test mailing) every tenth name as it randomly goes through the list.

A random nth name selection ensures that you get an average, unbiased sample that represents a typical cross section of the list.

This is much better than ordering the entire list and then picking the test names by hand. The danger of doing it that way is that you subconsciously select the names that will give you the best results (because you want your mailing to be a success). Test results are artificially elevated because of this favorable selection, and roll-outs don't bring the results you would have expected.

OTHER FACTORS YOU CAN TEST

Below, in no particular order, are numerous factors that can be tested via direct mail.

Be selective. Don't test everything. Don't overtest. Use tests only to ensure success or determine key information you really want or need to know.

You can test:

- products
- premiums
- formats
- sizes
- copy
- personalization
- brochure versus no brochure
- themes or sales appeals
- teasers
- colors
- first-class versus third-class mail
- business reply versus "place stamp here"
- 800 number versus regular phone number
- mail-back reply form versus fax-back reply form

TEN ESSENTIAL RULES OF DIRECT MAIL TESTING

1. Make every mailing a test.
2. Establish goals for each test. Determine the information you want to get out of the test . . . the degree of reliability needed in your data . . . and how much money you can afford to spend on the test.

3. Test significant factors that make a substantial difference in direct mail results. These include the list, the offer, and—in mail order—the price.

4. Also test to find out things you need to know or want to know. There may be issues specific to your industry, product, or market that have never been tested in direct mail before. If there is no reliable data from other sources, *you* have to be the pioneer in your field.

5. Use direct mail tests to settle questions, debates, and disagreements concerning strategy, format, lists, design, and copy. Instead of arguing theory, put ideas to the test.

6. Test even if you are using a small list with minimal or no roll-out. Try to split the list for an A versus B test of a mailing package or a direct mail element, such as letter length or offer.

7. Be consistent in your testing. For example, if you are testing a single factor, such as an envelope teaser, all other factors in the two test packages must be identical—including the mailing list from which the names are taken and the date on which the packages are mailed.

8. Don't *assume* you know what will work. Test to find out. More often than not, the results will shock you. Direct mail tests are great for shaking up so-called marketing and advertising "experts" who think they know it all.

9. Even if you don't have enough money or names for a statistically valid test, test anyway. Some information is better than no information. Just be aware of the fact that the test is not statistically valid—and act upon the results accordingly.

10. To learn more from a direct mail test, make a list of questions you want answered. Call up some of the people who did not respond, and ask them your questions. In addition to learning a great deal about why your mailing failed to motivate these people, you may be able to turn nonresponders into responders and generate a lot of additional inquiries or orders.

PART III

DIRECT MAIL FORMATS

▾ **10**

SALES LETTERS

THE POWER OF LETTERS

I don't know about you, but whenever *I* receive a direct mail package, the first thing I read is the letter. I may glance at the outer envelope, the insert slips, the order form. I'll probably skim the brochure. But I'll always read at least the first few paragraphs of the letter . . . more if it's a good one that holds my interest.

Why do we like reading direct mail letters better than brochures or ads? Perhaps it's a natural reaction—almost everyone likes getting mail. Even though direct mail is not personal mail, it *looks* much the same as a personal letter . . . and so we treat it as such. According to one recent study by Simmons Market Research Bureau, 97 percent of consumers surveyed said they opened some or all of the direct mail they received. Only 3 percent said they throw solicitations away without opening them.

"The letter is the most important part of a direct mail package," says the Direct Marketing Agency, a Connecticut-based ad agency, in a self-promotional ad. "A good letter will invariably outpull the most impressive brochure."

THE LETTER HAS THE TOUGHEST JOB

In any direct mail package, the letter has the toughest job, because it does most of the selling. The *outer envelope* carries the package, and it may be designed to stimulate interest in its contents—through use of teaser copy, illustrations, or see-through windows. The *brochure* informs and gives descriptive information. The *order form* encourages readers to respond and gives them an easy way to do so.

But the direct mail writer uses the *letter* for making his or her sales pitch. The letter must grab attention with a powerful, relevant, engaging lead paragraph. It must stimulate readers' interest in the product or what the product can do for them. It must create a desire for the product, by describing the product's benefits in an enticing fashion. And it must ask for action, by giving the readers reasons why they should buy *now*—and not tomorrow.

MY "SECRET WEAPON" IN DIRECT MAIL

If you have a small business with a limited budget, you may wonder, "How can I compete with the fancy, full-color, laser-printed, gimmick-laden, costly mailings my competitors send?"

The answer is that the simplest, least costly direct mail package conceivable—which is basically just a form letter with a reply card—can often produce profitable results for you.

Here's how to put together such a package:

• First, there's the outer envelope. You can use your regular number-ten business envelopes as they are—no need to imprint them with teaser copy or graphics. Just run them through the word processor or apply address labels.

• Next, write the letter. Type up a form letter on your office typewriter, then offset-print it on one or two sides of a sheet of paper. No need for special letterhead—just use your regular business stationery. And no need to personalize—the inexpensive form letter, if properly written, can work very well for you.

• Now add a reply card. It can be a business reply card, where *you* pay the postage for every card returned to you. But if you don't want to bother with this, you can require the recipient to put his own stamp on the card.

There you have it—plain outer envelope, form letter, and postcard. These three elements, if properly used, can bring back a good response for you.

But the real attraction of this package is low cost and simplicity. The letter can be typed by you, and offset at the local quick-print shop. The reply card can be typeset by the printer, and as I said, it's not mandatory that you use a business reply format. To print five hundred envelopes, letters, and reply cards will cost only seventy-five to 150 dollars. And you don't need a graphic artist, postal expert, or computer letter shop to help you.

Are you on a limited budget? Try this basic package and see how it works. Then, if it pays off, use the profits to upgrade your package, perhaps adding personalization to the letter, a business reply permit to the reply cards, a brochure, other inserts, or copy and graphics on the outer envelope. Start small, then work your way up.

HOW TO WRITE A DIRECT MAIL LETTER

Here are some things to keep in mind when sitting down to write your next direct mail letter:

1. Make your direct mail letter look like a regular letter. Use a typewriter . . . don't typeset. Copy it on your regular letterhead.
2. Write in a friendly, natural, conversational tone. Use personal pronouns—*I*, the letter-writer, talking directly to *you*, the

reader. Avoid pompous-sounding business-memo style or overly puffy "advertising" style. Just write naturally.

3. Think about how the letter looks on the page. Readers are turned off by long blocks of text. Use short paragraphs and short sentences. Underline phrases and indent paragraphs for emphasis. Use typewriter symbols as graphic devices. These can include asterisks (*), bullets (•), ellipses (. . .), dashes (—).

4. Make your letter lively and personable, not dull and boring. Be "up" and enthusiastic about your product. Let your enthusiasm and personality shine through in the copy.

5. Focus on the readers and their needs, rather than your product and your own interests. For example, instead of "Our new phone system" say "Your telecommunications needs . . ." or "Are your phone bills too high?"

6. Extremely short paragraphs and sentences in the beginning of the letter help hook readers and draw them into the body.

7. The best thing to talk about in the lead paragraph is readers' most important problem or pressing concern (health, security, money, happiness). Then you can get around to how you're going to help them solve this problem or address this concern.

8. Be concise. Most people would rather read a short letter than a long one. If a long letter is needed to tell a complicated story or make a complete sales pitch, make sure every sentence adds to the message, and cut out all unnecessary words.

9. Be clear. If readers have to struggle to figure out the letter, they will probably throw it away before too long.

10. Be direct. Get to the point right away.

11. Be specific. Explain exactly what it is you're selling and what it can do. Some writers try to arouse curiosity by being deliberately vague and by masking the nature of the product. Sometimes this can work. But more often it flops because it annoys people.

12. Be simple. Take pains to explain your product and your offer in terms that the reader will be sure to understand. If you

need to elaborate on a principle, theory, or technical point, consider using a brochure. The letter's job is to sell, not tell.

Following are examples of effective letters. There's nothing especially clever or creative about most of these letters. I picked them simply because I think they do a good job of getting the prospect to take the desired action—which is ultimately the goal of any successful direct mail piece.

INQUIRY FULFILLMENT LETTER: "BIG CLIP"

An inquiry fulfillment letter is sent to prospects who have requested more information on your product. It is usually mailed with a brochure or flyer, order form, and any other literature you normally send.

The BIG CLIP is an oversized plastic paper clip (five inches long) that can be imprinted with an advertising message and used as a novelty in mailings or as a giveaway.

When I saw the BIG CLIP advertised in a circular, I sent in for more information. Here is the letter that accompanied the brochure and order form.

> Enclosed, Mr. Bly . . .
>
> is the information which you requested on our "BIG CLIP."
>
> This low-cost advertising specialty never fails to get the attention of everyone who sees it. It has been particularly popular for use as an attention-getting letter gadget with mailings (one customer has already ordered 5 times).
>
> Use the "Big Clip" as an unusual convention or trade show handout, as a novel business card (it won't be

thrown away), or to add attention and longer life to your next mailing.

The prices shown on the enclosed literature include your advertising imprint in straight type. If we are to imprint with your artwork, engraving is about $8.00.

This is one of the lowest priced ad specialties that will keep your message *on top* of the recipient's desk.

Yours for advertising with **IMPACT**!

Richard R. Butler

Comments: This letter succeeds for a number of reasons:

1. Note how the writer uses the salutation line to begin the first sentence ("Enclosed, Mr. Bly . . .) and lead us directly into the first paragraph ("is the information you requested . . ."). This is more graphically dynamic than the conventional "Dear Mr. Bly."

2. It reminds me that this is not a "cold" sales letter, but that *I requested the information*. This gives the letter a better chance of being read.

3. The second and third paragraph use plain, concise, direct language to explain what the product is and its advantages, give some proof of its success, and suggest possible uses.

4. The fourth paragraph tells the cost. Price, often omitted from many mailings, is a key concern of almost every customer in every situation. Sometimes it may help to omit price, but not when asking for an order by mail.

5. The fifth paragraph gives additional benefits (low price and effectiveness in getting your message across). And the letter achieves all this with admirable brevity.

INQUIRY FULFILLMENT LETTER: SERFILCO

Serfilco is a supplier of pumps, filters, and waste treatment equipment for the chemical process industry. This cover letter was attached to their brochure, sent in response to my request for information.

> Dear Mr. Bly:
>
> Recently you requested information on chemical *pumps*, process *filtration* equipment or *waste water* treatment equipment.
>
> I would like to help you! If the literature we sent to you solved your problem, it's time to call me for a quotation.
>
> If you still own the problem, call me. I may solve it before the end of our conversation. I'll even pay for the call—(800) 233-3861.
>
> I am your Serfilco District Sales Manager. There is no charge to put me to work for you.
>
> Sincerely yours,

Comment: You can't help but be impressed with the friendly, sincere tone of this letter and the writer's helpful attitude. Yet he isn't afraid to ask for the order. A simple but effective message.

INQUIRY FOLLOW-UP LETTER: IBM

Some prospects do not, for whatever reason, respond to the inquiry fulfillment letter. Many companies send one or more follow-ups, either letters or postcards, hoping to get responses from people who ignored previous mailings. Here's a sample from IBM:

WE'RE BACK AGAIN BECAUSE WE HAVEN'T HEARD FROM YOU.

Will you do us a favor by answering a few questions on the enclosed reply card?

A while ago you inquired about our analytical instruments and we were glad to send you information about them.

Naturally, when a prospective customer contacts us, we are anxious to see that full information is provided.

Have we sent you all that you need? Can we help you with more?

Inquiries are important to us because they are often our first contact with a new customer. That's why we are asking the questions on the enclosed business reply card. It will only take a minute or two to answer them, but they will be very valuable to us in doing a better job with all who want us to send information—including you.

Would you fill out the card now, please, and send it back before it slips your mind? Many thanks.

Sincerely,

Gary L. Gisle
Director of Marketing & Service

P.S. We will be glad to send you additional information. Just jot your request on the enclosed reply card and we will respond promptly.

Comment: In a form letter, such as this, you can make the first sentence into a headline, typing it in all caps across the top of the letter, as is done here. Many direct mail writers feel this has more impact than simply typing "Dear Prospect" or "Dear Executive."

This letter is a nice, polite request for a reply. Phrasing the request as questions ("Will you do us a favor . . . ?" "Have we sent all that you need?") makes it seem that IBM is trying to help the reader, rather than the other way around. Perhaps the letter would have been stronger if the writer had described the product and its key benefits, reminding the reader what he specifically requested and why it is important to him.

LEAD-GETTING SALES LETTER:
BRIAN E. WEISS, D.D.S.

Here's a letter mailed to me "cold" from a dentist I didn't know:

Dear Mr. Bly:

You know how difficult it is to look your best if dental problems are causing discomfort and pain or if the appearance of your teeth needs improvement.

Have you been putting off a dental checkup or consultation on an existing problem? This note may encourage you to take the important step to help yourself feel better by making a dental appointment.

In our spacious comfortable dental offices our patients receive skilled and concerned care. Our equipment and techniques are among the most advanced. You will find us competent and understanding whether you need a simple filling, cleaning or require a crown, bridge or complete dental restoration.

We are expert in the modern "bonding technique"

which enables us to whiten discolored teeth, repair chipped teeth or reshape your teeth usually without injections or drilling.

You will find that our fees are very fair for fine complete dentistry with convenient appointment schedules.

My card is enclosed—please keep it. If you require fine dental care now or just want a checkup please call 977-7616.

Sincerely,

Brian E. Weiss, D.D.S.

P.S.: Neglecting your teeth and gums can create many problems. With this note as a reminder, why not call today for an appointment.

Comment: This letter follows a classic sequence for persuasive copywriting known as the "Motivating Sequence." It consists of five steps: (1) get attention, (2) show a need, (3) satisfy the need, (4) prove your superiority, and (5) ask for action.

1. The first paragraph gets our attention by talking about a problem that many of us face: bad teeth.
2. The second paragraph shows us the need to see a dentist to solve the problem.
3. The next three paragraphs demonstrate that the way to satisfy this need is to visit Dr. Weiss.
4. These paragraphs also give reasons why he is a good dentist (fair fees, convenient appointments, comfortable offices, skilled care).
5. Finally, the letter asks for action by suggesting that the reader call for an appointment.

A classic approach that works almost every time.

LEAD-GETTING LETTER: EUGENE A. HOSANSKY

A sales letter is an excellent way for an individual or organization offering professional services (public relations, legal, accounting, graphic design, editorial) to reach new prospects and get leads. Here's one from a freelance public-relations specialist:

Dear Mr. Blake:

Is freelance a dirty word to you?

It really shouldn't be, because in public relations, with its crisis-lull-crisis rhythm, really good freelancers can save you money and headaches. Use them when you need them and when you don't they don't cost you a cent.

Use me. I am a public relations specialist with more than 20 years of experience in all phases of the profession. I am presently working on various assignments for AC&R Public Relations and other organizations.

MY SERVICES ARE AVAILABLE TO YOU
ON A FREELANCE BASIS.

The enclosed fact sheet describes my capabilities and lists some of the clients I have worked for.

Think of me especially during those hectic times when you are short handed and could use a skilled person to immediately throw into the breach.

I hope you will feel it worthwhile for us to meet to discuss the possibility of my working with you on projects for your clients.

In this regard, I will call you in a week or so if I haven't heard from you by then.

Cordially,

Eugene A. Hosansky

Comment: This letter also follows the classic Motivating Sequence formula:

1. The first sentence grabs attention with a provocative question.
2. The second paragraph shows the reader that he has a need for freelance help.
3. The third paragraph satisfies the need by showing the reader where to get help.
4. The rest of the letter gives reasons why Mr. Hosansky is the person to call when you need help.
5. The last two paragraphs spell out what happens next.

REAL ESTATE LETTER: ROYAL ATLANTIC

A popular strategy for selling vacation or retirement homes is to invite prospects for a free or discount vacation at the resort or community—which is usually designed to give the seller a captive audience for his sales pitch. But the Royal Atlantic nearly hooked me with this very appealing letter:

If you love the city . . .

but long for cool ocean breezes and quiet moonlit beaches, then you should know that your dreams can come true with your own oceanfront vacation home.

Owning oceanfront property is a luxury that only a limited few will be able to enjoy. And today, even renting oceanfront property is becoming more and more difficult with the rapid conversion of vacation resorts (including our own) to cooperative ownerships.

But if you act now, you can invest in your very own

oceanfront home and build for your future at the same time.

The Royal Atlantic is making it possible for you to vacation on the ocean forever. Enjoy your own retreat by the sea with a heated swimming pool, private beach, full service restaurant, efficiency units, and much, much more.

APPRECIATION, DEPRECIATION, EQUITY BUILD-UP, TAX SAVINGS, and RENTAL INCOME are all considerations in the purchase of your vacation home. And we have experts to assist you in your decision.

We're so excited about this offer that we're extending a special invitation for you to come and see for yourself.

VISIT US AND RECEIVE A SPECIAL OVERNIGHT MINI-VACATION including accommodations, breakfast for two, and full use of our facilities for only $53 per couple. We want you to sample what the Royal Atlantic has to offer—beautiful sunrises over the Atlantic, our comfortable apartments, and the magic of Montauk.

If you cannot get away overnight, you are welcome to come out and spend the day with us. Enjoy a fine lunch and a leisurely afternoon in the sun, either on our beach or alongside our oceanside pool for only $20 per couple.

Whichever you prefer, *please hurry*. We have a limited number of accommodations available and we don't want you to miss your chance to enjoy this special offer.

Sincerely,

Joan Barbieri
Marketing Director

> P.S. CALL BEFORE October 31st to make reservations for your special mini-vacation on the ocean. The magic of Montauk awaits you! Remember accommodations are limited so call NOW 516-668-5597.

Comment: People buy vacation homes based on a combination of emotional and logical decisions. Thus this letter is effective because it combines emotional appeals ("cool ocean breezes," "quiet moonlit beaches," "Montauk magic") with hard-headed reality ("appreciation, depreciation, equity build-up").

Note the way the first sentence is graphically used as a headline, and how ellipses (...) lead your eye into the body of the letter.

Nearly everyone reads the "P.S." portion of a letter, so experienced direct mail writers almost always use a P.S. to get across an additional sales point or restate the offer, guarantee, or some other important message—as is done here.

A good direct mail letter gives the reader a reason to reply *now*, not tomorrow. Royal Atlantic creates a sense of urgency by stressing the need to make reservations today, and makes it believable with a logical argument ("a limited number of accommodations").

MAIL ORDER LETTER: NEW PROCESS COMPANY

New Process Company sells men's fashions by mail order. Their mailings contain numerous inserts with photos and descriptions of various items, plus a cover letter, which varies with each mailing. Here's one:

> Dear Mr. Bly:
>
> A memo recently crossed my desk that said I would have to RAISE MY PRICES—NOW—to offset our spiraling operating costs!

But I said, *"No! Not Yet!"*

I know that customers like you, Mr. Bly, expect the BEST VALUE for their money when they shop at NPC. And that's why I'm going to hold the line on higher prices just as long as I possibly can!

So, in the next few minutes, while you're looking through the enclosed group of Bargain Slips, please keep in mind that I may not be able to guarantee such terrific low prices in the future.

Now, my only problem is keeping enough of these fantastic Bargains in stock to handle the avalanche of orders we'll be receiving.

You see, Mr. Bly, my supplies are not unlimited and those I do have on hand are going to go F-A-S-T!

To be sure of your selections for a WEEK'S FREE TRIAL, mail your order TODAY in the postage-paid envelope attached.

Sincerely,

John L. Blair, President

P.S.: Please remember to fill in and sign the Preferred Customer Certificate above. Then, detach and return it along with your selected Bargain Slips.

Comment: When it comes to giving the reader a reason to order *today*, this letter packs a double punch: (1) prices are going to go up soon, and (2) supplies are limited. The writer has created a real sense of urgency here. In addition, the letter makes company president John Blair look like the good guy—I feel like he's making a real effort to hold down those prices for me *personally*, even though a faceless memo writer has decreed that he must raise prices soon. It works! A good model of a letter used to sell multiple items in a single mailing.

RENEWAL LETTER: NATIONAL REGISTER

A few years ago, I bought a copy of *The Standard Directory of Advertising Agencies*—a big, costly volume published by the National Register Publishing Company. Since staff, clients, and ad agencies come and go rather quickly, these directories soon become obsolete, and updated volumes are published three times a year. Here's a letter National Register sent me, urging me to buy a new edition:

R E N E W A L   T I M E

Dear Customer:

The "Bible of the Advertising Business" is coming off the press again!!!

The Agency "RED BOOK" is about to be published for June 1986. This means that your copy of the STANDARD DIRECTORY OF ADVERTISING AGENCIES is obsolete!

Consider these facts: over 50 new agencies added every four months—200 each year; 15,000 personnel changes; 10,000 account changes; hundreds of mergers, address and name changes.

Work with an up-to-date tool. Order your new June Agency "RED BOOK" now. Just check the form of service below that you wish to receive, fill in your name, company, etc., and return it in the postpaid envelope provided.

Cordially,

Russell F. Brown
Vice President—Sales

P.S.: Order three consecutive AGENCY "RED BOOKS" and keep up-to-date on all the merger activity!!

Comment: This letter is short, but it needn't be long, because the reader already owns a *Red Book* and knows all about it. Therefore, the letter's job is to convince the reader to order a new *Red Book* because his or her old one is out of date. If this letter were selling *Red Books* to people who did not already own them, it would have to go into more detail about what the *Red Book* is and the benefits of owning one.

SHORT MAIL ORDER LETTER: *BUSINESS WEEK*

Sometimes mail order marketers are successful with very short letters—mini-letters, I call them. Here's one I received from *Business Week*. It was computer-printed and attached to a tear-off subscription order form.

> Dear Robert Bly:
>
> Many of the sharper executives you're competing with are being briefed each week by *Business Week*. What we're doing for them, we could be doing for you—with reliable information, objective interpretation, perceptive analyses not found elsewhere (not in *Fortune*, *Forbes*, or *The WSJ*). Try *Business Week* on a free trial. Mail the certificate below!

Comment: The letter writer assumes that the reader is already somewhat familiar with *Business Week* and competing business journals. If this assumption is correct, the letter may well be a winner. If not—back to the drawing board! In any case, busy executives will appreciate the brevity of the message.

MAIL ORDER LETTER: THE STUART MCGUIRE CO.

Here's a letter selling shoes by mail.

> They said it couldn't be done.
> Yet here they are . . .
>
> Luxurious "rich men's" shoes—
> AT YOUR PRICE.
>
> Try a pair for 30 days <u>AT</u> <u>NO</u> <u>RISK</u>.

Dear Friend,

Ever eased your feet into luxury? Shoes with LEATHER uppers . . . LEATHER linings . . . even LEATHER insoles?

Never all three? Most men haven't. After all, these luxuries cost you an arm and a leg in stores these days.

Take leather insoles. 95% of American men have <u>never</u> felt the luxurious difference they make.

> Leather insoles <u>bend</u> easily—right out of the box. Leather insoles <u>soak up</u> perspiration, "<u>breathe</u>" naturally. Leather insoles add SOFTNESS.

Why don't ALL shoes have them? They cost too much. In stores, you'll pay $85, $95, even more for shoes with this "extra."

But not if you buy DIRECT—from Ortho-Vent.

See for yourself. Order at no risk. I'll rush you ON APPROVAL shoes with all the style, comfort, and craftsmanship rich men pay $95 for. All at YOUR price.

> They have genuine LEATHER uppers—shaped on true-to-your-size <u>combination lasts</u> for guaranteed perfect fit.

They have glove-soft LEATHER linings—often combined with cotton twill at the toe for even greater absorbency.

They even have LEATHER insoles—an "extra" offered by less than 5% of the shoes made today.

On top of that, they offer a luxury you won't find in ANY other shoes at ANY price . . .

OUR EXCLUSIVE SPRING-STEP® CUSHION.

I know the statement I'm about to make is pretty daring—especially in these days of grand juries, the FTC and all. But I've got millions of repeat customers who agree that SPRING-STEP® SHOES ARE THE MOST COMFORTABLE YOU CAN WEAR.

ORDINARY SHOES have an asphalt/cork "filler" between the outer sole and insole. It's hot, stiff. Resists every step, even after long wear.

SPRING-STEPS® have no stiff "filler." We've replaced it with a layer of bubbly foam cushion from heel to toe. It's 80% AIR!

Thanks to Spring-Step®, your feet no longer feel the pounding shock of each step. Instead, they're cradled by our supple leather insole and the resilient cushion beneath it. You've got to feel it yourself to believe the comfort.

PLUS—Spring-Step® makes our shoes so soft, so flexible, they need no "breaking in." Just order your usual size, and PRESTO! Right out of the box they feel natural as your shadow.

How can we do it? All this leather luxury, all this comfort, AND guaranteed fit—at your price?

By dealing with you DIRECT. From one central warehouse. You pay NO middleman's markup. NO costly store overhead. We've been saving customers money this way for over 80 years now.

YOU RISK <u>NOTHING</u> by trying a pair. Wear them a full 30 days. Compare looks, comfort and fit with ANY other shoe at ANY price. If ours aren't the most comfortable, the best value, I'll buy them back. No questions asked. Regardless of wear.

Order today—so I can rush your shoes by return mail. If you like, just say "charge it" to your favorite credit card.

Sincerely,

Pat Thomas

P.S.: To encourage you to give us a try, I've enclosed a special coupon that gives you $10 off your first order—<u>in addition to</u> the 30%–40% we already save you off store prices. But it's only good for the next 10 days—so redeem it right away!

Comment: When I got this letter, shoes were about number 2,788 on my priority list of "Things to Think About." But after I finished reading it, I began thinking that it would be nice to own a pair of luxurious, comfortable shoes . . . and maybe I should accept their free trial offer.

This letter does a number of things right:

1. Short paragraphs and short sentences make this long letter extremely easy to read.

2. The writer does a good job of building up the reader's perceived value of—and desire for—the shoes.

Freelance copywriter Burton Pincus says that good direct mail letters "dramatize the offer in a way that dwarfs the product's or service's cost when compared to the value of what is being purchased." This letter does just that.

3. Graphic devices—indented paragraphs, words in all caps, underlines—help make the letter appealing to the eye.

4. The letter is packed with reasons why you should try the shoes. The reader is given specific facts and benefits—not puffery or empty claims.

5. The last two paragraphs talk about a free, no-risk trial rather than "buy these shoes!" The copy makes it seem like the shoe company is loaning you a pair of shoes to try on rather than making a sale.

6. The P.S. gives a strong incentive to order *now*—a ten-dollar discount that will expire in ten days.

LETTER OFFERING FREE INFORMATION: MONY

Copywriter Sig Rosenblum calls this the "bait-and-switch" technique. Instead of talking about your product or company, you highlight the free information you send to prospects—whether it's a brochure, report, pamphlet, book, booklet, guide, or kit. Then, when the prospect responds, a salesperson takes over. Recently the Mutual Life Insurance Company of New York sent me a bait-and-switch letter:

Dear Friend:

We have reserved for you a free copy of Prentice-Hall's TAX SAVING STRATEGIES, a helpful book for Corporate Executives and Professionals. It contains practical, timely and useful ways for you to maximize the value of your deductions and save dollars.

Along with this gift, we'd like to acquaint you with

MONY's unique new Personal Financial Planning Service. This special service has been designed for successful people like you whose hectic schedules leave little time to properly coordinate investment strategy, insurance, estate planning, or even a day to day budget.

We'd like to help you in these areas and show you how you can save more resources to spend and invest through creative tax planning.

Again, all you have to do to learn more about our Personal Financial Planning Service and get your free copy of "Tax Savings Strategies" is mail the certificate below.

Act now! Find out how you can reduce your taxes starting today.

Sincerely,

Comment: The letter is brief, well written, and to the point. But I'm not sure the bait-and-switch strategy is appropriate here. If, as the writer points out in the second paragraph, the reader is too busy to plan personal investments, he or she will probably not have the time or interest to read a book on the subject. So the offer may not be right for this audience of busy executives and professionals.

Often an inexperienced writer will bury the key selling points within the body of the letter, rather than putting them up front in the lead. And I think that's the case here.

The second paragraph, for example, says that this service is designed for people who are too busy to manage their personal finances. Perhaps the letter could begin, "If you're too busy earning a living to manage your personal assets, here's a service that can help."

Another key benefit—tax reduction—isn't presented until the very last sentence. An effective letter might lead off with this:

"Now MONY can help you use *legal methods* to get you a bigger refund at tax time."

LIST-CLEANING LETTER: NEW PROCESS COMPANY

The longer a name on your mailing list remains inactive, the greater the chance that it no longer represents a hot prospect for your product or service. For this reason, it's a good idea to periodically send a letter to everyone on your list asking if they are still interested in receiving your mailings, newsletter, catalog, or whatever it is you send them. Those who don't respond are removed from your active list.

Recently I received one of these letters from John Blair of the New Process Company.

> Dear Mr. Bly:
>
> *The BAD news is*:
> I must take your name off my mailing list because you haven't placed an order with BLAIR for over a year.
>
> Why is that bad? It means you'll be passing up big savings and spending more than you need to for clothes—because I don't think anyone in the New Milford area can beat my prices.
>
> *The GOOD news is*:
> An order now will keep your name on my list— and assure you of regular news of all my money-saving fashion offers throughout the year.
>
> As always, there's no obligation to keep what you order. Try anything you like for seven days, absolutely free. If you're not 100% satisfied, just return your selections and owe nothing.

Are you sure you can afford to pass up my money-saving fashion values? Take advantage of these tremendous savings—send your order and keep your name on my list. You'll be glad you did!

Sincerely yours,

Comment: This letter does double-duty by (a) updating the mailing list and (b) asking for an order at the same time. Another example of brief but effective direct mail copy. Note the use of personalization: "Dear Mr. Bly" in the salutation and "the New Milford area" (a reference to my hometown) in the second paragraph.

CATALOG LETTER: HARRY AND DAVID

Catalog marketing is an effective way to sell a broad line of related products by mail. But catalogs—typeset, colorful, with lush photos and illustrations—are a rather impersonal medium. To add warmth, personality, and selling power to their catalogs, many marketers send a cover letter with their catalog mailings. The letter can either be printed in the catalog itself (usually on the inside front cover or the facing page) or on a separate sheet. You can use the letter to talk about your company, your products, your catalog, your service, your commitment to quality, your track record, benefits you offer to customers, or your guarantee. Or you can point the reader to specific features of the catalog, or to bargain items on various pages.

Here's an example of this type of letter. It's from Harry and David, a company that sells fruit and gourmet food by mail.

Dear Friend,

What do you think when you see a letter that starts

with "Dear Friend" . . . a letter from someone you've never met?

When we first started our mail order business back in the thirties, we wondered how people would feel about buying gourmet fruit gifts through the mail . . . from "friends" they had never met. Used to the operations of a family farm, Harry and I thought of "friendly" in terms of familiar faces, verbal agreements, handshakes—the very things mail order doesn't have.

Well, after more than forty years and thousands of new friends, our favorite dictionary definition of *friendly* is still: "showing kindly interest and good-will." We're sorry about the handshakes, but we'll see to it that you still find plenty of kindly interest and goodwill every step of the way you do business with Harry and David.

> Beginning with our catalog . . . we take particular pride in the accuracy, as well as attractiveness, with which we represent our gifts. The descriptions are as helpful as we can make them, giving dimensions and actual weight of the edible contents—not shipping weights—of the gifts you buy. In pictures and words you can see the quality, the attention to detail, the personal touches that are part of each one of these unique, original gifts. And in pictures and words we try to give a personality to our Christmas catalog that says how we feel about our business, our products, and you.

When you place your order with us, you receive a prompt acknowledgment, whether it's for one gift or a hundred. Every step in the process of filling your order receives the closest attention. We carefully check your order for shipping information and other personal instructions from you. Every gift is expertly packed to arrive safely, and looking as attractive as it does in the catalog.

> And behind every order there is always the famous Harry and David Guarantee—you, and the people we send your gifts to, *must* be satisfied. Period. If for any reason you are not satisfied, your money will be refunded or a replacement gift sent, whichever you prefer.

But all the guarantees, pretty catalogs, and "kindly interest" won't substitute for good products. *We're in the business of selling high quality gifts at prices that make them among the best values in the marketplace today—and we'd like to do business with you, today.* Please enjoy shopping through our catalog . . . then try us with an order this year, won't you? Filling out the postage-paid order blank enclosed and dropping it in the mail only takes a few minutes. But the goodwill can last for years.

Your friends,

Comments: Here, Harry and David use the letter to expound a company philosophy of goodwill and friendly service that I'm sure will win them many new customers. The tone is warm, folksy, and down-home—the exact image Harry and David are aiming for.

The beginning of the letter is especially effective because it anticipates and acknowledges the reader's response to a form letter labeled "Dear Friend." Here the writer has cleverly turned a potential negative into a positive selling point.

LETTER ASKING FOR AN APPOINTMENT: MASERATI IMPORT COMPANY

Another thing a sales letter can do for you is set up an appointment, either for your salesperson to visit the customer at his or her home or office, or for the customer to visit you at your store, office, or showroom. The letter below invites the reader to set up an appointment to test-drive a luxury car.

Dear Mr. McCoy:

One of a kind. Is that phrase a little trite?

I used to think so until I tried to find *you*.

Now I know what "one of a kind" really means.

The process of finding your name and address was the advertising equivalent of panning for gold.

The problem? How do I find the kind of person whom I could ask to test-drive (at their own home) the new Maserati Quattroporte?

How do I find the uniquely discriminating individual who would say "yes" to an offer of a complimentary bottle of French champagne . . . and the unparalleled experience of driving a one-of-a-kind automobile?

The solution? Well, I hope the solution is you.

Are you the type of person who would buy a Maserati?

People who choose the Maserati luxury sedan aren't the kind who buy the most expensive car they can find. Because the Maserati isn't. It's only about half as expensive as a Rolls, for example.

And people who choose the Maserati aren't the kind who are looking for a status symbol either.

Why buy for status when only one out of every thousand people you pass on the street will recognize what you're driving?

No, the Maserati owner is someone whose appreciation of a fine car goes beyond considerations of money, status, and even mere looks. This is an individual who truly appreciates automotive quality.

Like an excellent champagne on the sensitive palate of a connoisseur, the Maserati offers pleasures which are, to be honest, lost on most people.

Shall I be more specific?

From the moment you step into the Quattroporte and experience the unmistakable sensation and scent of genuine hand-tooled leather and briarwood paneling, you know you've encountered something worlds apart from every automobile you've ever driven before.

When you look under the hood, you will be looking into more than 50 years of automobile racing history.

But when you *drive* the Quattroporte . . . ah, that's when you'll learn what owning a Maserati is all about.

Feel it power its way through turns with complete stability. Wait until you feel the texture of the pavement beneath you as it hugs the road like no other luxury sized car you've ever driven.

If you weren't surrounded by so much spacious opulence, you'd swear you were in a sports car.

But I can't explain the Maserati to you any more than I could explain the taste of lobster or the pleasures of love.

You have to experience it.

And that's why I'm writing you with an offer which I believe has never been made by an automobile company before.

If you can't come to the Maserati, the Maserati will come to you.

Just dial (415) XXX-XXXX, or fill in the enclosed card to set up a convenient time with us.

And our representative will drive a brand new Quattroporte luxury sedan right up to your doorstep.

He will offer you a bottle of fine French champagne as a token of our gratitude for your interest.

Then, he will walk around to the passenger's side, beckon you to the driver's seat, and invite you to have the driving experience of your life.

There'll be no hard sell. This car either sells itself or it doesn't sell at all.

But our representative will not only be able to answer any questions you may have, he'll also be there for you to share your enjoyment with someone who . . . "understands."

You can take as long or as short a time with the car as you like. And, of course, there's absolutely no obligation.

For a little while at least, you'll know how it feels to own a Maserati.

So, just write your telephone number on the enclosed card and we'll call you within a few days to set up a perfectly convenient time—Saturdays and evening hours are fine with us.

Or, if you prefer, dial (415) XXX-XXXX (collect, of course) and make an appointment right away.

The bottle of French champagne is a good one, by the way, so this offer might be worth your while even if you don't like cars.

But I know you do.

And if you like cars, you'll love the Maserati.

Like you, it's one of a kind.

Sincerely,

Jeffrey Quale
President

P.S.: Do you already own a luxury sedan? Don't let that stop you from accepting my offer. Even if you're not in the market for another car right now, call us and test drive the Maserati Quattroporte. Compare it with your Jaguar, your Mercedes, even your Silver Spirit. You've got nothing to lose. And a bottle of French champagne to gain. How about this weekend? Call us today.

Comment: The sales appeals used here are exclusivity and flattery. The reader is made to feel special—and who among us does not enjoy being seen as "one of a kind"?

Short paragraphs and short sentences make this letter extremely readable. Note that the writer is selling the *offer*—the opportunity to test-drive a Maserati and get a free bottle of champagne—rather than the product itself. The more you sell your offer, the better your response will be.

This letter was written by freelancer Richard Armstrong, and it won the Caples Award for excellence in direct marketing.

KEEP-IN-TOUCH LETTER:
SALESMAN'S OPPORTUNITY

Also known as "cordial contact," the keep-in-touch letter is the soft sell of direct mail. It is used to build goodwill and keep your name in the mind of your customers, rather than make a hard pitch for a direct sale.

Which is better for ad response?

_____ A box number for address
_____ A street number for address

We keep getting calls and letters, particularly from new advertisers, asking which is better for getting greater ad results.

Frankly I didn't think it made much difference. After all what difference should it make; an address is an address, as Gertrude Stein would say.

But after making a far from scientific check with a number of advertisers, I must admit I'm surprised. Whether you choose a box number or a street number for an address does indeed have a great deal to do with ultimate ad response.

A street number address will almost always increase ad response. There appear to be several reasons: (1) It offers greater "size," "stability," "impact," as advertisers say. (2) It encourages more salespeople to visit the plant. And (3) it seems to encourage more phone calls (easier to look up a company's phone).

Perhaps the answer might be to include both in an address—especially if that will speed up mail delivery.

It appears that a street address makes your firm seem

"bigger," more "established," and "easier for people to deal with," as several said.

But some of our most successful advertisers use box numbers. The inference might be they'd be even more successful if they'd switch.

Whatever kind of address you use in your ad you're sure to make more sales over the last quarter, if you schedule an ad in OPPORTUNITY's "Key to Sale— Demonstrate!" OCTOBER ISSUE—which starts to circulate around Sept. 21st.

Deadline for ad copy for the *October issue* is *August 31st*. If you need an extension, or any other ad help, please call, collect, 312-346-4790.

Sincerely,

Barney Kingston
Merchandising Director

Comment: This letter is one in a series of cordial contacts that Barney Kingston sends to advertisers and potential advertisers for his magazine, *Salesman's Opportunity*. All the letters take a soft-sell approach, providing genuinely useful information and advice on how to improve your advertising. Only in the last two paragraphs does Barney discuss his magazine, and even then, it's more of a reminder than a sales pitch.

Cordial contacts using this informational approach are excellent for companies that sell high-priced products or services . . . or in situations where customers need to be educated or want a lot of information . . . or for selling professional services where a hard-sell approach would be inappropriate.

COMBINATION LETTER:
WOODBRIDGE MEMORIAL GARDENS

Sometimes one letter does two jobs. The letter below is a combination inquiry-fulfillment and appointment letter. It serves as a cover letter accompanying brochures which the recipient requested. And it also paves the way for an appointment with a company sales representative (called a "counselor").

Dear Friend:

Here are the brochures we promised you.

As president of our company, I want to thank you personally for your interest in Woodbridge Memorial Gardens. I also want to congratulate you on your wisdom and foresight in planning ahead. Thousands of families are now recognizing that planning all burial arrangements in advance is the only way to save money and anguish.

What most people do not realize is that it is easier and more economical to own a majestic mausoleum than to go through the rapidly growing costs of plots, vaults, monuments, gardening, and perpetual care bills.

Our organization has served over 100,000 families in our memorial parks, and believe me, with over 50 years of experience, we have learned, and can show you, how to avoid the costly pitfalls of old type cemetery and funeral arrangements.

I have asked our neighborhood counselor to pass this valuable experience on to you with our free family counseling service. There is absolutely no obligation, and you will soon learn, among many other things:

* How to avoid the high cost of burial arrangements.
* How our new mausoleums compare with old cemetery burial.
* Complete prices and payment plans for the mausoleum.
* How to register for a free, 24-HOUR, 365-day Emergency Service.

Remember, too, that Woodbridge Memorial Gardens, conveniently located from all parts of New Jersey, Staten Island, and Brooklyn, is considered by many to be the most beautiful mausoleum in the entire area.

Its architecture is reminiscent of the grandeur of Pompeii. The rich Italian marble, the sunlight streaming through the trees in the glass-enclosed gardens, the plush carpets, the inspiring works of art give Woodbridge beauty and serenity that defy description.

And our four-seasons climate control, comfortable seating, and friendly atmosphere make this the ideal family shrine. One that the whole family will visit willingly and often to remember loved ones. And you will have the peace of mind in knowing that the Woodbridge Mausoleum alleviates the disturbing problems associated with ordinary earth burial.

BUT ONE WORD OF CAUTION: Because families like yours are entitled to a 30% savings before new construction is complete, it is important that you act without delay. This way, locations you prefer at prices designed to suit your budget will still be available.

Our counselor will also make sure you receive your

personalized, free Family Planning Portfolio, which cannot be bought anywhere. It is designed to save you hundreds of dollars and great emotional anguish. I promise you that this portfolio and our free family counseling service will give you information and insight on how to easily solve one of life's most difficult and inevitable problems.

So I urge you to take 15 minutes of your time for our counselor to explain how to use your Family Planning Portfolio and to pass on to you the benefits of our 50 years of experience.

And please remember you are under no obligation— only our sincere hope that you wil avail yourself of our guidance and counsel.

Sincerely,

Comments: Death is a delicate subject. This well-written letter has a sincere, dignified, proper tone, yet it also does a good job of selling the benefits of Woodbridge Memorial Gardens, advance planning, and the counseling service. The writer seems genuinely interested in helping us take care of an important matter, even though we know he is selling a product.

A CHECKLIST FOR LETTER WRITERS

Galen Stilson, a Florida-based freelance direct response writer, offers the following checklist of sales-letter writing techniques.

▾ A High-Performance Techniques Checklist

[ ] Shift your letterhead to the bottom of the letter to avoid distraction

[ ] Lead with a benefit or promise headline

[ ] Use the salutation to target your primary audience

[ ] The first sentence should make the recipient want to read more

[ ] Format your letter for the perception of easy reading

[ ] Use lots of benefit-loaded subheads

[ ] Place the basics of your offer up front on page one

[ ] Focus on the perception of believability

[ ] Always write from a "you" orientation

[ ] Always typewrite the sales letter

[ ] Use emotional copy in the sales letter

[ ] Justify the desire to buy with proof of your promise

[ ] Choose one primary copy theme and wrap others around it

[ ] Include precise user benefits by audience type to increase sales

[ ] Remember that specifics are much more potent than generalizations

[ ] Prompt action in the last paragraph and sentence

[ ] Use command/suggestion copy throughout the letter

[ ] Never complete a sentence on an odd-numbered page

[ ] Keep words and sentences short and vary paragraph length

[ ] Add some sell to the closing

[ ] Always use a postscript and treat it as a headline

[ ] Choose a logical spokesperson as the signatory

Source: *Circulation Management*, December 1986. Reprinted with permission.

TO TEASE OR NOT TO TEASE?

A big decision you must make is whether to mail your letter in a regular envelope or a special envelope imprinted with teaser copy.

Most mailings use short teasers set in large, heavy type. Others use lengthy teaser messages that involve headlines, subheads, body copy, and notes written in fake handwriting. You can even use photos, drawings, or graphics to illustrate your teaser and draw more attention to your envelope.

Obviously, you want your mailing to get the greatest possible response. So the question is, "If I add a teaser, will the response increase, decrease, or stay the same?"

Test results reveal that the answer to this question varies depending upon the product, the offer, the mailing, and the teaser itself.

Sometimes, adding a teaser increases response—dramatically. Other times, a blank envelope does *much* better than an envelope with a teaser.

Why is this?

Teasers have both a positive and a negative aspect.

The negative is that the teaser identifies the package as direct mail. It says to the recipient, "This envelope contains an advertising pitch, not important business or personal mail, so feel free to throw it away if you want to." And many people do.

The positive aspect is that a well-executed teaser can actually *increase* response by whetting the recipient's appetite for more information, or arousing curiosity about what's inside the envelope. This type of teaser says, in effect, "Hey, this is something you'll really be interested in!" If the material inside delivers what the teaser promises, you'll have your reader hooked!

Here are some examples of effective teasers:

THE INVITATION INSIDE COULD HELP SAVE YOU HUNDREDS OF DOLLARS . . . and provide *better* financial security for your family. Please open and respond . . .   (Geico/Life Insurance)

Announcing great savings on the IBM Personal Computer. Plus convenient financing . . .   (IBM)

CAN 193,750 MILLIONAIRES BE WRONG?
Answer by August 5, 1986. Get two FREE previews from *Financial World*   (*Financial World* magazine)

INSIDE:
The true story of how a 31-year-old computer consultant stumbled upon a discovery so fascinating and ingenious, it has literally stunned the investment community—and how you could have turned a $100 investment in each of certain low-priced stocks into $27,566 in less than a year.   (Stock advisory service)

3 business forecasts *Forbes* believes are certain to come to pass.

How will they affect your company . . .
your investments . . .
your career?   (*Forbes* magazine)

Also inside:
A money-saving trial
  subscription offer.

HERE'S AN OPPORTUNITY FOR   (computer graphics service)
  YOU TO GET *FREE SOFTWARE*
  THAT LETS YOU CREATE
  CHARTS, GRAPHS, TABLES,
  AND OTHER BUSINESS
  GRAPHICS . . . IN MINUTES . . .
*RIGHT ON YOUR OWN PERSONAL
  COMPUTER, without* help from
  ad agencies, graphic artists, or
  other expensive outside
  vendors.
FOR DETAILS, see inside . . .

Your telephone bill refund is   (telecommunications consulting
  coming . . .   service)

CHEMLAWN HAS A $10 GIFT   (CHEMLAWN lawn-care service)
  FOR YOU.

If You Think $2.00 Doesn't Buy   (Mutual of Omaha accident
  Much Anymore, Look Inside   protection insurance)
  . . . You'll Be Amazed!

WARNING: (Client Advisory)
In 1986, competitive pressures
  on accounting professionals
  will *increase.* INSIDE: A
  practice-building tool that can
  help you meet the challenge,
  grow and *profit.*

HIGH ACHIEVERS!   (*Human Potential* magazine)
In every field, a few individuals
   consistently excel. They seem
   to possess some extraordinary
   power. They chalk up *success*
   after *success*—even in the
   face of overwhelming
   obstacles.
WHAT'S THEIR SECRET?
Find out inside—and discover a
   unique new tool to help you
   unlock *your* full potential.

Here are some rules for writing good teaser copy:

1. Identify the target audience ("A money-saving tool for the plant engineer . . .", "An announcement of unprecedented importance to PDP-11 users who want to be VAX users").

2. Talk about the reader's problems. Then say that the solution to the problem may be found inside the envelope. ("COMPUTER CRASHES. Now you can end them—*Forever*. How? See inside . . .").

3. Tell the reader that something free or valuable is inside the envelope. Or at least hint at it. ("INSIDE: Free Gift Worth $25," "TEAM UP, AMERICA! Your official decal of the 1984 Olympics is enclosed.")

4. Use language that refers to the contents of the envelope ("See inside," "For details, see inside," "Here's your invitation," "Enclosed is your . . .").

5. Promise the reader a benefit. ("INSIDE: A new way to save money on mailing lists.")

6. Mention that the envelope contains something new or exclusive.

7. Use the word FREE on the envelope. This never fails to

get attention. ("HERE'S AN OPPORTUNITY TO GET *FREE SOFT-WARE* . . .").

8. Make a provocative statement. This arouses curiosity and gets the reader to tear open the envelope. For example, conservative fund raisers write on their envelope, "Ted Kennedy doesn't want you to read this."

9. Create a sense of urgency ("LAST CHANCE to renew your CCMC Membership and receive a FREE gift").

10. Don't mislead the reader with the teaser, or make the teaser sound so great that the contents of the envelope can't live up to it. If you do, the reader will be disappointed when he gets into your letter, and will throw the package away in disgust.

ENVELOPES WITHOUT TEASERS

As I said, one disadvantage of teasers is that they tag your package as "direct mail." One advantage of plain envelopes is that they hide the fact that they contain direct mail.

"A perfectly blank white envelope with no teaser and a blind return address is bound to be opened," writes freelance copywriter Bob Matheo in *Direct Marketing*. "Does anybody throw away a piece of mail without at least finding out who it's from or what it's about?"

The key to using a nonteaser envelope is to maximize its resemblance to personal mail. Here's how to do it:

1. Don't use even a single word of teaser copy, or graphics, or illustration. The envelope should be 100 percent teaser-free.

2. Don't use your regular letterhead, which is imprinted with your corporate logo and thus identifies the mail as coming from your company.

3. Instead, make the return address (printed in the upper left corner of the envelope) a plain street address or box number, or

use the name of an individual rather than your company. And have this printed in black in a plain typeface.

4. Better still, if you're not worried about returns, omit the return address and mail in a completely blank white envelope. This type of mailing never fails to get opened.

5. Use a better-quality paper stock for your envelopes.

6. Try to word process or computer-address the envelopes so they look as if they were personally addressed on a typewriter. Avoid labels or windowed envelopes, if possible.

7. If you use a window envelope, use matching stock for your letter and brochure. You don't want gaudy, colorful artwork to show through and identify your package as advertising matter.

8. Some mailers have had great success with envelopes that resemble invoices, bills, bank statements, or legal notices. But be careful. This can backfire. Many people get scared by official-looking envelopes, and become angry when they realize they've been tricked.

9. The same goes for envelopes that look like telegrams or overnight-delivery-service packages. Again, this type of approach angers many people.

11

DIRECT MAIL BROCHURES

THE BROCHURE TELLS

Remember that old direct mail saying from chapter 10, "The letter sells, the brochure tells"? This chapter is about how to create effective direct mail brochures that tell your story in an interesting, attention-grabbing, meaningful fashion.

With the cost of production so high, why do so many mailers include expensive brochures, folders, and flyers with their letters? For the same reason we do *anything* in direct mail: to increase response.

If the brochure can increase the response level to the point where the extra sales more than pay for the cost of printing and mailing the brochure, then it is profitable and worthwhile.

Testing is the only way to know for certain whether your response will increase, decrease, or remain the same when you include a brochure with your letter.

In one test, a company created a full package complete with letter, reply card, and brochure. The response was pretty good, but it was expensive to send the full package.

So, they tested a small quantity without the brochure. And guess what? Response didn't change! From then on, they mailed a letter with reply card only, since the brochure wasn't helping to increase the package's pulling power.

In many other cases, however, I've seen letters that bombed until they were backed up with a strong illustrated brochure giving detailed information, illustrations, and additional benefits. Once the brochure was included, response soared, and the additional profits far exceeded the cost of producing the literature.

Of course, you've got to make a decision *before* you test: Should your initial mailing include a brochure or not?

WHEN SHOULD I USE A BROCHURE?

Here are some of the situations where you'll need a brochure to supplement your letter:

• *For more information.* In some selling situations, customers need a lot of detailed or highly technical information to make a decision—more than you would want to pack into a letter. Here, the letter is used to state the main benefits, while the brochure presents the details. In a mailing selling computer equipment, a detailed list of technical features and specifications might be printed on a sheet of paper separate from the letter. In a package selling a book by mail, I will always list the author's biography and a detailed table of contents on a separate flyer. Such lengthy, dry information would detract from the sales pitch if inserted into the middle of a letter.

• *To teach.* A brochure is an excellent way of educating your readers about a topic. In a mailing I sent to dentists, my letter asked the dentist to request a sample order of a new type of dental post. Problem was, the procedure for using this new post was a little different from what the dentists were used to doing. The solution was to include a small illustrated booklet showing, in simple words and pictures, the new technique.

When the dentists saw that the procedure was easy, and very similar to current practices, it overcame their resistance to the new product.

• *To impress.* A company that electroplates gold, silver, and other metals onto metal parts sends prospects a brochure showing pictures of scientists working in research labs. The pictures don't inform or explain; they *impress* by showing how modern and sophisticated the plating company is. In the same way, a package promoting a get-rich-quick book includes a photo of the book's author posed next to a Rolls Royce—so we will be impressed with his wealth. Pictures and words working together can sometimes be more impressive than a mere typed letter working alone.

• *Proof.* Sometimes a brochure is needed to prove claims made in the sales letter. For instance, a letter from a vitamin manufacturer says that his formula has given new health and vitality to thousands of people. Included with the letter is a brochure packed with pictures of satisfied customers; underneath each picture is a testimonial from the customer saying how much better he or she feels after taking the vitamins. Another way to prove his claim would be to send reprints or excerpts of papers from medical journals testifying to the medical benefits of the vitamins.

• *Establish credibility.* Because it is a somewhat more expensive and more permanent form of communication than a letter, a brochure does a better job of saying to the reader, "Hey, this is a real company, not just some fly-by-night operator." After all, reasons the reader, *anyone* can pay fifty dollars to have some letters typed. But if you've sprung for the cost of a fancy brochure, you must be a substantial company with real money. People are skeptical, and if you have any reason to feel that people would hesitate to do business with you or respond to your mailing, a brochure can help establish credibility.

• **Dramatize.** An illustrated brochure can sometimes make a point more dramatically than an all-copy letter. For example, a brochure for a hair-replacement center shows before and after photos of men who have had hair transplants. A brochure for a diet center shows a picture of a two-hundred-pound woman. Next to this picture is another photo of the woman at 130 pounds, six months after starting the diet program. A fund-raising brochure for a humane society could dramatize the plight of animals by showing photos of animals abused in laboratory research. A foster-parents program mailing could show a heartrending photo of a hungry, poverty-stricken child.

• **Demonstrate.** If you can demonstrate your product in print, you stand a much better chance of making the sale. In a brochure selling a new piece of equipment, you might use a series of photos with captions to show step-by-step how your product works. For a brochure on a facsimile machine, the sequence might be (1) turn on the machine, (2) connect to your telephone, (3) place the document in the feeder, (4) press the start button, (5) remove the document, (6) a facsimile is printed on the recipient's machine across the country.

• **Explain.** If your product or service is unfamiliar or complex, the brochure can be used to give a lengthy explanation of what it is, how it works, and why the reader should be interested. The letter concentrates on getting the reader to respond to the offer, and refers the reader to the brochure if he wants the detailed information.

• **Visualize.** Rather than just show pictures of the product, you can show pictures of people enjoying the benefit or end result of the product. A brochure advertising a new food processor shows delicious food prepared with the processor, rather than the machine itself. A brochure on a home-study course designed to help people become richer shows vacation homes, luxury cars, cruise ships, swimming pools—the end result of becoming wealthy, rather than the workbooks and cassette tapes that help you get there.

BROCHURE CONTENTS

What type of information and illustration goes into a direct mail brochure?

In general, the brochure contains written information too detailed or lengthy to include in the letter. It can also show photos, drawings, diagrams, charts, graphs, and tables—something a letter usually cannot do.

Your brochure can include any of the following:

- testimonials of satisfied clients and customers
- list of clients and customers
- photos of clients and customers
- photos of your staff
- capsule biographies of key company personnel
- photo series demonstrating use of your product
- product photos
- photos of people using your product
- photos of people enjoying the benefits or end result of your product or service
- typical applications of your product
- certificate of warranty or guarantee
- order blank
- toll-free number
- list of local offices or sales representatives
- technical specifications
- list of product features
- descriptions of related products or services
- descriptions of accessories and supplies
- brief description of your company
- sample news clips from articles about you in the press

- sample letters from satisfied customers
- diagram of product with call-outs pointing to specific features
- quiz or other checklist the reader can fill out
- graph showing product performance
- bar chart, pie chart
- map showing location of plants, offices, other facilities
- table of data or information
- list of product specifications
- cartoon
- photo of facilities (manufacturing plant, offices, etc.)
- list of key benefits
- picture of premium or free gift offer
- cover of booklet, brochure, report, or other information sent in response to inquiry

Use this checklist as a springboard to stimulate your own thinking, but don't let it limit you. Perhaps your product or service lends itself to some unique illustration or approach that I haven't thought of here.

SIZE AND FORMAT

The size and format of the brochure determines, in large part, how you design and write the piece.

In a brochure, each page is a self-contained unit. Unlike a book or report, in which the text just runs onto the next page, the text in a brochure must be written to fit the space available. Also, the way the brochure unfolds determines the sequence in which the reader sees each section. Copy must be written with that sequence in mind.

Here are a few things to consider when planning your brochure.

First, your regular product brochure should not be used as

your direct-mail brochure. It probably contains too much detail for someone who is receiving a "cold" (unsolicited) sales pitch. Also, it's probably too expensive to mail "blind," when you consider that 90 percent or more of the people who receive it will throw it away without a second glance.

You need a separate, smaller, less expensive brochure to accompany your direct mail letter. The direct mail brochure should concentrate on enhancing the selling message of the letter. Save lengthy detail for your regular brochure, which will be sent to people who respond to the mailing and ask for more information.

Second, direct mail brochures are usually created by folding a large sheet of paper to form panels. For example, if you take a sheet of typing paper and fold it once, horizontally, you've created four panels (pages).

Larger brochures are formed by stapling a number of sheets of paper together, as in a booklet. This is rarely done with direct mail brochures. First, most direct mail brochures are short rather than lengthy. Second, folded brochures have more of a sense of immediacy, of "read me now." A stapled brochure gives an impression of detailed information that may be filed for later reference. And you don't want the reader to file your brochure away for later—you want him to read and respond *now*.

Third, your brochure, when folded, should fit standard-size envelopes. Otherwise, you have to pay a lot of money to have special envelopes printed to hold your odd-size brochure.

Fourth, weight is important, because the heavier your brochure, the more it costs to mail. This is another reason to keep the brochure small. Lightweight printing stock also helps keep mailing costs down.

HOW TO FIND A FORMAT YOU LIKE

A brochure is a three-dimensional physical object. You hold it, feel it, unfold it.

It's difficult for me to show or describe various brochure formats on the pages of this book. Fortunately, there's a better way.

Right now, get two file folders and label both of them "DIRECT MAIL BROCHURES." Keep one in your office and take one home. For the next month, open every piece of direct mail you get at the office or at home, remove the brochure, and drop it into your file.

At the end of a month, dump all the brochures onto your desk. Go through them, and separate into three piles: (a) great brochures that really leap out and grab your attention, (b) those that are OK but nothing special, and (c) those that are ho-hum and don't excite you.

Now, look through your a, b, and c piles and analyze what makes each piece exciting or ineffective. Is it the way the artist takes advantage of the format, having a new and exciting message presented as you unfold each page? Is it the paper stock, the colors, the typeface? the use of catchy headlines and subheads?

Keep the best examples as models for when you have to design your own brochure. Save good examples in the three basic sizes: number ten, six-by-nine, and nine-by-twelve. Now, when you're trying to figure out how to lay out a brochure, you can turn to your sample file for ideas and inspiration. If you come across an interesting new brochure in the mail, add it to your reference file.

Don't be afraid to copy a layout or format. The secret to successful direct mail, as one successful practitioner once told me, is to know what works and use it.

When writing and designing your brochure, it's helpful to create a "dummy." The dummy is a full-scale mock-up of the brochure made from blank sheets of paper. It shows the page size, the folds, the panels, and any other special techniques such as a cut-out or pop-up.

Using scissors and tape, make a dummy—or better yet, several dummies. Then, with a pencil, start to sketch in your rough ideas for possible headlines, subheads, photos, illustrations, and other graphics. Experiment until you're satisfied with the flow of the piece—the way your message presents itself to the reader as he or she unfolds your brochure. Once you're satisfied, you can polish the headlines, write body copy, and determine what the final visuals will be.

BROCHURE COVERS THAT SELL

The first thing the readers see when they look at your brochure is the cover. (Sometimes they see the back cover first. But because we are trained to read from beginning to end, they will quickly flip to the front and start there.) For this reason, it pays to start selling right on the cover.

One technique is to use a cover headline that gives the reader a self-contained message. For example: "THE NEW HITACHI CHILLER-HEATER CAN CUT YOUR HEATING AND COOLING COSTS UP TO 50% OR MORE."

The reasoning behind this technique is that many people will only glance at the cover and not bother to turn the page. And those who do get past the cover may only skim the brochure without really reading it. So headlines, especially cover headlines, should present the key benefit up front.

A second technique is to use the headline to lure the reader inside. For example: "HOW ARE COMPANIES IN YOUR AREA PAYING UP TO 50% LESS IN HEATING AND COOLING COSTS THAN YOU ARE? See inside for details. . . ."

The logic here is people who just skim aren't really interested anyway, and *real* prospects will want the information in the brochure. The headline is used to grab the attention of real prospects and direct them toward your detailed sales pitch.

A third technique is to combine both approaches. For example: "HITACHI CHILLER-HEATERS CAN CUT HEATING AND COOLING COSTS UP TO 50% OR MORE. For details, see inside. . . ." This headline delivers a complete message *and* encourages the reader to turn the page.

Here are some examples of strong selling headlines, taken from the covers of direct mail brochures I've received over the past year or so.

Here's the free cup of coffee you missed . . . [packet of instant coffee was affixed to front of brochure]	(Palmer House Conference Center)
Now you can have a FREE branch office in Canada.	(CHANNELS Computer Sales Network)
HOW TO PRINT, STUFF, SEAL, STAMP AND SEND 100,000 LETTERS OVERNIGHT.	(TELEPOST mail service)
In a comparison test, which card do you think would win? [VISUAL: side-by-side photos of Citibank VISA card and American Express Card]	(Citibank)
Are these some of the communication problems you face?	(Pitney Bowes 8100 Facsimile System)
SELL MORE . . . SELL MORE EASILY. "I don't care how hot, cold, or lukewarm you are now. If you are *selling*, you can do *much* better—the easy way!"	(Sandler Sales Institute)
THE HARDEST THING ABOUT BECOMING A *MILLIONAIRE* IS *BELIEVING* YOU CAN DO IT. Next hardest is getting *started*. We'll help you do both . . .	(Hume Publishing, home study course)

GREAT IDEAS THAT SHAPED OUR WORLD
The classic thinkers you always *intended* to read (but never had time for) are now available on *audio cassettes*

(Knowledge Products audio cassettes)

Get a fascinating new view of the exciting world all around you . . . with NATURAL HISTORY, The Magazine of the American Museum of Natural History. It's yours as a benefit of Museum Membership with the invitation enclosed.

(American Museum of Natural History)

TIPS FOR DESIGNING DIRECT MAIL BROCHURES

1. Pick a size to fit the envelopes you will be using in your mailing.

2. Be sure to use a standard size. Custom envelopes are expensive.

3. Make a dummy. This makes it easier to visualize what the final piece will look like.

4. Keep cost considerations in mind. A two-color printing job is about 15 percent more expensive than one-color. Four colors can add 50 percent or more to the job.

5. Using a professional photographer to take new photos or commissioning an illustrator to do a drawing is also expensive. Are there existing photos and illustrations you can use in your brochure?

6. You can often save money by reusing photos and drawings created for other mailings, ads, slide presentations, or brochures.

7. You'll get greater response by designing the brochure as a separate piece from the letter, rather than combining letter and brochure into a single piece of literature.

8. It's also better to have the reply card or form separate from the brochure, rather than have a reply form you have to tear off or cut out of the brochure. However, if there's room, you might consider having *two* reply forms—one separate, one as part of the brochure.

9. Guarantee and warranty statements should be surrounded by a certificate-like border, to make them look more "official" and valuable.

10. Pop-ups, die-cuts, and embossing can add visual appeal, but they also add cost. Use with caution.

11. Use full color only if budget is not a constraint or when your product or service *must* be illustrated in color—such as collectibles, clothing, gourmet food, fine art.

12. Be creative with one-color and two-color jobs. For example, you can achieve a colorful appearance with a one-color job: Instead of printing black ink on white stock, print black on *yellow* paper. Or blue on gray. Or dark brown on light biege.

13. But unless you're striving for a dignified approach or image building, it's best to use bold, "hot" colors. Red is very good as a second color in hard-sell direct mail. So are green and blue.

14. Use borders, boxes, tints, and other graphic devices to break the copy up into short sections. Arrows, bursts, asterisks, and handwritten notes can help draw the reader's eye to a particular message.

15. Readability is vital. Don't use a creative color scheme or complex design if it makes the copy difficult to read.

16. Make headlines and subheads big and bold.

17. Underlining, tints, and printing in a second color can help highlight phrases or paragraphs of copy.

18. If there's a toll-free number, put it in large type and place a sketch of a telephone to the left of the number.

TIPS ON WRITING DIRECT MAIL BROCHURES

1. Cluster your thoughts. For example, when using testimonials, put all the testimonials on the same page rather than spreading them throughout the brochure. When giving biographies of key personnel, put them all in the same section. Having similar thoughts in a cluster makes a much greater impression on the reader.

2. Use plenty of headlines and subheads. Many readers will only scan your brochure without reading the body copy. A glance at headlines and subheads should give the reader the gist of your story.

3. Make headlines and subheads sales-oriented, not just descriptive. For instance, instead of "Here's how it works," say, "Here's how the Financial Advisory Service increases investment income by 20 percent or more." Put benefits in every headline and subhead. Make them persuasive, not just informative.

4. Use short sections of copy. Readers would rather read many short sections than one long one. (This is why books are divided into chapters.)

5. If you want to highlight a particular section, instruct the artist to put it in a separate box, surrounded by a border and printed on a light color tint. For example, you may want to highlight a special service (such as a telephone hotline) or a premium (such as a free gift or report).

6. Use a two-part headline to lure the reader inside the brochure. The first half of the headline is printed on the front cover; the second half on the inside spread. For example: "Here's the free cup of coffee you missed . . .

. . . if yours wasn't one of the 2,513 meetings held at Conference Center 7 in its first year."

7. If you have a lot of benefits or sales points to discuss, simply list them in 1-2-3 fashion. The headline of such a brochure might be, "10 reasons to buy Universal Life Insurance" or "6 steps to a happy retirement."

8. If you have a lot of explaining to do in your brochure, consider a question-and-answer format, where each subhead is a question, and the answer is given in the body copy below it. Such a brochure might be titled "Questions and answers about Universal Life Insurance" or "6 questions to ask before you select a retirement plan—and the answers."

9. If you have a lot of miscellaneous features, sales points, or technical specifications to present, put them in a separate area of the brochure. List them in table or "bullet" form rather than as straight text. This makes it easier to scan the brochure.

10. Be sure to include your company name, address, and phone number on every enclosure in the direct mail package. Highlight toll-free numbers by setting them in large, bold type.

USING MULTIPLE BROCHURES

A direct mail package isn't limited to one letter or one brochure or one order form. You can put in as much as you want. The question then becomes, "Is it better to use a single brochure or several smaller enclosures?"

It really depends on what you are selling. The New Process Company sends a letter with many small pieces of literature (called "Bargain Slips"), each describing and illustrating a different item of clothing you can order by mail. Each item has its own minibrochure to ensure enough room for a complete description. Multiple brochures make sense here.

On the other hand, we've all opened mailings that we thought were too cluttered with too many different pieces of paper. Sweepstakes mailings often take this approach, using half a dozen or more different slips, sheets, folders, and other enclosures.

Why do companies continue to use this approach when so many of us find it so annoying? In his book *Tested Advertising Methods*, John Caples offers an answer:

Much direct mail advertising goes directly to the wastebasket. However, a prospect will rarely throw all of your mailing pieces into the wastebasket without at least glancing at them. If your entire advertising message is contained in a single circular or a single booklet, the prospect will devote a few seconds to it and if it doesn't arouse his interest, he will throw it away. On the other hand, if your envelope is stuffed with half a dozen different mailing pieces, the prospect will probably glance at each piece before throwing it away. People hate to throw things away without at least glancing at them. They want to avoid disposing of anything valuable. Therefore, your six different inserts give you six opportunities to catch the interest of the prospect instead of only one opportunity.

This explanation makes sense. But please keep in mind that Mr. Caples wrote it in 1974. Today's prospects are far busier than people were in the 1970s. Half of all adult women work today. Everyone gets much more direct mail. And they have less time to read it. So this approach of cramming the envelope full of different slips of paper may not work so well anymore. You have to test to be sure.

I generally recommend a single brochure unless there is some sales point or body of information so important and so different from your main message that a separate brochure or flyer is needed to make it stand out. For example, let's say your product has a unique feature, and that for a limited time you are offering 25 percent off the regular price. Your first flyer might highlight the feature, while a second flyer stresses the 25 percent off and the details of the offer.

As a rule, use a single brochure unless you feel a compelling need to do otherwise. And remember, each piece of paper in the direct mail package must pull its own weight. Before you create another brochure or flier or letter, ask yourself, "Does this really increase the selling power of my package? Will I get more orders if I add this to the envelope?" If not, discard it.

HOW TO USE BUCK SLIPS

A *buck slip* is a small (usually four-by-nine-inch) slip of paper used to highlight an additional sales point or feature in the mailing. Not really a brochure, the buck slip is approximately the same size as the outer envelope. It is not folded. And it has a minimal amount of copy—usually printed on one side only.

A buck slip might highlight the offer. It may stress a deadline or a time limit after which the offer is void or the price goes up. It might feature the "premium"—the free gift you get when you place your order. It might be imprinted with testimonials from satisfied customers. It might be designed as a warranty or certificate of guarantee. Or, it can reprint recent newspaper or magazine articles that deal with the topic of the mailing.

12

ORDER FORMS, REPLY CARDS, AND BUSINESS REPLY ENVELOPES

ASKING FOR THE ORDER

Direct mail always calls for action on the part of the readers. It tells the readers what the next step is—and urges them to take it.

A good direct mail package not only asks for a response, it makes readers feel they would be making an error by *not* responding. It also creates a sense of urgency, or gives some other compelling reason why a response is required *today*, and not tomorrow or next week.

A good direct mail package boldly asks for the order or some other response, such as a request for information. The focal point, then, becomes the *reply element*. The reply element is the part of the package the reader mails back to the advertiser to place an order or request more information.

The reply element is usually a reply card (in the case of lead generation) or an order form and reply envelope (in the case of mail order). But it can take other forms, such as a certificate, questionnaire, token, or other device. And there's no law that says you must stick with a single reply element. Some mailings use two or three different reply elements in the hopes of boosting response.

Should you include a reply element in your mailing? Yes, for two reasons.

First, the reply element makes it easier to respond. Instead of writing a letter, the reader simply fills in a form. Instead of typing out an envelope and hunting for a stamp, the reader uses the postage-paid, self-addressed envelope you've thoughtfully provided. And the easier it is to respond, the more responses you'll get. So a reply element almost always results in a better response.

Second, the mere presence of a reply element sends a message to the recipient, saying in effect, "This is direct response mail, and we would appreciate a reply from you." Thus, readers are alerted to the fact that a response is desired. This increases overall response, both from people who use the reply element and those who prefer to respond by phone!

HOW TO DESIGN A REPLY ELEMENT

Here are some basic rules that apply to all types of reply elements, including reply cards and order forms:

• ***The reply form should be easy to fill out.*** The reply form should be clear, never confusing. Tell the reader what to do next in simple 1-2-3 fashion. The form should be designed so that anyone who receives it can follow your directions without assistance. If the reply form is complicated, or unclear, or difficult to complete, people will throw it away.

For example, make it crystal clear how much should be added for sales tax, shipping, and postage. If the recipient isn't sure, he will throw away the order form rather than risk the embarrassment of asking for help. Complex order forms can actually *lose* orders for you!

• ***A clean design.*** The design should be simple, clean, and uncluttered. Don't cram too much into a limited space. If you have a lot of information, use a larger order form. A cluttered piece of paper turns readers off. And you don't want an order form that repels potential customers.

• ***Leave enough room for people to write in the information you ask for.*** This rule seems obvious and easy to follow. Yet I see it ignored in hundreds of mailing each year. Surely you've been frustrated by order forms that ask for your full name, then give you one half inch of space to write it . . . or force you to cram your address, city, state, zip, apartment number, *and* phone number on a single line.

When designing your order form, give the reader plenty of room to write. A good test is to fill out your own reply card or order blank. Do you find yourself writing in tiny, cramped handwriting to make it all fit? If so, redesign to give your prospects more "breathing room."

• ***Fewer steps.*** The less work the reader has to do to complete your order blank and get it in the mail to you, the better. Remember, the more time it takes to prepare an order form, the less likely people are to bother.

There are a number of things you can do to make it easier for the reader. A self-addressed, postage-paid "business reply envelope" (BRE) saves the reader the trouble of addressing and stamping his own envelope. A toll-free phone number printed on the order blank gives people the option of phoning in their order, rather than writing.

If you're mailing to businesspeople, tell them they can attach their business card to the reply form, eliminating the need to fill in name, company, address, and phone number. Better still, if you use an envelope with a transparent window, the mailing label can be affixed to the reply form (which shows through the window) rather than the outer envelope. Thus, the reader doesn't need to fill in his name and address on the reply card, because you've already done it.

• **Headline your offer.** The first sentence of the reply form should be a headline that restates the offer and acknowledges the reader's desire to take advantage of the offer. Some examples of how to phrase this headline are presented below:

YES, I would like to receive a complimentary information kit about the *Thomson McKinnon Investment Trust*

(Thomson McKinnon Securities)

YES! I want to help bring an end to this vile sport and stop the suffering for thousands of loyal pets!

(Humane Society)

I accept your invitation to become an Associate Member of the American Museum of Natural History at the low introductory rate. . . .

(American Museum of Natural History)

YES, enter my trial subscription to *Forbes* as checked below.

(*Forbes* magazine)

YES, show me how SureBind will make my Plastic Binding System even better . . .

(GBC binding machines)

Please send the free, full-color brochure on the Contour Chair.

(Contour Chair Lounge)

YES, I want my free telephone and a demonstration of the new Pitney Bowes 8100 Facsimile System.

(Pitney Bowes)

• **Give a short sales pitch.** In the most concise language possible, your reply form should restate the nature and terms of the offer, and highlight the key benefits stressed in the letter and brochure. In a few sentences, you want to summarize your whole sales pitch, so that the reader can get the essence of your story just by reading the reply form.

Although it's important to be concise, it's even more important to be complete. Don't leave out information that the reader must have in order to make a proper response. For example, if your minimum order is one hundred dollars, the form should specify, "Minimum order—$100." Otherwise, you will have a lot of explaining to do to people who send you checks for twenty-five or fifty or seventy-five dollars.

• *No risk, no obligation, no sales calls.* People who might otherwise send in an order or a reply card requesting more information are reluctant to do so because they think that either you will somehow trick them into buying merchandise they didn't order, or your salespeople will put pressure on them, either in person or by phone.

Reply copy should reassure prospects that this isn't so. It should make the ordering process as painless, as pressure-free, and as nonthreatening as possible.

If there is no obligation for requesting free information or a free gift, say so. If you offer a money-back guarantee, say so. If the customer has thirty days to return the merchandise for a full refund, say so. If no salesperson is going to call on your prospects, say "No salesperson will call." These messages go a long way toward putting prospects at ease.

Of course, you shouldn't make these statements if they aren't true. If your order form says "No salesperson will call," and then the customer gets a sales call, you will be branded a liar and your credibility will be destroyed.

• *Make it look valuable.* People are reluctant to throw away anything that looks valuable. The more "important" your order form looks, the greater its power to get people to stop, examine, and use it.

There are two ways to make your order form seem more valuable.

First, never call it an "order form." The word *order* is a negative, because it involves spending money. Instead, give the reply form a title that implies value and, if possible, savings (if yours is a money-saving offer) or some other benefit.

For instance, if your reply form entitles the user to a discount, call it a CERTIFICATE OF SAVINGS. If the form opens an account or credit line, call it an ACCOUNT OPENER FORM. If it entitles the user to a money-back trial, call it a TRIAL REQUEST FORM. If it brings the reader a free gift, call it a FREE GIFT CHECK. If it brings the reader free information, such as a brochure or report, call it an INFORMATION REQUEST FORM. If it is used to set up an appointment for a product demonstration, call it a FREE DEMONSTRATION RESERVATION FORM. (These are suggestions only. Be imaginative!)

Second, design the form so that its appearance gives the impression of importance and value—or at least, urgency. A common technique is to put an ornate border around the order form, giving it an appearance similar to that of a stock certificate or other valuable paper.

• *Phone number.* Put your phone number on every order form, and encourage those who prefer to call to do so.

People are different. Some people are impatient with filling in order blanks and find the phone a tremendous time-saver. Other people are shy about phoning and feel less threatened by putting down their order or request on paper. By giving recipients both options, you increase your chance of closing the sale.

• *Use visuals.* If you are offering a free color brochure, illustrate your reply card with a picture of the brochure's front cover. If you are giving away a free gift, show a picture of the gift. Illustrations catch the eye and enhance the appeal of your reply forms.

• *Ensure privacy.* In cases where the reply form is small enough to fit on a postcard, you can use a postage-paid "business reply card" (BRC), eliminating the need for a separate reply envelope. The reader just fills in the back of the card and drops it in the mail.

However, if the reply form asks for confidential or sensitive information, it's best to include a reply envelope to ensure the prospect's privacy. For example, let's say you ask the prospects to indicate their annual income on the reply form. Most people would not want the postal carrier or other people to be able to read this information off the back of a postcard. By mailing back the card in a sealed reply envelope, the prospect can respond to your questions while maintaining privacy.

• *Multiple response options increase response.* You can often increase your response rate by giving prospects more than one response option.

• *Use the reply form to prequalify prospects or gather market research information.* By asking a few simple questions you can separate good prospects from bad and learn a lot about your target market.

These last two points are so important that they deserve extra attention. Let's start with multiple response options.

THE MAGIC OF YES-NO-MAYBE

This is amazing, but true.

Some time ago, smart direct marketers discovered that they got a better response by asking for a reply from people who *weren't* interested in the offer as well as from those who wanted to buy.

This changed the way most reply forms are structured.

Previously, we only asked for a response from those who wanted more information or were ready to make a purchase. There was one box to check off, and it read something like, "[ ] YES, please send me _____ copies of THE MAGIC OF SAYING 'NO' for $12.95 each plus $1 a copy postage and handling."

Now, many reply forms offer the reader two or three options for responding. This has two advantages.

First, it can, in some cases, bring in more orders or inquiries from people who are interested, by presenting a wider range of offers appealing to a wider audience. Having a "NO" option actually increases the number of "YES" responses!

Second, the people who respond "NO, not interested" are valuable prospects in themselves. People who have no interest whatsoever in your product or service will throw the reply form away without a second glance.

But there are also many people who are genuine prospects and have *some* interest, but aren't ready to order for any of a number of reasons.

Why did the people who almost bought not send an order? Perhaps the price is too high. Or the offer isn't right. Or your sales letter just didn't sell them. A "NO" option captures their response and allows them to indicate some interest without committing to a purchase. Any good sales trainer will tell you that the salesperson's job is basically to turn a "NO" into a "MAYBE" and a "MAYBE" into a "YES." The multiple option reply form gives you an opportunity to get "NO" and "MAYBE" responses that would otherwise be lost.

A classic Yes-No-Maybe order form was included as part of a mailing package I received from *Financial World* magazine. I've reprinted it below so you can see how it works:

FINANCIAL WORLD
Free Introductory Offer Expires August 5

YES! Send me 2 free issues of *Financial World*, enroll me as a subscriber and bill me later at the low rate of $18.95 for 12 additional issues (making a total of 14 issues). I'll save 45% off the single-copy price, 21% off the regular rate. If not pleased with my 2 free issues, I'll just write "cancel" on the bill and owe nothing. Either way, the 2 issues are mine to keep and use—free!

MAYBE! Send me 2 free issues of *Financial World*. Let me look them over before I decide to subscribe. If I do,

I'll pay the same special rate. If not, the 2 issues are mine to keep with your compliments.

NO! Offer my 2 free issues to another serious investor on your list.

SEND NO MONEY NOW:
Mail in postpaid envelope to: Financial World, P.O. Box 0745, Des Moines, Iowa 50350

See how this works? The YES option is the "hard" offer. It is for people who are relatively certain they want the magazine.

The MAYBE option is an intermediate offer. It allows prospects to examine the product, and then decide whether they want to buy. Actually, the specifics of this offer are the same as the YES option; it's the way it's phrased that's different.

The NO option is the soft offer. It encourages prospects to reply even though they are not buying.

I use this same three-level approach when writing a reply card for a lead-generation mailing. My *hard* offer asks the prospect to make some sort of a commitment—usually to attend a sales presentation or product demonstration or to agree to speak with a sales representative.

My *soft* offer lets the prospect request literature or other information by mail only. This eliminates the stress and pressure of personal contact.

My *negative* offer allows the prospect to say he is not interested and asks him to tell us *why* he is not interested. This gives us a lot of useful information that would otherwise be lost.

And gathering information is another job the reply form can do for you.

THE REPLY FORM AS RESEARCH TOOL

In addition to bringing back orders, checks, and inquiries, the reply form is a powerful tool for research. By asking prospects to tell you something about themselves, you can gather a great deal of information about your market at no additional cost.

This information can be used to prescreen and qualify prospects. Or as pure market research.

In prescreening, you ask questions that help you determine whether the person replying is a genuine prospect for your product. For instance, let's say you sell commercial printing services to large companies that do a lot of printing. You don't want small jobs or clients, just large ones. To prescreen leads, you ask on your reply card, "How much do you spend per year on printing?" The answer instantly tells you whether the person is a qualified prospect for your service.

Other questions used to qualify prospects include:

- How many employees in your organization?
- Do you own a personal computer?
- How many photocopies do you make per month?
- What is your annual advertising budget?
- Check here if you own your own home . . .
- How many overnight packages do you send in a week?
- Do you use an IBM mainframe? [ ] model number [ ] operating system
- Do you [ ] recommend [ ] specify [ ] approve purchases for your company?
- When will you consider purchase of this type of equipment? [ ] next 6 months [ ] 6–12 months [ ] no immediate plans

By asking these questions, advertisers learn which leads represent potential customers and which are a waste of time. For example, you are going to have a tough time selling your new software package to a person who does not own a computer. And it is not profitable to sign up customers for your overnight package-delivery service if the customers never send packages overnight.

Another reason to ask questions on the reply form is to gather information that is useful either in helping solve the customer's present needs or learning about customer needs for future product development.

Here are some common research questions advertisers ask on the reply form:

- Which of these products are you currently using?
  [ ] modems [ ] printers [ ] surge protectors
  [ ] power supplies [ ] hard disk drive
- Which of these publications do you subscribe to? . . .
- Would you be interested in attending a seminar on [specify topic]?
- If you were buying a new telephone system, what feature or features would you look for?
- Who else in your organization would be interested in learning more about our product/services?

Asking which publications the prospect reads tells you where to advertise. Asking what features a potential customer would look for in a new phone system gives you an indication of which features to discuss in your next ad or mailing.

REPLY FORM FORMATS

There are four basic types of reply forms:

1. Business reply cards used for lead generation.
2. Business reply cards used for mail order.
3. Questionnaires/spec sheets used for lead generation.
4. Order forms used for mail order.

Let's take a brief look at each.

BUSINESS REPLY CARD: LEAD GENERATION

In a lead-generating package, you are not asking for an order or a check; you merely want the prospect to request more information. Therefore, the reply element can be much simpler than in a mail order package, and the entire message can fit easily on a small postcard.

A *business reply card* (BRC) is a postcard imprinted with a business reply mail permit number. The front of the card is addressed to the advertiser. No postage is required to mail the BRC; postage costs are paid by the advertiser on each card they receive. For information on how to get a business reply permit and use business reply mail, contact your local post office. The permit is only forty dollars a year or so and anyone can get one.

The back of the card has space where the prospect can fill in his name, address, and phone number. He can also check off a box to indicate his level of interest. By filling in the card, checking the appropriate box, and tossing the card in the mail, prospects can quickly and easily respond to your mailing. Below is a model business reply card for you to use.

YES, I'd like to know how to improve my business presentations and reports with the QuickBind report-maker.

[ ] Please call to arrange a free, no-obligation demonstration. The best time to call is: _____.

[ ] Send a free copy of your booklet, "12 Ways to Make Your Reports and Proposals Stand Out From the Crowd," by return mail.

[ ] Not interested right now. Try me again in _____
(month/year)

Name _____ Title _____
Company _____ Phone _____
Address _____
City _____ State _____ Zip _____

IS THE PHONE FASTER? FOR AN IMMEDIATE
APPOINTMENT CALL US TOLL-FREE 800-XXX-XXXX

Is it absolutely necessary to use a business reply card? No. Although business reply cards and envelopes generally generate a greater response than cards and envelopes that require a stamp, you can require the recipient to provide his own stamp, if you wish. If you do this, be sure to print the phrase "PLACE STAMP HERE" in a small box in the upper right-hand corner of the front of the card or envelope.

Some advertisers worry that offers of free information will attract "brochure collectors" who are not genuine prospects. Ross Anderson came up with copy aimed at discouraging this type of inquiry:

YES, ROSS, I am interested in the opportunity to sell Diamonds as outlined in your letter. Please send your complete Diamond Wholesaling Program to me so I can decide if I want to join you in this program. I'm not obligated by asking for this information, but I AM GENUINELY INTERESTED, NOT JUST CURIOUS. Send it as soon as you can.

Name _____
Address _____
City _____
State, Zip _____

BUSINESS REPLY CARD: MAIL ORDER

In a mail order package selling a single product, a postcard is usually sufficient for presenting all the information the prospect needs to place an order. On page 288, copy from the reply card for a mailing selling subscriptions to *Financial World* magazine is given.

How can you get more orders from this type of card?

One way is to add a tear-off stub. The prospect keeps this portion of the card as a reminder of his order. Typically, copy on the stub restates the offer, summarizes the guarantee, or describes the free premium. Another way to use the stub is to provide space for the customer to write in the date, number, and amount of his check.

As a consumer, I'm not fond of stubs. They're a pain to tear off, and who needs more paper? However, advertisers who use stubs say they *work*, so you should probably use them.

A second way to boost response is to add a business reply envelope (BRE) to your package. Even though the reply card can be mailed without the envelope, using the envelope boosts response. Why? Some people like the privacy an envelope provides. Others prefer to pay by check rather than credit card, and use the envelope for mailing their checks.

Business reply envelopes have traditionally been plain and devoid of teaser copy or other advertising messages. Nowadays, smart advertisers are realizing that the BRE presents yet another opportunity to do some more selling—one last chance to send the consumer a message before he places his order and drops it in the mail.

A fund raiser writes on his BRE, "Your stamp saves the farm workers money." (If you put a stamp on the BRE, the fund raiser won't be charged by the post office.) In a hand-written message on his BRE, a newsletter publisher reminds subscribers, "For SAME DAY SERVICE call 1-800-XXX-XXXX toll-free. We will send your first issue—and the bonuses—TODAY!" The teaser on a sweepstakes BRE reads, "Beat the Gold Bonus Seal Deadline Date and you could be eligible for an EXTRA Prize of $25,000!"

BREs are big response boosters when used in conjunction with BRCs and order forms. Busy consumers really appreciate the convenience of an envelope that is already addressed and postage-paid. In a recent ad campaign, Revlon pre-addressed envelopes with attached, perforated order forms bound into magazines opposite their direct response ads for European Collagen Complex, a skin-care product. The results? Response *quadrupled*, zooming from 0.5 percent to 2.0 percent.

QUESTIONNAIRE/SPEC SHEET: LEAD GENERATION

In some selling situations, the advertiser needs a lot of information about the customer before he can sell the customer the right product for his needs or come up with a solution to the customer's problems.

An ideal way to get this information is through direct mail. You send the customer a questionnaire, survey, or specification sheet. The customer is asked to fill it out and mail it back to you (usually in a business reply envelope you provide). You can then give a firm price quotation or proposal to the customer.

Instead of calling this type of reply form a questionnaire, give it a name that implies value. For example, you can call it a "Free Analysis Form," "Problem-Solver," or something similar. Letter copy should stress that you are offering a free analysis of the customer's problem, rather than trying to make a sale.

ORDER FORM: MAIL ORDER

For complex offers, or mail order packages selling multiple items, a reply card is insufficient. You'll need a full-blown order form, which can be one or more pages, usually 8½ by 11 inches.

Such an order form should contain complete instructions and solicit all the information you need to fill the customer's order. The order form should contain the following:

- instructions telling the customer to print or type (handwritten orders can be hard to read)
- space for the customer to fill in name, address, and apartment number (United Parcel Service does not deliver to box numbers)
- space for both work and home phone numbers (in case you have to contact the customer about his or her order

- a request to verify and correct address if a mailing label is affixed to order form
- space to fill in shipping address if different from billing address
- space to indicate the desired merchandise, including quantity and price
- instructions on methods of payment
- indication that payment may be tax deductible (if this is the case)
- a notice to Canadian and overseas customers that all prices listed are in U.S. dollars
- notice of additional charge for overseas shipments
- notice that credit cards are accepted
- notice of minimum order for credit card
- space to indicate credit card being used, number, expiration date
- space for signature for credit card orders
- toll-free number for orders by phone
- local number (if toll-free number doesn't work for in-state calls)
- information on the guarantee
- information on the return and exchange policy
- description of the discount schedule
- descriptions of last-minute sale items
- information on packing, shipping, and delivery
- information on whether gift wrapping is available
- information on shipping and handling costs and sales tax
- a thank-you to the buyer for the order
- a request for the names and addresses of friends who would like to receive your catalog or be put on your mailing list
- information as to whether the customer objects to your giving his or her name to other companies for mail solicitations
- code number (so you know which mailing generated the order)

- expiration date (date after which your offer is no longer valid)
- clean, easy-to-follow layout
- sufficient room to write in all information requested
- statement notifying readers, "This offer void where prohibited by law."

SEVEN WAYS YOUR ORDER FORM CAN INCREASE YOUR AVERAGE ORDER

Freeman F. Gosden Jr. points out that the best way to increase profits is to increase the dollar amount of your average order. And what better place to do this than on the order form? After all, by the time readers get involved with your order form, they have already decided to buy. Why not sell them *more*?

Here are Freeman Gosden's seven ways to use the order form to increase the size of your average order (reprinted, with permission, from his book *Direct Marketing Success* (New York: John Wiley & Sons):

• *Last-minute news/hot item flash.* Readers always have greater interest in what is the latest. An order form is a natural place to reinforce a "last-minute" item.

• *President's or merchandiser's favorites.* Most letters from presidents or owners of catalogs are very dry and don't take the opportunity for a strong call to action. If the respected merchandiser singles out a few items he feels are important, they will sell.

• *Liners.* By adding twenty to one hundred items to your catalog order form, just line listed like a laundry list, you will generate impulse sales. The secret is to use only those items that are fully explained by their names or by three or four additional words, with no illustrations. Examples are "Four Titlist Golf Balls," "Apple Corers," "Vice Grip Pliers," and so on.

• ***Volume discounts.*** If you have done your math correctly, you can afford to spend more to increase your average order because you have already covered most of your overhead and expenses. Incremental costing makes sense. "Ten percent off on all purchases over $100" can make sense to the reader. It is also a justification for him to spend more money with you.

• ***Gift packaging.*** Very special packaging does work at specialty retail stores. It can work just as well with mail. That special package, priced right, can generate more gross profit than an item of merchandise.

• ***Sale-sale-sale.*** The order form, with expanding pages, is ideal for sale merchandise. The lesser quality of most order form paper makes the placement of items on sale a natural.

• ***Simple and smooth-flowing order form.*** If your order form is simple and easy to fill out, you not only increase your chances of large orders but also decrease the chance for errors.

▾ 13

PROFITS FROM POSTCARD DECKS

POSTCARD DECKS: DIRECT
MARKETING'S SECRET WEAPON

Years ago, when I worked as the advertising manager for an industrial manufacturer, a product manager asked me to create a full-page advertisement for a new product. "And oh, yes," he added, at the end of our meeting, "I'll also want to run a postcard, too."

I discovered that the magazine in which our ad would run, *Chemical Engineering*, also published a "card deck"— something I'd never heard of before.

Frankly, I was unenthusiastic about the deck. Who, I wondered, would want to leaf through a bunch of postcard advertisements—especially when they already received *Chemical Engineering* magazine?

I paid our ad agency to create a brilliant ad. And slapped together the postcard without too much fuss and bother . . . almost as an afterthought.

The ad ran and the postcard ran, and the results shocked me. The full-page ad, which cost over $2,500 to produce and more than four thousand dollars per insertion, pulled maybe a hundred or so inquiries.

But the postcard, which cost less than three hundred dollars to produce and approximately one thousand dollars or so to run, generated more than five hundred replies!

At this point I began to think, "These postcard decks are worth looking into!" And maybe you're saying the same thing now, too.

WHAT IS A POSTCARD DECK?

Postcard decks are packs of loose postcards, sealed in a paper, poly (clear plastic), or foil wrapper, and distributed to a mailing list of prospects who, we hope, will be interested in the products and services advertised on the cards. (A few publishers mail decks of postcards bound into booklet form. An example of this is the Executive Mart, published by Hamel Publishing Company, Inc. But the majority are loose decks.)

Although I've seen postcard decks with as few as a dozen cards and as many as a hundred, the average deck probably contains forty to sixty separate cards.

The typical card, which measures 3½ by 5⅜ inches, is black and white—although larger folded formats and color cards are available.

The front of the card, or *mailing side*, usually contains the advertiser's address, business reply imprint, and permit number . . . so that when the prospect drops it in the mail, the card will be returned directly to the advertiser.

The back of the card, or *advertising side*, generally contains a miniature ad. In this tiny space, you must fit a headline, some brief copy, and, if appropriate, a visual. You must also leave a space for the prospect to write in name, address, company, and phone number.

Because the space is so limited, copy must be brief, visuals small. There is no room for complex diagrams or explanations or a detailed listing of features. You have to quickly state your offer, highlight a few key benefits, and prod the reader to respond.

ADVERTISING IN POSTCARD DECKS

The first step is to locate postcard decks that are right for your offer.

This process is similar to choosing which magazines to advertise in. The difference is that there are only six hundred or so postcard decks that accept outside postcards, against more than six thousand magazines that accept outside ads. Also, all postcards in a deck are basically the same size and format, while magazines offer a greater variety of sizes and shapes to choose from. This makes it a little easier to plan postcard advertising.

In addition, most postcard decks are mailed only three times a year. This limited mailing schedule, combined with the limited number of decks being published, makes it nearly impossible to rely on postcard decks as your *sole* method of direct marketing. So, despite the low cost of postcard decks, postcard promotion will only be part of your overall effort. You will have to supplement postcards with other inquiry and sale-generating activities, such as direct mail and print advertising.

How do you select the right postcard decks? A good place to start is with postcard decks you receive or know about. Take a look at the postcards in these decks. Do they seem to be aimed at the market you are trying to reach? Are their postcards advertising products similar to yours? Also ask your customers which postcard decks they receive.

SRDS (Standard Rate and Data Service) published a directory of postcard decks and their publishers. The listings include the name of the deck, description, price to insert a card, publication schedule, and contact information. SRDS is available in the reference rooms of larger libraries, or call (708) 256-6067 for more information.

One alternative to running a postcard in an existing deck is to create your own deck and mail it to your customers and prospects. John Wiley, a book publisher, regularly mails decks featuring business and technical books. The Wiley decks feature only Wiley books and Wiley does not accept outside advertising. If you have many related products and a large mailing list, creating your own postcard deck may be an option for you. But for most of us, with limited product lines and budgets, it is more likely that we will run postcards in one or more of the existing decks.

CHOOSING A POSTCARD DECK

First find those postcard decks that are mailed to people who are likely to be potential prospects for your product.

If you advertise in a magazine, for example, you might also want to run a postcard in their card deck. There's a possibility that if people receiving the deck have read your ad in their magazine, response to your postcard may go up.

Postcards are segmented by markets in one of three different ways:

• *Industry.* Many postcard decks are aimed at specific industries, such as chemical processing, pulp and paper, food processing, pollution control. Most of these are published by companies that also publish trade journals in these fields.

• *Affinity.* A second category is postcard decks aimed at people with similar interests, such as investors or personal computer users.

• *Geographic.* Perhaps the fastest-growing segment of the postcard deck industry is card packs aimed at businesses within a specific geographic market region, such as Boston, New York, Atlanta, Chicago, Houston, Los Angeles, San Francisco, or Miami. An example is Business-to-Business, Inc., which publishes a card deck mailed three times a year to seventy-five thousand prospects in Manhattan.

CALCULATING COST-PER-THOUSAND

Once you've found the card decks that reach your industry, you have to determine which one is the best buy—in other words, which card deck reaches the most prospects for the lowest cost?

One important measure is *cost-per-thousand*, which is how much it costs to reach one thousand prospects with your message. The formula is:

$$\text{Cost-per-thousand} = \frac{\text{Cost of advertising in the card deck} \times 1{,}000}{\text{Number of people card deck is mailed to}}$$

Let's say a publisher with a deck mailed to thirty-two thousand business executives charges advertisers $1,200 to run a card in the deck. The cost-per-thousand is:

$$\frac{\$1{,}200 \times 1{,}000}{32{,}000} = \$37.50 \text{ per thousand.}$$

To put it another way, the cost-per-contact . . . the amount of money you have to spend to put your postcard in the hands of *one prospect* . . . is:

$$\frac{\$37.50 \text{ cost-per-thousand}}{1{,}000} = \$0.0375.$$

Thus, using this postcard deck, you can send a postcard mailing to your prospects for about four cents per person. This is about ten times less expensive than a regular direct mail package.

COMPARING RESULTS

The cost-per-contact, however, only tells you how much you'll have to spend to reach people who receive the postcard deck. It does not tell you whether they will read your postcard. It does not tell you whether they will respond to your offer.

The real measure, then, of any postcard deck, is how many leads or sales it produces for you—and at what expense. But this varies widely based on several factors, including whether you are running in the right deck and the quality of the mailing list receiving the deck.

As with anything else, there are good postcard decks and not-so-good decks. Some will perform for you. Others won't. Of course, you can't know how well your card will work in a particular deck until you test it.

After running your postcard in a deck, count up the sales or leads. Then divide the cost of advertising in the deck by the volume or orders or leads generated. This gives you cost-per-lead (or cost-per-sale) ... an accurate yardstick by which to measure performance of the deck.

$$\frac{\text{Cost of advertising in the deck}}{\text{Number of leads generated}} = \text{cost-per-lead}$$

$$\frac{\text{Cost of advertising in the deck}}{\text{Number of orders received}} = \text{cost-per-sale}$$

Total sales generated − *Cost of advertising* = *profit.*

How many responses will you receive? It depends on whether your product and offer appeal to most of the people receiving the deck or just a fraction of them. And some decks are more responsive than others.

"In terms of numbers, your company can expect a statistical response of between ¼ and 1 percent in returned cards and telephone inquiries—all within a month," states a promotional brochure for the postcard deck published by Business-to-Business Inc. I would say those figures are fairly typical of the industry.

Once you know which postcard decks generate the most leads

or sales per dollar, postcard success becomes a matter of refining and testing different headlines, visuals, and layouts to come up with the postcard that will pull the most response for you every time you run it.

Note that many postcard decks allow "split testing," which means they will mail two versions of your card (or two different cards) to each half of their mailing list. This provides an easy, inexpensive means of testing card A versus card B.

Items you might consider testing include price, headline, offer (free gift versus no free gift), benefit headline versus free-booklet headline, one-color versus two-color cards, one-color versus four-color, visual versus no visual, or format (number of panels, address block on front of card versus on back of card).

HOW PEOPLE READ DECKS

People read postcard decks the way *you* read them: quickly.

I picture my prospects flipping through the deck with a waste-basket positioned between their knees.

As quickly as they can, they go through the deck, pitching cards into the trash. After all, they are busy. They have many other things to do. At best, they view reading postcard decks as a necessary evil—something they would avoid altogether except for the fact that they occasionally find an interesting or helpful offer or two buried in with the rest of the cards.

One study estimates that the average prospect spends one minute going through the entire deck—approximately one second per card. Others say that readers spend up to three seconds scanning each card.

The point is that your card is glanced at, not studied in detail. Just as a highway billboard has only five seconds to gain attention and deliver a message before drivers speed by it, a postcard has but a few seconds to catch the reader's eye and say, "Hey, stop a minute. Here's something worth paying attention to."

The studies also show that people do not stop and read cards of interest. Rather, they pick out those cards that get their attention and set them aside for later reading.

I have found that I usually create two piles when reading through a card deck: one for cards I want to respond to, and a second pile for cards I want to pass on to other people.

"I hypothesize that card scanners do not fully read the cards of interest as they scan but put them aside for later scrutiny," says Wayne Hepburn, a writer and consultant specializing in card deck advertising, writing in *Direct Marketing*. "There is a subtle self-induced pressure to go through the entire pack and react to each card before getting serious about any of them. This is the opposite of magazine reading."

The most important factor in getting attention as people scan cards is a headline that leaps off the card and grabs the reader. A good visual can also help, especially if it is a picture of something the reader can identify with. Body copy is less important, although some is needed to provided supporting evidence for those readers who like to know a little more about a product before responding. And you need to use a portion of the card as a coupon in which the reader can fill in name, address, and phone.

Since the headline is the most crucial element, let's take a closer look at some successful postcard deck headlines.

HOW TO WRITE A POSTCARD DECK HEADLINE

Unlike an advertisement, which seeks to build image or awareness over an extended period of time, the postcard headline's main mission is to grab attention so that the reader pauses long enough to decide to remove the card from the deck for immediate response or later consideration.

There are a number of different approaches you can take when writing postcard headlines.

• *Free offer.* The word "FREE" is pure magic in postcard headlines. I'm sure there are a large number of people who are attracted to postcard decks because of the numerous free offers. (I'm one of them! I love to get things for free.)

If you give away a free gift, a free product sample, or a free booklet, stress the free offer—not the product itself—in your headline and body copy. Show a picture of the free sample, gift, or booklet—not the product. Sell your offer, not the product.

Here are some examples of successful free-offer headlines. (Please note: I say "successful" because most of these cards have run repeatedly in card decks. I assume the advertisers would not continue to run the cards unless they were pulling well.)

FREE ISSUE OFFER	(*Fact* magazine)
FREE ISSUE	(*Computer Shopper* magazine)
WRITE FOR FREE BOOK: "HOW THEY WIN AT COMMODITIES"	(Murlas Commodities)
FREE CATALOG SUBSCRIPTION	(Cabela's)
SEND FOR YOUR FREE REPORT: "HOW TO PROFIT IN PRECIOUS METALS"	(Murlas)
AMAZING FREE OFFER *THINK & GROW RICH*	(SMI International)
FREE PENNY STOCK MARKET REPORT	(Stuart James Company)

• *Benefit headline.* Another powerful technique is to state the key benefit of your product in a crisp, to-the-point headline. This benefit can be a low price, cost savings, wealth-building opportunity, productivity, or the ability to do something you couldn't do without the product.

Advertising writers sometimes write vague or coy headlines.

The purpose is to arouse curiosity, then explain the payoff in the body copy.

But in postcards you don't have this luxury, because body copy is limited to a few well-chosen sentences. When writing a postcard headline, make your headline as direct, as specific, and as clear as possible. Try to tell the whole story in the headline. Leave nothing to imagination.

Here are some postcard headlines that do an admirable job of getting right to the heart of the key product benefit.

UP TO 75% DISCOUNT ON COMMISSIONS WHEN YOU TRADE WITH CHARLES SCHWAB . . .	(Charles Schwab)
35mm PRINTS AND SLIDES FROM THE SAME ROLL	(Seattle FilmWorks)
YOUR INVESTMENT CAN GROW FROM $7,500 to $20,000	(Federal Mailers)
REDUCE PAYROLL UP TO 8% WITH THE SMART CLOCK	(Coastal Data Products)
HOW TO SAVE MONEY ON OFFICE SUPPLIES	(Quill)
AVIS WANTS YOU TO SAVE TIME AND MONEY	(Avis)

Don't worry about whether your headline is similar in content and style to another card in the deck. People do not sit and comparison-shop between one postcard and another. Rather, they respond to any card in the deck that has a headline and offer that appeals to them. If your main benefit is saving time and money, stress time and money savings in your headline. If you offer a free booklet, say "free booklet" in the headline.

• **Question.** A proven response-getter in print advertising and direct mail is to ask a provocative question in the headline.

You don't see this technique applied much in postcards, but I suspect it would work well.

The key is to ask a question that promises a benefit, a reward for reading the postcard, or arouses curiosity on the part of the reader.

Some examples:

HOW LONG MUST YOU KEEP IMPORTANT PAPERS?	(*destroyit* paper shredders)
HOW MANY *SLIDES* DO YOU KEEP? HUNDREDS? THOUSANDS?	(Multiplex Display Fixture Co.)
APPLYING ADDRESS LABELS BY HAND?	(Heyer, Inc. labeling machine)
MOVING YOUR OFFICES?	(Relocation Management Systems)
DO YOU USE FEDERAL EXPRESS?	(Citipostal)
PRINTING CRISIS? WE CAN HELP!	(Penn Copy Center)

• **Command headline.** A classic example of a command headline is Exxon's famous slogan, "Put a Tiger in Your Tank."

Command headlines generate action by literally telling the reader what to do. Another example from a recent print ad: "Buy Scott Towels."

This type of headline is a logical choice for postcards, because our main job is to tell (or rather persuade) the reader to mail our card back to us.

Here are some examples of command headlines used in recent postcards:

PROTECT YOUR COMPANY'S VALUABLE ASSETS	(Seton Name Plate Corporation)
DEVELOP A WINNING BUSINESS PLAN WITH THIS EASY-TO-FOLLOW GUIDE	(American Management Association)
DISCOVER THE EXCITING WORLD OF DIRECT MARKETING	(Hoke Communications)
LEARN TO THINK AND GROW RICH	(SMI International)
BE A PRINTER . . . WITHOUT A PRESS	(Norco Printing Corp.)
INCREASE VALUABLE STORAGE CAPACITY	(Office Efficiency Systems, Inc.)
DISCOVER THE POTENTIAL OF OVER-THE-COUNTER INVESTING	(OTC Stock Journal)
EARN INSURED TAX-FREE INCOME	(Clayton Brown & Associates)

• *News headline.* Postcard decks bring people news of new products, new ideas, new ways to save time and money. As with other forms of direct response, postcards are especially successful when offering products or information that the readers perceives they cannot get elsewhere.

If your product or idea is new, stress the news aspect in your headline. You can do this by using such words as *new, discover, announcing, now, it's here, at last,* and *just arrived.*

Here are some postcard headlines containing news:

ANNOUNCING A BREAKTHROUGH IN COMPUTER POWER PROTECTION	(Best Power Technology)

OPTICAL SCANNING: THE FUTURE IS HERE TODAY!	(Skan Technologies, Inc.)
DISCOVER NEW WAYS TO SCHEDULE PERSONNEL	(Methods Research Corp.)
NEW OLYMPUS FLEXIBLE FIBERSCOPES	(Olympus Corporation)
NEW . . . ANTI-SLIP PVC DUCKBOARD	(Tepromark International)
NEW! MURPHY'S LAW SLIDES, POSTERS, OVERHEADS	(Visual Horizons)

I know that the first headline announcing the future of scanning technology pulled a large number of leads for the advertiser.

• *Mail-order headlines.* When going after sales rather than leads, many advertisers state the offer directly in the headline. This includes the name of the product, the price, the discount being offered, and, if space allows, a statement summarizing the key product benefit. In selling directly from a postcard, it pays to be direct. Here, subtlety is the enemy of sales. Some examples:

1000 FULL COLOR BUSINESS CARDS ONLY $53.50	(Southern Color Corp.)
80 FROSTED WRITE-ON SLIDES SAVE $4.00 Off List $8.00/BOX PLAN YOUR SLIDE SHOWS ° Easy to Write-on and Type-on!	(Visual Horizons)
RECHARGEABLE AEROSOL SPRAY CAN! $29.95 each Includes at no extra charge 5 nozzles	(Abbeon Cal, Inc.)

Save 50% on ESQUIRE and get this important book—A MAN'S BODY—FREE!	(*Esquire* magazine)
16-CENT CUSTOM TOTE BAGS. FAST DELIVERY. LOW QUANTITIES. For trade shows, meetings, promotion, retail— any occasion	(Art Poly Bags)
IMPRINTED GOLF TEES & BALL MARKERS 2⅛″ WOOD GOLF TEES 500—$22.50	(Highlander Company)

• **Headlines to avoid.** Avoid headlines that are generalizations, vague, boastful, or involve broad claims or word-play. Ineffective in ordinary print ads, these say-nothing headlines can dramatically *surpress* response in a postcard deck. Some examples from actual postcards:

Headline	*Comment*
A NEW BREED OF FLEXIBILITY . . .	Says nothing; could apply to virtually any product.
ARKANSAS. WHERE AUTUMN IS THE BEST BARGAIN YOU NEVER BOUGHT.	I call this one, "What did he say?" Unclear and confusing.
THE MOSTEST FOR THE LEASTEST.	This from a major business manufacturer selling a costly facsimile machine. Says nothing!
COPIER UPTIME. IT'S PART TECHNOLOGY, PART PEOPLE, AND ALL KODAK!	Appropriate for a corporate brochure or image campaign (maybe), but not for a response-getting postcard. Where's the hook?

GAIN UNIVERSAL ACCEPTANCE. This postcard offered a microfilm/microfiche reader/copier. But the headline could just as easily apply to a Dale Carnegie course on how to be popular.

SMALL IN THE OFFICE, BIG ON THE JOB. For a card offering details on a copier. A better headline might read, "MINI-DESKTOP COPIER TURNS OUT 11 COPIES A MINUTE!"

THE SIX SECRETS OF
WRITING EFFECTIVE POSTCARD COPY

• *Keep it short.* You don't have much room on a 3½-by-5⅜-inch postcard panel. Copy must be brief and to the point. Maximum length is approximately one hundred to 150 words.

Don't use an overly verbose or descriptive style. Write in terse, almost clipped prose. Make sure each sentence gives the reader a new piece of information; you don't have room to repeat yourself. Avoid transitional phrases, warm-up paragraphs, and other stylistic habits that waste words.

• *Design your copy.* Do a rough layout showing how your copy should be positioned on the card.

Don't just write copy in ordinary paragraph format. Use headlines, subheads, captions, bullets, bursts, arrows, underlining, boldface type, and graphic devices to highlight various components of your copy.

• *The promise of the headline should be fulfilled in the body copy—immediately.* Your first few sentences should immediately explain, elaborate on, and support the promise made in the headline.

Here's an example from a postcard selling a $69.95 book, *Tests for Hiring Office Personnel*:

HIRING THE WRONG PERSON
CAN BE A VERY EXPENSIVE MISTAKE!

Now you can avoid it with *The Complete Portfolio of Tests for Hiring Office Personnel*. Be sure the person you hire has the *right skills* for the job.

Don't guess anymore! Use these scientifically designed tests to:
° Differentiate between similar candidates
° Identify a person's strengths and weaknesses
° Predict success or failure on the job
° Make a more objective hiring decision
° Know you hired the right person for the job. . . .

• **Stress benefits, not features.** Highlight the benefits of what you are selling. For example, if you are selling a machine that folds papers into booklets, don't say, "Stainless steel hopper, 10 inches wide." Say, "Makes up to 600 booklets per hour."

Of course, if you are after a direct sale instead of a lead, you have to give a description of exactly what the reader is getting for his money. But these features should be secondary to a discussion of the benefits of your product or offer.

If you are selling a simple product the reader is already familiar with, such as office supplies, stress the benefits of your offer rather than the product itself. Talk about your low price, volume discount, free catalog, or fast shipment.

Postcards are inadequate for explaining complex products and concepts. If the reader needs a basic education in your product before he can make a buying decision, postcards may not work well for you. Of course, you can write a booklet or report presenting the background information, then offer it free through a postcard.

• **Include a fill-in blank.** As if the postcard's advertising side wasn't small enough, between a quarter and a third of that area is taken up by a name-and-address block where the prospects fill in their name and address, answer any questions you've asked, and might also check off a box to indicate their area or level of interest.

In addition to bringing back an inquiry or order, the name-and-address block can also be used to ask questions for market research purposes or to prequalify prospects. For instance, a card offering free information on computer security might ask the prospects how many computers they have or how many people have access to their system.

If you use your card for survey purposes or to screen leads, ask only one or two questions and keep it simple. Don't ask too many questions or you'll discourage readers from responding.

Some advertisers free up this space for more copy by putting the name-and-address block on the front of the card (the business reply side). This is something you may want to test.

My feeling is that the name-and-address block should be integrated with the headline, visual, and copy on the selling side, just as it is in the reply card or order form included in a regular direct-mail package. The name-and-address block is more than just a means of capturing orders or requests for information; it is a visual device that says, "Hey, I'm a response card. Fill in your name here and then drop me in the mail!"

Without this name-and-address block, the card doesn't *look* like a response device . . . and that may hurt results. Remember, the reader only glances at the advertising side of the card for a second or two before trashing it or putting it aside for later consideration. Almost no one turns cards over to look at the mailing side because they know it merely contains a standard business reply mail imprint.

• *Include instructions.* Even though it may seem obvious, don't assume the reader knows what to do with your card. Include instructions on what to do next. Copy should tell the reader, "For more information, fill out the space below and mail this card today." A card that doesn't ask for the order just sits flat in the pack. Tell the reader what to do.

VISUALS

Because you need room for headline, copy, and name-and-address block, the space for your visual is extremely limited: usually no more than 2½ inches wide by 1½ inches high.

Most postcards are illustrated with either a picture of the product or, if you are offering free information, a picture of the front cover of your free booklet, catalog, or brochure.

Take a look at some postcard decks. The quality of photo reproduction may not match a glossy magazine or annual report, but it's much sharper than a newspaper. So it pays to use good-quality photographs in your card.

Diagrams, charts, graphs, schematics, and other complex visuals do not work well in postcard decks. The reason is that the original must be reduced in size to fit the space, rendering fine detail unreadable.

If you are advertising a cassette program or book, and the author is well known to people in the field, you might increase response by showing a photo of the author in addition to the cover of the book or cassette album.

Although some advertisers are successful with postcards that are all-copy, I recommend you include a visual. The picture gives the postcard the graphic appeal needed to catch the reader's eye as he rapidly flips through the card deck.

Product photos already taken for slide presentations, print advertisement, or press releases are usually ideal for card-deck advertising. Many advertisers routinely create postcard versions of all of their product ads using the same visual plus an abbreviated version of the ad headline and copy.

SELF-MAILERS

A BAD RAP

Self-mailers have traditionally gotten a bad rap from direct marketing consultants, writers, and ad agencies.

"Self-mailers don't work," these professionals tell us. "They generate low response. People don't read them. They are thrown away because they look like brochures—advertising matter. A letter and reply card will nearly *always* outpull a self-mailer."

But many clients feel differently. "Self-mailers are easy to produce and wonderfully inexpensive. And we do get good results with them in many situations," one client recently told me.

Are self-mailers the sure road to direct mail disaster . . . or a powerful secret weapon? Let's find out the truth.

THE ECONOMIES OF SELF-MAILERS

First, it's true that a standard package consisting of a letter, brochure, and reply element will often outpull a self-mailer.

One company, a tool manufacturer, decided they would use a double-postcard (a simple self-mailer consisting of a four-panel postcard) to offer their mail order catalog to consumers. The price of the catalog was one dollar.

At the insistence of their ad agency, they tested this double postcard against a package consisting of a letter and reply card. Same graphics and copy. The only difference was the format.

The results? The letter and reply card generated three times as many orders for the catalog as the double postcard. Demonstrating once again that letters usually do pull better than self-mailers.

Then why would anyone ever want to consider a self-mailer? *Cost.*

SELF-MAILERS ARE INEXPENSIVE

Self-mailers are *much* cheaper to produce and mail then standard direct mail packages.

With a self-mailer, you have only one piece of paper to print. A standard direct mail package has at least five: outer envelope, letter, brochure, order card, and reply envelope. Plus, all these elements must be coordinated, folded, and stuffed. And they are often computer-personalized. All of which costs money.

Depending on size and format, the self-mailer can be produced for a small fraction of the cost of a full-scale package. Creative costs are also lower. Copywriters and art directors charge much less to produce self-mailers than what they charge for a full package.

As a result, even though the direct mail package might generate a greater amount of total leads, the self-mailer might give you a lower *cost*-per-lead, because it is so inexpensive to produce and to mail.

In a case where the direct mail package pulls only a little better than a self-mailer, but costs a lot more to produce, the self-mailer may be the more economical choice.

WHEN SHOULD YOU USE A SELF-MAILER?

When should you consider using or testing a self-mailer? There are several situations:

• *Mailings to customers.* Bob Milroy, an executive vice president with Alexander Marketing Services, a Michigan-based ad agency, recommends self-mailers for mailing to your in-house list of customers and prospects.

"Your customers and prospects—people who already know you—are more likely to read whatever you send them than people who don't know you, such as names on outside rented lists," says Milroy. "Even though a self-mailer is obviously promotional material, your customers will probably read it, because it's from you. You don't have to overcome obstacles to readership."

If you mail regularly to customers and prospects, try switching to self-mailers on half your list and see how it works. Remember, there is less need to grab attention and persuade the reader to open the envelope as when mailing cold to prospects. You might create a standard letterhead and call your monthly mailings "sales bulletins" or "bargain-of-the-month announcements" or use some other title that indicates value.

Some companies produce monthly self-mailers that resemble newsletters. Because they look like information, these quasi-newsletters get higher readership than regular direct mail packages.

• *Continuity.* Jim Alexander, president of Alexander Marketing, has another suggestion. "Self-mailers are good for continuity in a series of mailings," Jim observes. In a series of mailings, for example, you might alternate between letters and self-mailers.

In a self-promotional mailing series for his agency, Jim mailed a series of letter and nonletter packages over eighteen months. Total response was 30 percent.

• **Short message.** Jim also recommends self-mailers for communicating a short, pithy message to readers. Perhaps you just want to announce a change of address, a price change, a special sale, or some other event that doesn't require a lot of explanation or embellishment. You can do it on the back of a postcard for much less than sending a letter package.

• **Low-response offers.** If your type of offer typically pulls a small response, using an expensive mailing package may not allow you to break even. Self-mailers can be an economical alternative. This is why they are so popular for seminar promotion. The typical seminar mailing pulls only ¼ to ½ of one percent. But it can be profitable if promoted with a low-cost self-mailer.

• **The elusive target.** In certain business-to-business marketing situations, we are sometimes not sure who in a company is the right person to sell our product to.

In such a case, a self-mailer may do better than a standard package for the simple reason that self-mailers get passed along from person to person until they end up on the right person's desks. Envelope packages, on the other hand, are usually thrown away by the recipient if he or she is not interested in the offer.

Some direct marketers actually encourage pass-along by printing specific instructions under the address label. A self-mailer for an IBM seminar on project planning and control contains these instructions:

ATTENTION MAIL ROOM PERSONNEL (OR ADDRESSEE):
This announcement about important seminars should go to the person who works *with* the DP department, such as: manager of operations, manager of production, vice president of planning, administrative vice president, vice president of finance, etc. DP managers should also receive this announcement.

• *Mail order.* Double postcards and other inexpensive self-mailers are being used by publishers and mail order companies to sell products directly through the mail. Because a double postcard is so much simpler than the usual lengthy mail order package, you can mail to many more potential buyers at far less cost. Even if overall response rate per thousand pieces mailed is lower, the self-mailer may actually generate more orders for the same amount of money spent.

However, self-mailers don't give you the opportunity to do as thorough a selling job as you can in a complete mail order package. With a self-mailer, you only have one piece of paper to work with. A standard mailing package gives you a larger, more flexible forum for selling.

For this reason, self-mailers aren't effective with complex offers or products that require a lot of explanation and selling.

If you are going to try to sell directly from a self-mailer, make sure the following conditions exist:

- the use and nature of the product are already familiar to the reader;
- the mechanism for ordering the product is greatly simplified;
- the price is low enough that the purchase of the product could be considered an "impulse" buy; and
- the bargain is readily apparent.

For example, I recently received a small self-mailer offering me a discount price and free gift for subscribing to *Business Week*. Since I am already familiar with *Business Week*, I don't need to be sold on the magazine. Telling me the price, offering a gift, and giving me a reply element might be enough to get me to write a check.

On the other hand, if someone sent me the same simple self-mailer offering an accounting software package for my computer, I would not order based on price and a free gift. I would need to know a lot more about the product—how it works, what it can do for me—before placing an order. A traditional mailing package could provide that information better than a self-mailer.

• **Large volume.** If you have an extremely large mailing list, and no way of separating the most likely prospects from so-so prospects, you may simply not be able to afford to send a full-blown mail package to the list. A self-mailer is the only economical way of reaching everyone on the list with news about your offer.

On the other hand, if you can segment the list, and pick out your prime prospects, you might consider mailing a full-scale package to the better portion of the list. Then use a self-mailer to cover the remainder.

Xerox did this with a mailing selling its Conference Copier, a $3,295 piece of office equipment. (The Conference Copier is a blackboard that produces a hard copy of whatever is written on the board at the touch of a button.)

The cream of the list, consisting of five hundred key corporate decision makers, received a series of costly three-dimensional mailings announcing the product. The theme of the mailing was how communications in meetings have evolved from primitive writing tools to modern office technology (such as the Conference Copier). Mailings contained such elaborate objects as a miniature Rosetta stone and a quill pen and parchment.

The second group consisted of fifteen thousand intermediate-level prospects. They received a simpler mailing, which invited them to attend a demonstration of the product at a local hotel.

Then, to cover the rest of the list, Xerox sent out 200,000 four-color self-mailers offering a free fifteen-day trial of the product.

The self-mailer has generated many sales. "We have learned that it is possible to sell high-priced equipment directly by mail and phone," says Dick Martin, manager of advertising and sales promotion for Xerox Direct Marketing. "And we do."

Other companies have had similar results. Macmillan software uses a color self-mailer to generate qualified inquiries for two expensive software packages, Asyst and Asystant. Used by scientists for analyzing laboratory data, these products are priced from $495 to two thousand dollars. The Macmillan self-mailer generates a respectable 4 percent response when mailed to Macmillan's in-house prospect list—names of people who responded to past advertisements and promotions.

Mark Toner, who runs the direct mail program for Amano, a manufacturer of computerized time-recorder and data-collection equipment, also favors self-mailers for their low cost. He uses an 9½-by-11-inch sheet, folded twice to form six panels. One third of the mailer consists of a perforated tear-off business reply card designed to bring back an inquiry. The balance has descriptive copy and color photos of Amano's product line.

Toner says his response from outside mailing lists ranges from less than 1 percent to 3 percent. When mailing the same piece to his in-house list, he can get as much as 5 percent.

Joe Michaels, president of Michaels Advertising in Fort Lee, New Jersey, points out that response varies greatly with two factors: (1) size of the potential market and (2) the price of the product. And the two often go hand in hand.

He tells of doing two separate mailings, for two different products, to the same list. The first mailing was for a glass-lined chemical reactor costing approximately $160,000. The second offered more information on a pH probe costing $1,500. The results? The reactor mailing generated twenty to thirty replies, while the mailing for the less costly probe brought back several hundred replies.

"With big-ticket items, there is a limited market," says Joe. "Once a company buys a $160,000 glass-lined reactor, they may not need another for twenty years. There are likely to be many more people on the mailing list in the market for the less expensive $1,500 pH probe."

Joe, who handles mainly industrial clients, says it is "standard operating procedure" at his agency to turn all print ads into self-mailers. The primary purpose of these self-mailers is not to generate a response, but to "maintain top-of-the-mind awareness," according to Joe. The self-mailers are mailed at the same time the ad is running, giving the ad double exposure—a "one-two punch," as Joe calls it.

WHY IT WORKS

Why does the self-mailer work so well for large lists, especially where you cannot segment "hot" prospects from the rest of the list?

Think about the people you are reaching, and you realize that people on the list fall into one of three categories:

• *People who are not interested in your product and would not buy it for any reason.* This group also includes people who do not respond to direct mail for *any* offer.

You are not going to get response from these people no matter how good your mailing package. Yet you cannot identify them in advance. So it's cheaper to miss the mark with a self-mailer that costs a few pennies, rather than a full-blown piece costing thirty to forty cents per package.

Most of the people on your list fall into this category. As you know, in mail order, response rates of 2 percent are typical. Even with a dynamite mailing piece and a great offer, more than 90 percent of the people on the list are probably not going to respond.

• *People who want your product and are predisposed to buy it.* There are certain people—again, you can't identify or separate them in advance—who are practically sitting around and *waiting* for your offer. Getting them to buy is a simple matter. All you have to do is say, "Here's the product, here's the price, here's the order form." They would, if you could preidentify them, respond as well to a note scribbled on toilet paper as they would to a costly four-color mailing with all the bells and whistles.

Because they are ready to buy, a self-mailer tells them the basic information as well as the full-blown package. In fact, they probably won't bother reading a detailed letter or brochure, because they are already sold.

This group represents a profitable but extremely small portion of the list . . . perhaps only 1 percent or less.

• *Another small but important group is the fence-sitters.* These people don't have a preference either way. They have not made up their minds and can be swayed either way. They are prime candidates for being sold through persuasive advertising.

Here, the full-scale mailing package, with its superior persuasive abilities, is much more effective than the self-mailer, which is limited to presenting a much abbreviated sales pitch. If you could preidentify the fence sitters, and separate their names from your list, the full-scale mailing package would probably outpull the self-mailer dramatically . . . enough to make a real difference in sales and profits.

The self-mailer, in effect, allows you to "skim" the list and inexpensively convert a large percentage of the people in the second category—those who are in the mood to buy from you—into paying customers. "Your self-mailer 'skims the cream,' allowing you to reach prospects at low cost and capture those customers who are ready to buy," explains copywriter Richard Armstrong. "Fund raisers use this approach, sending simple, inexpensive packages to people who are predisposed to make a donation to their organization or cause." Richard notes that self-mailers are also widely used by magazine publishers and seminar companies to "skim" large lists of potential subscribers or attendees.

Of course, if you were somehow able to separate the category 3 prospects—people who need to be sold and will buy if you can persuade them—you might send a separate, more elaborate package to them, as Xerox has done with its Conference Copier.

WRITING SELF-MAILER HEADLINES

The first thing the reader sees is the headline, or teaser, on the outer panel of your self-mailer.

Unlike a direct mail package, which can be "disguised" to resemble personal mail, a self-mailer immediately identifies itself as advertising material. Therefore, you have no choice but to try and grab the reader's interest with the strongest headline you can.

(The one exception I can think of to this rule is in business-to-business direct mail aimed at executives. If you put two folds in an 8½-by-11-inch sheet of white stock, you can create a self-mailer that is approximately the same shape and color as a number-ten business envelope. By printing the company logo and address in the upper left-hand corner of the address panel, you can achieve a look that resembles, at first glance, the outer envelope of a regular business letter.)

A good friend of mine who runs a successful direct marketing ad agency specializes in seminar promotion and uses self-mailers to get people to register by mail. His theory, in seminar mailings, is that the headline of the mailer should not be clever, cute, or long-winded. Rather, it should state, in large, heavy type, and in the fewest possible words, the nature of the seminar.

Some examples:

HOW TO WRITE AND DESIGN SALES LITERATURE A One-Day Seminar	(Performance Seminar Group)
HOW TO SHARPEN YOUR NEGOTIATING SKILLS	(Fairleigh Dickinson University)
FINANCIAL MANAGEMENT FOR NEWSLETTER PUBLISHERS	(The Newsletter Association)
EFFECTIVE SALES MANAGEMENT	(The Dartnell Institute of Management)

| MAIL ADVERTISING PROFIT SEMINAR | (Rene Gnam Consultation Corporation) |

Here are some additional mailer headlines that work:

Headline	*Comment*
HERE'S A SIMPLE BUT POWERFUL INVESTING TECHNIQUE—THAT ANYONE CAN UNDERSTAND	Some people will believe it; others will be immediately skeptical. But don't you at least want to open the mailer to find out what the story is?
NEED CHEMICAL OR BIOCHEMICAL INFORMATION IN A HURRY? START YOUR SEARCH HERE . . .	If I needed chemical or biochemical information, I would read further.
STOP WATER DAMAGE IN YOUR BASEMENT *BEFORE IT'S TOO LATE!*	Fear is always a powerful motivator. Water damage in the basement is something homeowners do worry about. And the phrase "before it's too late" adds a real sense of urgency.
INTRODUCING THE WORLD'S FIRST ANTI-STATIC DISKETTES. And Verbatim Will Pay You To Try Them.	As a diskette user, this announcement got my attention. And the offer of payment for trying the product was a strong incentive to find out more.
RECEIVE VALUABLE FREE PRESENTATION TIPS WHEN YOU REQUEST INFORMATION ON GBC'S COMPLETE LINE OF PRODUCTS AND SERVICES. Offer expires December 31, 1986.	"Free" is still the most powerful weapon in the direct mail copywriter's arsenal. More people respond to free offers than any other kind. Having an expiration date also helps boost response.

INSIDE! FIND WHAT COULD BE YOUR KEYS TO SUCCESS . . .	Borders on being too vague and general, but somehow manages to make a strong enough promise and arouse enough curiosity to get you to take a look inside.
RADIO SHACK COMPUTER CENTERS—JUNE SAVINGS SALE!	Using a well-known company name in the headline increases readership. And using the self-mailer to announce a sale is effective because it makes it apparent that your offer is a bargain.

CHOOSING A FORMAT FOR YOUR SELF-MAILER

The best way to get a feel for which formats and sizes would work best with your offer is to collect and study samples of self-mailers.

In particular, you should note:

- which sizes are most popular
- how many folds are used
- use of two-color versus full color
- layout of copy and illustrations
- format and positioning of reply element
- offers being used (lead-generation vs. mail order)
- methods of payment for mail orders
- type of paper stock mailer is printed on
- theme and format of self-mailers used by companies selling products or services similar to yours
- formats and layouts of self-mailers that might be adapted to your own offer.

Self-mailers come in all sizes and shapes. Some of the more common ones include:

- 11-by-17-inch sheet folded once to form four panels
- 11-by-25-inch sheet folded twice to form six panels
- 11-by-25-inch sheet folded twice to form six panels, with one-third of the sheet cut in half to form a short fold-over panel
- 8½-by-11-inch sheet folded twice to form six panels
- 8½-by-14-inch sheet folded three times to form eight panels
- single postcard (3½ by 5½ inches or larger)
- double or triple postcard
- newsletter format
- minicatalog
- magalog (sixteen-to-twenty-page self-mailer designed to resemble a magazine)

SIXTEEN WAYS TO IMPROVE
YOUR NEXT SELF-MAILER

• *Use a powerful headline.* The headline on the outside panel is usually what decides whether the reader will open your self-mailer or throw it away. Make sure your headline delivers the most powerful selling proposition possible. The headline should be immediately clear and in no way confusing or vague. And it should give the reader a powerful reason why he should look inside.

• *Set the headline in large, bold type.* Draw attention to your headline. Make it bold. A headline in large letters catches the eye of people who walk by and see your self-mailer on a table, desk, or the top of the pile in someone's in-basket.

Also, put the headline on both the front and back panel. This way the selling proposition is visible whether the reader sees the mailing piece from the front or from the back.

• *Break copy up into sections.* Use subheads, bullets, borders, boxes, and color tints to segment and highlight various portions of your copy. Experience shows most people only skim self-mailers; few read them through thoroughly. One expert estimates that the maximum amount of reading time given to self-mailers is ninety seconds. The reader should be able to tell, at a glance, what you are selling and the key benefits of your offer.

• *Use short sections of copy.* The total length can be long or short, depending on product and offer. But each section of copy should be brief. Each copy block should cover only one sales point or feature. When you want to discuss another sales point, insert a subhead and start a new section.

• *Use bullet format.* Use numbered points, lists, and bullets to make your copy easy to scan. The reader should be able to pick out the selling points that interest him by quickly scanning the inside panels of your mailer. Don't bury key points in long-winded paragraphs of text.

• *Use visuals to identify the product or service.* If you're selling computer training, show pictures of people sitting at computer terminals. If you're selling a lawn-care service, show photographs of lush, green lawns. The pictures are a visual device that help the reader instantly identify the nature of your offer and prepare him to listen to a sales pitch on the subject.

• *Highlight free offers.* If you are offering something free to people who respond, highlight the free offer in a separate block of copy. Use a subhead that says, "Yours FREE" or "Special FREE offer." Show a picture of the item you are giving away.

• *Highlight features.* List the features of your product or service in a separate copy block. Don't elaborate on them. A simple listing of the facts in bullet form will suffice.

This is especially important in selling books, seminars, or technical equipment. You never know which feature of your product or which chapter in your book will appeal to a particular reader. By including a comprehensive listing, you are certain that you have at least mentioned everything a potential buyer might be looking for.

• *Use testimonials from satisfied customers.* These can be grouped together or sprinkled throughout the margins of the self-mailer. I prefer to put all testimonials in one section because I think it makes a greater impact.

Dartnell, a book publisher, finds this technique so effective that they devoted an entire page in a recent self-mailer to reprinting a single letter of testimonial from a satisfied customer!

• *Use a toll-free telephone number.* Highlight the phone number on the reply element and throughout the body of the mailer. You might even consider putting it on the cover; this may prompt calls from "impulse buyers" who are too busy or don't want to bother reading through your mailer.

• *Stress the offer.* Unless your mailing is designed merely to build awareness or make an announcement, you should tell readers exactly what you want them to do and what will happen when they do it. Are you offering more information, a free product sample, a free analysis or consultation? Make your offer clear and highlight it—both in the closing paragraphs of your copy and again in the reply card.

• *Make bargains apparent.* Highlight sale prices and discounts offered. Provide an incentive for immediate response, such as a cash discount or free gift. This discourages the readers from their natural inclination, which is to put the mailer aside or file it for later consideration—actions which seldom result in a sale for you.

• *Highlight the guarantee.* State your guarantee in a separate box. Highlight it with a certificate-like border or by printing over a tint. A self-mailer for Barefoot Grass Lawn Service of Fair Lawn, New Jersey, makes this guarantee:

SATISFACTION GUARANTEED

This is our promise to you: If for any reason, you are not pleased with the results of the treatment, simply notify us and we will retreat your lawn at no extra cost. So you have nothing to lose, and a better lawn to gain.

• *Put a place and date reference on the outer panel.* In a mailing inviting someone to attend a trade show, put the location and date of the show on the outer envelope. If you are advertising a sale, specify the month of the sale.

There are two reasons for highlighting the date. First, it tells readers whether they can take advantage of your offer. (If they read that your seminar is on August 15, they can quickly check their calendars to see whether they can make it.) Second, it alerts them to the fact that they have limited time in which to act.

• *Consider using a series of self-mailers.* The price of self-mailers is so low that you can afford to mail your prospects a series of two or three mailings for the price of one full-scale direct mail package. Try it.

• *Emphasize the reply element.* Use graphics that draw attention to the reply element. For example, print a heavy dashed line along the border where the reply card is to be teared off or cut out. Show a little picture of a scissors along the dashed border. Use a certificate border or other design element to make the reply element look official and important. Give it a title that implies value, such as "FREE TRIAL RESERVATION CARD" or

"FREE INFORMATION REQUEST FORM" or "EXECUTIVE VIP INVITATION RESPONSE FORM."

The point is to make the reply element leap off the page when the reader opens your mailer. Unlike regular direct mail, where the reply element is separate, in most self-mailers the reply element is attached to the main selling piece. Therefore you must take extra pains to make it stand out. A reply card that isn't begging to be clipped and mailed is one that won't generate a lot of replies for you.

Index

About the Author

ROBERT W. BLY is an independent copywriter and consultant specializing in industrial, high-tech, business-to-business, and direct response marketing. He has written copy for more than one hundred advertising agencies and corporations including RCA, Grumman Corporation, On-Line Software International, IBM, AT&T, M&T Chemicals, Prentice-Hall, the Philadelphia National Bank, and Edith Roman Associates.

Mr. Bly is the author of twenty-seven books, including *The Copywriter's Handbook, Targeted Public Relations,* and *Selling Your Services,* published by Henry Holt. His articles have appeared in such magazines as *Writer's Digest, Cosmopolitan, Amtrak Express, Business Marketing, High-Tech Marketing, Computer Decision,* and *Direct Marketing.*

Bob Bly has taught copywriting at the New York University School of Continuing Education. Before becoming a freelance copywriter, he was advertising manager of Koch Engineering Company, Inc. and a staff writer for Westinghouse. He currently presents in-house seminars on direct marketing for corporate clients nationwide.

Questions and comments on *Power-Packed Direct Mail* may be sent to Mr. Bly at this address:

Bob Bly
22 E. Quackenbush Avenue
Dumont, NJ 07628
(201) 385-1220